The IC Toolkit

The IC Toolkit

Jim Knight

Jessica Wise

Michelle Harris

Amy Musante

A joint publication

FOR INFORMATION

Corwin

A SAGE Company

2455 Teller Road

Thousand Oaks, California 91320

(800) 233-9936

www.corwin.com

SAGE Publications Ltd.

1 Oliver's Yard

55 City Road

London EC1Y 1SP

United Kingdom

SAGE Publications India Pvt. Ltd.

Unit No 323-333, Third Floor, F-Block

International Trade Tower Nehru Place

New Delhi 110 019

India

SAGE Publications Asia-Pacific Pte. Ltd.

18 Cross Street #10-10/11/12

China Square Central

Singapore 048423

Vice President and
  Editorial Director: Monica Eckman

Acquisitions Editor: Megan Bedell

Content Development Editor: Mia Rodriguez

Content Development Manager: Lucas Schleicher

Senior Editorial Assistant: Natalie Delpino

Production Editor: Tori Mirsadjadi

Copy Editor: Michelle Ponce

Typesetter: C&M Digitals (P) Ltd.

Proofreader: Lawrence W. Baker

Indexer: Integra

Cover Designer: Scott Van Atta

Marketing Manager: Melissa Duclos

Printed in the United States of America

Library of Congress Cataloging-in-Publication Data

Names: Knight, Jim, author. | Wise, Jessica, author. | Harris, Michelle (English teacher), author. | Musante, Amy, author.

Title: The IC toolkit / Jim Knight, Jessica Wise, Michelle Harris, Amy Musante.

Description: Thousand Oaks, California : Corwin, [2025] | Includes bibliographical references and index.

Identifiers: LCCN 2024033970 | ISBN 9781071971581 (spiral bound) | ISBN 9781071971604 (epub) | ISBN 9781071971611 (epub) | ISBN 9781071971635 (pdf)

Subjects: LCSH: Mentoring in education. | Teachers—In-service training. | Communication in education. | Effective teaching.

Classification: LCC LB1731.4 .K55 2025 | DDC 371.102—dc23/eng/20240730
LC record available at https://lccn.loc.gov/2024033970

This book is printed on acid-free paper.

24 25 26 27 28 10 9 8 7 6 5 4 3 2 1

Contents

Note From the Publisher: The authors have provided video and web content throughout the book that is available to you through QR (quick response) codes. To read a QR code, you must have a smartphone or tablet with a camera. We recommend that you download a QR code reader app that is made specifically for your phone or tablet brand.

Foreword

It is with great joy and admiration that I introduce this remarkable work by Jim Knight and the team at the Instructional Coaching Group. Throughout my decades-long friendship with Jim and my own journey as a teacher, principal, and professional learning leader, I have come to appreciate the way Jim addresses how coaching ultimately leads to student success: describing practical strategies for coaches, sharing the evidence about how instructional coaching improves teaching, and calling on systems to create conditions to support effective coaching. Jim's books stand out as invaluable resources.

This latest book, *The IC Toolkit*, is no exception. This book explores Jim's Seven Success Factors that are essential for effective instructional coaching. Readers will appreciate how Jim—along with coauthors Jessica Wise, Michelle Harris, and Amy Musante—emphasizes the need for true partnerships between coaches and educators, alignment among the many roles involved in effective coaching, and supportive environments where systems, schools, coaches, teachers, and students all thrive. This book is a unique resource for the people who carry out essential work in our schools every day.

Jim's writings are not merely insightful; they serve as historical markers that capture and help clarify major moments in our educational journey. They take us through the foundations of modern-day instructional coaching, new learning evidence about how coaches can spend their time to have the greatest impact, and even illuminate critical junctures such as coaching through the COVID-19 pandemic. In each phase of the journey, Jim prompts us to reflect on our approaches to support student learning and well-being and consider how to make adaptations if we need to re-center the student.

As I reflect on the writings in Jim's new book, many of which have been featured in Learning Forward's *The Learning Professional*, I see the throughline of humanity and a recognition of the dignity of educators. I also see themes from Learning Forward's Standards for Professional Learning woven throughout the pages. The Standards serve as our profession's cornerstone for high-quality professional learning, describing the content, processes, and conditions that lead to effective, high-quality professional learning. The Leadership standard, for example, underscores the critical role leaders play in creating spaces and structures that ensure coaches can learn and thrive as they develop skills to meet teachers' learning and instructional needs—a theme throughout Jim's writing.

We also see the three equity-focused Standards reflected throughout this book. These Standards encourage professional learning leaders to attend to the content (Equity Practices), the learning processes (Equity Drivers), and the systems and conditions (Equity Foundations) that lead to increased access to learning for both educators and students. These themes run throughout this book's discussion of how instructional coaching builds teachers' skills and capacity to create classrooms where the assets and experiences that every child brings to the classroom are recognized and celebrated.

By integrating equity, we create conditions for all students to have access to learning and invite educators to examine their own beliefs and biases as they work to understand our students, their families, and their communities so that we can pave the way for positive change. As coaches and teachers collaborate, it becomes crucial to navigate conversations with sensitivity to biases, ensuring that our educational practices remain inclusive and equitable.

Jim and I recently reflected on our long partnership and what the connection represents. In our conversation, it became clear that, like our respective organization's visions, we are here to do great work for children all over the world. Our collaboration represents a dedication to prioritizing students above all else. This goal of creating meaningful, rigorous, and engaging learning experiences for children is our collective responsibility as educators. The depth of this relationship has not only enriched our collective understanding of instructional coaching but also reinforced our commitment to modeling the partnership principles in every facet of our work. More than that, though, is our deep appreciation for each other. We see the impact of professional learning and instructional coaching. It is with great pleasure that we both get to play a part in the outcome of those efforts.

As you embark on the journey of this latest book, I hope you embrace the opportunity to reflect on the past, engage with the present challenges, and envision a future where instructional coaching continues to evolve and adapt to meet the needs of all learners. This book is a testament to how Jim and the Instructional Coaching Group have continuously seen educators as professionals. I commend Jim and his colleagues for their new work and find it hard to imagine where we would be as a field without their unwavering dedication to instructional coaching.

As you continue your professional development, I hope you find as much value in this book as I have. May this book inspire and empower you to champion the transformative power of coaching in creating brighter futures for our students.

With deep appreciation,

Frederick Brown

Acknowledgments

At the Instructional Coaching Group, we aim for excellent instruction, every day, in every class, for every student. To do that critical work, we recognize that effective professional development is necessary. The team at ICG works on six continents to facilitate learning for adults so that our world's students reap the benefits. While working with these distinguished educators, we often hear questions about how coaches can continue learning, how administrators can partner with coaches, and requests on how facilitators of coaching programs could lead meaningful learning opportunities using the research and work from Jim Knight and the Instructional Coaching Group. Because of the questions and the many partnerships that have fueled our work, we were inspired to compile a resource that might aid the support of implementation of coaching long after the training ends.

This book would not be possible without the gracious collaboration of several publications where many of these articles were first written. We would like to thank Anthony Rebora from ASCD and Educational Leadership, Suzanne Bouffard at Learning Forward (formerly the National Staff Development Council), Jennifer Dubin at Principal Leadership, and Deirdre Kinsella-Biss at Principal Connections. Thank you for partnering with us to share these articles with our audience.

As we compiled this book, we leaned on many learning partners who shared their thoughts, tested different components for us, and even contributed insight on how to make this as user friendly as possible. Those learning partners include Lauren Bernstein, Tricia Burbank, Leah Dowd, and Laurie Higgins from the Wilkins Coaching Team in Stoughton, MA; Coach Champions in Jefferson County schools in Alabama, and Instructional Coach Marquitis Adams in Gwinnett County Public Schools. Our wonderful teammates at ICG also poured into our ambitions endeavor and shared invaluable time with us. Thank you to Jennifer Hlavka, Christina Ortega, and Jamie Pitcavage for reading and rereading the various book elements we sent you. Thank you to everyone at the Instructional Coaching Group who supported the product we are so excited to share with the world. A special acknowledgement also goes out to our families. They loved us through many phone calls, late nights of collaboration and work, and time spent on this manuscript. Your support means everything.

Finally, thank you to the many instructional coaches, coaching teams, coaching champions, and administrators who will use this book to do incredibly important work. We are so grateful you have chosen to learn with us and encourage you to keep moving forward. We believe in you and are here for you in every page of this toolkit. As you implement these activities and explore the resources, just know that you have a little bit of us there with you.

About the Authors

Dr. Jim Knight, founder and senior partner of Instructional Coaching Group (ICG), is also a research associate at the University of Kansas Center for Research on Learning. He has spent more than two decades studying professional learning and instructional coaching. Jim earned his PhD in education from the University of Kansas and has won several university teaching, innovation, and service awards.

The pioneering work Jim and his colleagues have conducted has led to many innovations that are now central to professional development in schools. Jim wrote the first major article about instructional coaching for the *Journal of Staff Development*, and his book *Instructional Coaching* (2007) offered the first extended description of instructional coaching. Jim's book *Focus on Teaching* (2014) was the first extended description of how video should be used for professional learning. Recently, writing with Ann Hoffman, Michelle Harris, and Sharon Thomas, Jim introduced the idea of instructional playbooks with their book on that topic.

Jim has written several books in addition to those described previously, including *Unmistakable Impact* (2011), *High-Impact Instruction* (2013), *Better Conversations* (2015), *The Impact Cycle* (2018), and *The Definitive Guide to Instructional Coaching* (2021). Knight has also authored articles on instructional coaching and professional learning in publications such as *Educational Leadership*, *The Journal of Staff Development*, *Principal Leadership*, *The School Administrator*, and *Kappan*. Jim is also a columnist for *Educational Leadership*.

Through ICG, Knight conducts coaching workshops, hosts the Facebook Live Program "Coaching Conversations," and provides consulting for coaching programs around the world.

Dr. Jessica Wise is a virtual consultant with the Instructional Coaching Group. Beginning her career in education in 2007, Jessica has held various roles including a classroom teacher, school-based instructional coach and intervention/gifted teacher, district literacy specialist, and then leadership and staff development instructional coach. Jessica received her doctoral degree in school improvement from the University of West Georgia where her focus was facilitation of adult learning. When not working, Jessica enjoys hiking, movie night with her family, and reading. She lives in Georgia with her family.

Michelle Harris has been in education since 1993, starting as a special education para, then a teacher, coach, and administrator. She is the coauthor of *Instructional Playbook: The Missing Link for Translating Research Into Practice* and *Evaluating Instructional Coaching: People, Programs, and Partnership.* Michelle is a seasoned staff developer and has presented and keynoted in the United States, Canada, Africa, Asia, and Europe. She lives in Portland, Oregon, with her husband, two sons, a corgi, and two cats.

Amy Musante is a consultant with the Instructional Coaching Group. She began her journey in education in 1998 and has served in many roles to support students and diverse school communities. Her experience as a language arts teacher, secondary schools intervention specialist, and district director of coaching programming (UPK-12) has provided her with experience that informs her work continuously. She received her MA from Teachers College, Columbia University and has done considerable work partnering with the university postgraduation. In her free time, Amy loves spending time in nature, traveling with her family, and cheering on Buffalo sports teams.

Introduction

Excellence always comes at a price, and that price is practice. Whether we are watching a virtuoso violinist, eating a perfectly created meal, or cheering on our favorite athlete, the excellence we see, hear, or taste, is possible because someone practiced so that they could get better. Practice, focused on honing the art and craft of a profession, is just as important for instructional coaches as it is for master chefs or hockey players.

For more than twenty-five years, researchers and consultants at the Instructional Coaching Group (ICG) have been studying what excellence in coaching looks and sounds like. We've organized our findings around Seven Success Factors, and we've produced a number of books, articles, and workshops that help people learn about those factors. This book, however, is different. We have designed *The IC Toolkit* so that coaches can refine the art and craft of being an instructional coach. This book is packed with tools that coaches can use in a variety of ways to become highly proficient in the Seven Success Factors.

We designed this book so that over the thirty-six weeks of an academic school year, coaches, either individually or preferably collectively, can practice, reflect, and learn. If you're a coach who wants to improve or a leader who wants to set up meaningful learning activities for coaches, this book will give you tools that you can use every week.

In their book *The Knowing-Doing Gap* (2000) Robert Sutton and Jeffrey Pfeffer wrote that "one of the main barriers to turning knowledge into action is the tendency to treat talking about something as equivalent to actually doing something about it" (p. 29). Certainly, there is value in reflecting on and exploring the Seven Success Factors, and there are many articles in this text that can function as thinking prompts for meaningful dialogue. However, there are also many other tools that coaches can use to practice and improve so they can bridge the knowing-doing gap. And when coaches becoming highly proficient in the art and craft of coaching, good things will happen for educators and, most importantly, students.

What Is Included in This Book?

This book has an introduction, seven chapters, and a conclusion. The seven chapters represent the Seven Success Factors from Jim Knight's research. The following are the Seven Success Factors:

1. The Partnership Principles

2. Communication Skills

3. Coaches as Leaders

4. The Impact Cycle

5. Data

6. The Instructional Playbook

7. System Support

What Is Included in Each Chapter?

- One-page description of the Success Factor

- A table that lists all resources in the chapter

- Learning Paths

- End-of-chapter reflection questions

What Are Learning Paths?

Learning paths are our ideas on how to use the provided resources to explore each Success Factor in a meaningful way. Each Learning Path begins with a guiding question to focus your learning. Then, you will find the names of the resources that align with that path.

RESOURCES	
Articles written by Jim	
Activities to use as you read the articles	
Case studies or scenarios that allow you to apply your learning	
Checklists for coaching skills	
Videos from the Instructional Coaching Group's video collection	

To guide and support you through the Learning Paths, we have also included steps to use to engage in each Learning Path's activity.

How Do I Use This Book?

We wrote the book with *you* in mind. Our mission was to provide a toolkit made for learning, collaboration, discussion, and growth, all focused on the work of Jim Knight and The Instructional Coaching Group. If you are curious about how you might interact with these resources, we invite you to explore the following three scenarios. While this is not an exhaustive list of how you might learn with us, we hope the scenarios ignite ideas for how to proceed. Happy learning!

The Coach Champion

Christina is a Coach Champion, a facilitator of professional development who aims to build instructional coaches and support them as they coach within schools. Each month, Christina meets with a group of instructional coaches to facilitate their

(Continued)

(Continued)

learning and conversation about instructional coaching. The coaches go back to their schools and implement their learning, then continue to return to the monthly sessions with Christina to learn, reflect, and practice their coaching. Christina intentionally uses *The IC Toolkit* to choose learning paths for her coaches that align with their monthly topics. For example, at the start of the school year, Christina used Chapter 1, The Partnership Principles, to discuss the foundational beliefs we hold as coaches. After moving through that chapter, she realized that the coaches were still new to the Impact Cycle. Therefore, in the next few gatherings, Christina used Learning Paths from Chapter 4, The Impact Cycle, to enrich the coaches' understanding of the process of coaching. The Learning Paths provide Christina with articles for her coaches to read, videos to show her coaches, and activities she can facilitate as the coaches interact with the learning path resources. Christina writes down the date next to each learning path, so that she can see what she has used and where she might need to go next.

The Instructional Coaches

Jamie and four other coaches within his cluster of schools are all implementing the Impact Cycle with their teachers. Since coaching is new to their district, they try to keep in touch and help each other as they implement what they have learned about instructional coaching. Once every month, they meet on Zoom or in one of their schools to learn together, but they were not sure exactly *what* to learn about or even how. When Jamie discovered *The IC Toolkit*, he realized that the group of coaches could pick Learning Paths about topics they were working on with teachers and learn together as a group. The coaches take turns leading Learning Paths each time they meet, allowing the group to learn together with all the resources already planned for them.

The Solo Coach

Jenn recently moved out of the classroom to serve her school as an instructional coach. She has heard of coaching before and knows that there are some coaches in her district, but she does not know who they are. Jenn's principal recommended *The IC Toolkit* to her to invest in her own professional development as she adjusts to her role as a coach. Each week, Jenn designates one to two hours in her calendar for professional development. During that time, she looks through the Seven Success Factors, Chapters 1 through 7, and decides which factor she would like to explore during her learning time. Once she chooses a chapter, she uses the Learning Paths to experience self-guided and sacred time to learn and invest in her coaching skills. Jenn leverages the margins of the pages to annotate her articles and the reflection questions to jot her new learning. As a bonus, she is using the activities provided in each chapter as activities she can use when she eventually begins leading professional development at her school. The Learning Paths allow her to learn on her own and give her ideas about how to facilitate learning for others, too.

One More Tool

In the following section is a needs assessment survey you may choose to use along with this book. To maximize your learning experience in *The IC Toolkit*, you might choose to take this survey as a way to gauge where you, your coaching program, or your system is in the journey toward coaching proficiency with the Seven Success Factors. For example, you can take this survey, then see in which areas you have the lowest scores. That could inform you or your team where to begin in the book. A team might score high in the Partnership Principles, but they might score lower in the use of data. This team might choose to begin in Chapter 5: Data, so that they could target their specific area of need. We hope you find this tool helpful as you self-assess or reflect on the current needs of your coaching program.

Needs Assessment

Rank each success factor on a scale of 1 to 10 (1 = totally disagree; 10 = totally agree).

1. Partnership Principles

   - I believe my collaborating teachers' ideas, beliefs, opinions, and knowledge are just as important as mine.

   - I am 100 percent okay with teachers selecting goals that are different than the ones I would choose for them.

   - My collaborating teachers know that I think their voices are just as important as mine.

   - I willingly share my ideas when they are helpful, but I also refrain from trying to talk my collaborating teacher into adopting those views.

   - My coaching leads to deep implementation and sustained changes by collaborating teachers.

   - I expect to learn from each teacher I partner with, regardless of how much experience they do or do not have.

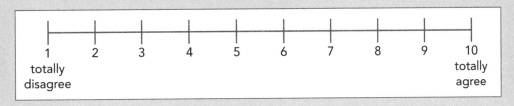

2. Coaching Skills/Communication
- I do not ask leading questions.
- I have a list of effective questions and use the questions differently depending on the progress of the coaching conversation.
- I prepare myself for coaching conversations by considering which questions I might ask during the coaching session.
- My questions effectively invite teachers to think more deeply about their situation.
- During the identify and improve stages of the Impact Cycle, my collaborating teacher talks at least 80 percent of the time.
- I stay focused on what my collaborating teacher says during coaching.
- I don't interrupt (except when necessary) during coaching conversations.
- My eye contact and nonverbal communication demonstrate to my collaborating teachers that I am listening to them.

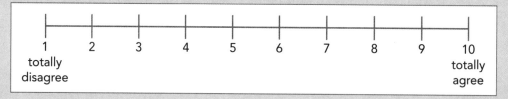

3. Leadership
- I can clearly describe my purpose.
- I manage my time so that I can focus on actions that help me achieve my purpose.
- I take care of myself and treat myself with the same compassion I would show to a good friend.
- People can count on me to do what I said I would do.
- I interact with collaborating teachers in ways that amplify their intelligence, capabilities, and efficacy.
- I balance personal ambition with humility, focusing on the greater good rather than on self-interest.

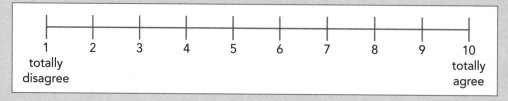

4. Impact Cycle
- I partner with teachers
  - to ensure they get a clear picture of reality before they set a goal,
  - to set PEERS goals,

○ to identify teaching strategies teachers can try to meet their goals,

○ to explain and model strategies so they can implement the strategies with confidence, and

○ to make adaptations until goals are met.

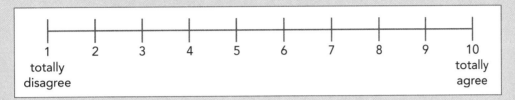

5. Data
   - I fully understand the difference between behavioral, cognitive, and emotional engagement.
   - I can gather valid, objective, reliable data for assessing behavioral, cognitive, and emotional engagement.
   - I fully understand the difference between content, procedural, and conceptual levels of knowledge.
   - I fully understand the difference between measuring the acquisition, connection, and transfer kinds of learning.
   - I can apply a variety of assessment tools (selected response, brief constructed responses, checks for understanding, rubrics, and others) to ensure that the right level and kind of learning is validly and reliably being assessed.

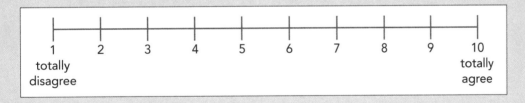

6. Teaching Strategies
   - I know the top fifteen highest-impact strategies teachers can use to hit goals in our district.
   - My organization has created an instructional playbook that I use frequently to identify and explain strategies teachers can use to hit their goals.
   - I confidently, clearly, and dialogically explain teaching strategies.

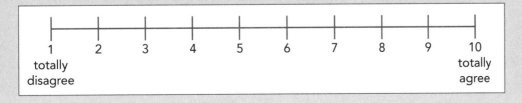

7. System Support

- My principal clearly understands my role as a coach and communicates regularly with stakeholders regarding my role.

- I spend at least 70 percent of my time partnering with teachers on the Impact Cycle.

- Our district has clearly identified the standards we use to assess coaches and the coaching program.

- I am evaluated by someone who has a deep understanding of instructional coaching.

- I am evaluated by a tool created for instructional coaches.

- We have a clear policy or agreement on confidentiality.

- All administrators in our district understand what instructional coaches do.

- All administrators understand the Partnership Principles at the heart of instructional coaching.

- I understand what I am to do and not do in my role as a coach.

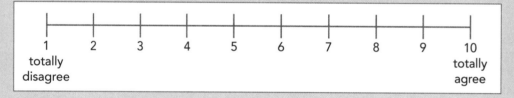

Needs Assessment Survey

Interested in completing the needs assessment online? You can use the following link:

https://qrs.ly/42g4p6q

An Example of How to Use a Learning Path

Sample Learning Path

Guiding Question: What are the Seven Success Factors?

Resources: *Teach to Win* article, The Chunk and Chew 10-2-2 activity

Activity:

1. Read through the Chunk and Chew 10-2-2 activity to become familiar with the process.

2. Engage in reading the *Teach to Win* article.

3. Use the Chunk and Chew 10-2-2 activity to discuss and share your thinking about the text.

4. Wrap up this Learning Path by answering the reflection questions that follow the article.

Teach to Win

Originally published in *Principal Leadership, 15*(7), 24–27. March 2015.

Seven Success Factors for Instructional Coaching Programs

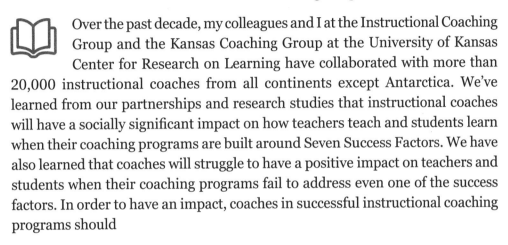 Over the past decade, my colleagues and I at the Instructional Coaching Group and the Kansas Coaching Group at the University of Kansas Center for Research on Learning have collaborated with more than 20,000 instructional coaches from all continents except Antarctica. We've learned from our partnerships and research studies that instructional coaches will have a socially significant impact on how teachers teach and students learn when their coaching programs are built around Seven Success Factors. We have also learned that coaches will struggle to have a positive impact on teachers and students when their coaching programs fail to address even one of the success factors. In order to have an impact, coaches in successful instructional coaching programs should

1. Understand the complexities of working with adults

2. Use an effective coaching cycle

3. Know effective teaching practices

4. Gather data

5. Employ effective communication strategies

6. Be effective leaders

7. Be supported by their schools and districts

Working With Adults

Coaches can know a lot about teaching, but if they don't understand the complexities of working with adults, they might prompt others to resist what they're offering. As I've written in *Unmistakable Impact: A Partnership Approach to Dramatically Improving Instruction* (Knight, 2011a), helping adults is more complex than simply giving expert advice. Professionals want to make decisions for themselves and be recognized with the status they feel they deserve. They take it personally when others criticize their personal work, and they are motivated to reach their goals only when they see them as personally relevant.

For these reasons, coaches should position themselves as partners by respecting teachers' professional autonomy, seeing teachers as equals, offering many choices, giving teachers voice, taking a dialogical approach to interactions, encouraging reflection and real-life application, and seeing coaching as a reciprocal learning opportunity (Knight, 2011b).

The Partnership Principles

1. Equality

2. Choice

3. Voice

4. Dialogue

5. Reflection

6. Praxis

7. Reciprocity

Coaching Cycle

If teachers are to be positioned as professionals, they need to have a lot of autonomy, but coaching must also be accountable. Within coaching, we see accountability as both coaches and teachers getting a clear picture of reality, setting powerful, student-focused goals, and then collaborating until those goals are met. Effective coaching is more than a few conversations; effective coaching leads to socially significant improvements in teaching and learning. Indeed, if student learning is not improving, instructional coaching isn't working.

For the past six years, my colleagues and I at the Kansas Coaching Project at the University of Kansas Center for Research on Learning have used design research to study and refine an instructional coaching cycle that honors teacher autonomy and is accountable (Knight et al., in press). Working with coaches in Beaverton, Oregon, and Othello, Washington, we developed and tested an instructional coaching cycle that incorporates three stages: identify, learn, and improve.

During the **identify** stage of the instructional coaching cycle, the coach and teacher get a clear picture of the current reality in the collaborating teacher's classroom, often by recording a video of a class (Knight, 2014), looking at student work, reviewing assessment data, or some combination of these methods. The coach then guides the teacher to a student-focused goal. Usually student-focused goals deal with student achievement (e.g., for 90 percent of students to score five out of five on a paragraph-writing rubric three times in a row), behavior (e.g., for students to be on-task an average of 95 percent of the time), or attitude (e.g., for 90 percent of students to read for pleasure as measured by students' journal comments). Once a goal has been set, the teacher and coach identify a teaching strategy to be implemented in an attempt to hit the goal.

During the **learn** stage of the instructional coaching cycle, the teacher learns the teaching strategy with the help of the coach. Often, instructional coaches describe teaching practices through the use of checklist, and then suggest various ways the teacher can see the practice in action. For example, a coach might model the practice in the teacher's classroom, the teacher might visit another teacher's classroom where the strategy is being used, or the teacher might watch a video or see the practice in some other way. Once the teacher has learned the practice, it's time to try it out.

During the **improve** stage of the instructional coaching cycle, the teacher tries the new strategy in the classroom. Often the coach video records the lesson and gathers data on students' progress toward the goal. The teacher and coach can make adjustments as necessary, sometimes even choosing another teaching strategy, until the goal is met.

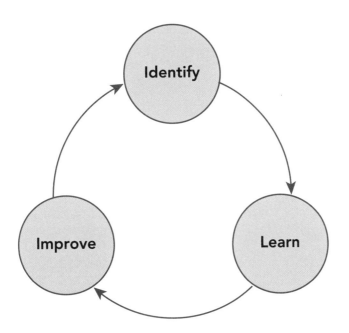

Teaching Practices

Instructional coaches help teachers improve student learning by improving teaching, so instructional coaches need a deep knowledge of a set of strategies that they know will help teachers hit their goals. We refer to this as the "instructional playbook." Strategies included in one's instructional playbook can be found in my book *High-Impact Instruction* (2013), Marzano's (2007) *Art and Science of Teaching*, John Saphire et al.'s (2008) *The Skillful Teacher*, or other publications focused on particular teaching strategies. What counts, though, is that the strategies described in the instructional playbook have all been proven to help teachers meet their goals.

An instructional playbook usually includes a one-page document that lists the teaching strategies teachers most frequently use and checklists that describe the various elements of each instructional strategy.

Thus, for example, a coach's instructional playbook that includes cooperative learning might contain a checklist that describes some general guidelines for implementing cooperative learning, another that describes a specific cooperative learning structure such as the jigsaw classroom technique, and a third that describes what students should do when they are participating in the learning structure.

An effective instructional playbook is (a) comprehensive and addresses planning, assessment, instruction, and community building; (b) focused, including a small number of powerful strategies (ideally described on a single page); and (c) precise, containing a complete set of checklists for all of the included teaching strategies.

Gather Data

Coaches guide teachers to set and achieve goals, so it is essential that they know how to gather basic observational data so that it can be used to set goals and monitor progress. Not all goals require observation. For example, if a teacher has set an achievement goal based on results on formative assessment, they may just need to review the assessments. However, goals do frequently involve coaches observing a class, gathering data, and sharing the data with teachers.

Some of the most important data that coaches can gather include on-task time (i.e., the percentage of students who are doing the learning task that the teacher has assigned); instructional versus noninstructional time; the type, kind, and level of question asked; and the ratio of interaction (i.e., a comparison of how often teachers attend to students when they are on task and learning compared with how often teachers attend to students who are off-task or disruptive).

Communication Skills

Coaching is relational, and coaches need to know how to build healthy relationships. Teachers rarely learn from collaborating coaches unless they see them as people they can trust.

Since teaching is so connected to personal identity, coaches need to be especially adept at a few critical communication issues. Good communicators know that speaking the truth is only half the battle; the challenge is to speak the truth in such a way that it can be heard. We have found that coaches are more effective when they have particular communication skills and habits. Effective coaches usually are good listeners, ask good questions, build emotional connections, find common ground, build trust, and redirect destructive interactions.

Leadership Skills

In addition to communication skills, coaches need to have leadership skills. While leadership certainly involves communication, we have found that the coaches who lead change successfully have two additional attributes. First, they must be deeply respectful and responsive to the teachers with whom they collaborate, adjusting their approach depending on the personality and needs of the teachers and their students.

Second, they must be assertive and disciplined, leading change in an organized, ambitious, forceful manner. Both are necessary.

Coaches who are responsive to teachers but undisciplined will waste teachers' time and often lose sight of the end goal before the coaching cycle is complete. Coaches who are ambitious and disciplined but unresponsive often push teachers away. The most effective coaches, as Jim Collins found when he studied effective leaders in great organizations, "are a study in duality: modest and wilful, humble and fearless" (Collins, 2001, p. 22).

System Support

Instructional coaches who make an impact work in districts that create the conditions that help them be effective. In part, this means that there is district-wide agreement about the coaches' roles (which often means that coaching is understood as a nonadministrative role), what information is and is not confidential, a shared understanding of how coaches will relate to teachers (we suggest the partnership approach), and agreement on how coaches will use their time.

Principals play an incredibly important role in shaping the success or failure of coaches. The most effective principals are instructional leaders who understand the positive impact professional learning can have on student learning. Principals who support coaches walk the walk by leading professional development sessions and agreeing to be coached themselves, perhaps by video recording model lessons and being coached during a staff meeting. Most importantly, principals who support coaches understand the power of coaching and communicate that frequently. If a principal does not speak out about the value of coaching, something needs to be changed, or a coach will struggle to succeed.

When it comes to instructional coaching, little changes can have a big impact. Teaching expectations, using rubrics, increasing positive attention, and using checks for understanding are just a few of the ways teachers working with coaches can dramatically increase student learning. When teachers learn, students learn. Such powerful positive changes won't happen, though, if coaching programs are thrown together carelessly. Effective coaching programs provide professional development, ensuring that the Seven Success Factors described here are in place. When those factors are addressed, truly positive improvements can happen quickly and frequently.

Reflection Questions for "Teach to Win"

1. On a scale of 1 to 10 (1 being at the very beginning and 10 being far along), where are you on your journey to implementing these success factors into your coaching program?

2. What is a new discovery you made about how to ensure success with coaching programs?

3. How important is it that everyone (teachers, coaches, leaders) understands these success factors?

4. What is your next action after exploring the success factors?

NOTES

CHUNK AND CHEW 10-2-2 ACTIVITY

 Purpose: To engage in reading, reflection, and discussion about a text in small chunks

Process:

1. Select a text of focus for a group to read and discuss together.

2. Establish a timekeeper for the group.

3. Before beginning, gather copies of the text and something to record thinking on for each person (a journal, paper, etc.).

4. The timekeeper will set a 10-minute timer (time can be adjusted to 5 minutes if need be), and each person will begin independently reading the text.

5. When the 10-minute timer goes off, the group will spend 2 minutes independently recording their thinking about what they have just read.

6. At the conclusion of the 2 minutes of independent reflection, the group will turn in and spend 2 minutes (time can be adjusted for bigger groups) discussing what they have read so far and their ideas about that material so far.

7. The group will continue this process of 10-2-2 minute sections until the text has been read in its entirety.

Modifications:

– Adjust the 10 minutes of independent reading time if the group has a short time for the protocol.

– Adjust the 2 minutes of independent reflection if the group wishes to have more time to write or reflect on what they have read.

– Adjust the 2 minutes of group discussion if the group is larger or if the group decides 2 minutes is not long enough to share their thoughts. If the group has a longer chunk of time to gather for this protocol, the recommendation is to extend the group discussion to 4 minutes, making the protocol 10-2-4.

How Might Christina Use This Learning Path?

As a Coach Champion, Christina sees the benefit of using this Learning Path with all the instructional coaches she supports. She reads through The Making Meaning activity, gets familiar with the process, and then ensures that she has read the article ahead of time. Then, when her coaches arrive for their monthly professional development, Christina shares the guiding question and all the coaches turn to the article in their copy of *The IC Toolkit*. As the coaches read, they are marking up the text and making brief notes about what they notice. When the timer goes off, Christina calls them back together and facilitates The Making Meaning activity, moving through the steps that include describing the text, asking questions about the text, speculating about the text, and discussing the implications for the coaches' work. Christina facilitates a meaningful discussion with her coaches, inviting them to turn in and talk through each part of The Making Meaning activity to encourage dialogue. As Christina closes out the Learning Path, she invites all the coaches to look at the reflection questions that follow the article. During this moment of individual reflection, the room full of instructional coaches silently answer the questions and consider what they will do next after learning about the success factors.

How Might Jamie Use This Learning Path?

Jamie and his colleagues meet on Zoom for their two-hour monthly learning and discussion. After coaching all week and continuing to build their school's instructional coaching program, they are left wondering what more they can do. Since it was Jamie's turn to choose a Learning Path for the group to use in their gathering, he shares that he has selected a path that will help them see what other factors they can consider taking back to their schools and even share with their respective principals. Jamie and his coach colleagues read the article together, silently reading their own copies and muting their Zoom microphones while they read. Jamie's timer goes off for them to unmute and come back together, and he moves them through the steps of The Making Meaning activity. With each step of the activity, Jamie turns to his coach group and invites them to share. Everyone engages, sharing what they read, asking each other questions, and discussing how this is significant for their schools. After moving through the activity, Jamie shares that they will use the reflection questions to wrap up their discussion. His group prefers to think out loud, so he asks the reflection questions that appear after the article one at a time, and the group shares their ideas together.

How Might Jenn Use This Learning Path?

Jenn is excited that it is time for her Tuesday learning time. She heads back to her classroom after working with a teacher and settles down with her copy of *The IC Toolkit*. Jenn and her principal have been talking a lot about how to continue building their school's coaching program, so Jenn is on a mission to explore how to make that happen. She discovers this Learning Path about the success factors for coaching programs and decides this is exactly what she is looking for today. She notices that the activity has multiple steps to it, so she begins by reading the article and making notes as she goes. Then, she guides herself through the stages of The Making Meaning activity, individually reflecting on what she read, the questions she would like to take back to her principal for discussion, the significance of the success factors, and the implications for her work. As she reflects, she is also gathering ideas for her next meeting with her principal. To wrap up the Learning Path, she uses the lined space in her book to reflect on the article and activity, making the most out of her time to invest in her professional growth. She gathers her notes and emails her principal to schedule their next meeting so she can share what she is left thinking. Jenn also tucks The Making Meaning activity away in her mind: She thinks this would be a great activity to use with teachers in future professional development sessions!

One Last Note

Which scenario most closely fits your context? Use this sample learning path to begin your learning with us, dive into the Seven Success Factors, and practice using *The IC Toolkit*.

Additionally, these are suggestions on how to use Learning Paths. While we have provided you with optional ways to learn, we also encourage you to make this book work for you. Thank you for committing to learn and grow, and for making an unmistakably positive impact on the world around you. Enjoy!

Chapter 1

The Partnership Principles

"I've learned that people will forget what you said, people will forget what you did, but people will never forget how you made them feel."

—*Dr. Maya Angelou*

Success Factor #1: The Partnership Principles

Coaches who invest in their foundational knowledge, beliefs, and approaches to coaching are thinking deeply about **Success Factor #1: The Partnership Principles**. This idea of partnership comes first in the list of Success Factors intentionally. It represents the underlying theory and beliefs coaches have and carry with them into each coaching interaction, serving as a point of reference that guides our actions when partnering with teachers (Knight, 2007, 2022). The seven principles are equality, choice, voice, reflection, dialogue, praxis, and reciprocity. Coaches who actively show up as partners and live by these principles can increase coaching success (Knight, 2022).

So Why Should We Be Talking About The Partnership Principles Within Schools and Systems?

The principles are our "theoretical framework," serving as a lens through which we can view each person and interaction as we coach (Knight, 2022, p. 20). They offer instructional coaches a chance to have a shared vocabulary from which to discuss how they go about coaching teachers (Knight, 2007). When schools and systems explore these principles, they are prioritizing a fundamental element to their coaching from which healthy and productive conversations can flourish.

Resources Included in This Chapter

ARTICLES	ACTIVITIES	SCENARIO	VIDEOS
"Seven Principles for True Partnership"	Text Scramble	Praxis Scenario	The Partnership Principles:
	Storytelling		1. Equality
"Why Teacher Autonomy Is Central to Coaching Success"			2. Choice
	In Closing		3. Voice
			4. Dialogue
"Five Habits of Humility"	Video Reflection: The Partnership Principles		5. Reflection
			6. Praxis
"Dialogue & Trust"			7. Reciprocity
			The Principles of Coaching:
"When Times Are Tough, Show Compassion"			1. Moralistic Judgment

Optional Learning Paths

Learning Path #1

Guiding Question: What are the principles that guide my coaching?

Resources: "Seven Principles for True Partnership" article, Text Scramble activity, The Partnership Principles YouTube videos

Activity:

1. Use the Text Scramble activity to read about and watch videos on The Partnership Principles.

   a. Each scramble group can be assigned one Partnership Principle to explore using the article and the video. For example, one person or group might read about equality and watch the equality video.

2. Wrap up the learning by using the reflection questions that appear after the article.

Learning Path #2

Guiding Question: What role should choice and teacher autonomy play in instructional coaching?

Resources: "Why Teacher Autonomy Is Central to Coaching Success" article, Chunk & Chew activity

Activity:

1. Use the Chunk & Chew activity to read the article "Why Teacher Autonomy Is Central to Coaching Success."

2. Wrap up the learning by using the reflection questions that appear after the article.

Learning Path #3

Guiding Question: How can humility contribute to the Partnership Principle of reciprocity?

Resources: "Five Habits of Humility" article, Storytelling activity

Activity:

1. Read through the Storytelling activity to become familiar with the process.

2. Read the article "Five Habits of Humility," and then use the Storytelling activity to discuss humility and reciprocity.

3. Wrap up the learning by using the reflection questions that appear after the article.

Learning Path #4

<u>Guiding Question:</u> What are the components of the Partnership Principle of dialogue?

<u>Resources:</u> "Dialogue & Trust" article, In Closing activity

<u>Activity:</u>

1. Read through the In Closing activity to become familiar with the process.

2. Read the article and then participate in the In Closing activity to share what stood out about the elements of dialogue.

3. Wrap up the learning by using the reflection questions that appear after the article.

Learning Path #5

<u>Guiding Question:</u> How can the equality Partnership Principle help us avoid moralistic judgment when working with teachers?

<u>Resources:</u> "When Times Are Tough, Show Compassion" article, Principle of Coaching video: Moralistic Judgment

<u>Activity:</u>

1. Watch the video about moralistic judgment. After the video, discuss or think about how this might align with the Partnership Principle of equality.

2. Then, engage in reading about compassion with the article.

3. Wrap up the learning by using the reflection questions that appear after the article.

Learning Path #6

<u>Guiding Question:</u> What role does the Partnership Principle of praxis play in coaching?

<u>Resources:</u> Praxis scenarios

<u>Activity:</u>

1. Use the Praxis scenarios to learn, discuss, and reflect.

2. Wrap up the learning by discussing how praxis will play a role in your coaching.

Learning Path #7

<u>Guiding Question:</u> How can I reflect on *my* use of the Partnership Principles?

<u>Resources:</u> Video Reflection: Partnership Principles

<u>Activity:</u>

1. Use the Partnership Principles Video activity to reflect on your practice.

2. Wrap up the learning path by discussing how video can continue to inform your coaching.

Guiding Question: What are the principles that guide my coaching?

Resources: "Seven Principles for True Partnership" article, Text Scramble activity, The Partnership Principles YouTube videos

Activity:

1. Use the Text Scramble activity to read about and watch videos on The Partnership Principles.

   a. Each scramble group can be assigned one Partnership Principle to explore using the article and the video. For example, one person or group might read about equality and watch the equality video.

2. Wrap up the learning by using the reflection questions that appear after the article.

The Partnership Principles

1. Equality
2. Choice
3. Voice
4. Dialogue
5. Reflection
6. Praxis
7. Reciprocity

Seven Principles for True Partnership

For deep professional learning, create the conditions for dialogue.

Originally published in *Educational Leadership, 80*(1). August 29, 2022.

 When I started out as a professional developer, I wasn't very good. My biggest problem wasn't my large folder of overheads or my limited presentation skills, it was the way I approached my audience. I assumed teachers would see how compelling the research was that I presented and then simply do what I told them they should do. When they didn't embrace my ideas, I labeled them as resistant.

During my presentations, however, I couldn't shake my suspicion that I was the problem, not the teachers. To better understand why my workshops were failing, I read authors from a wide variety of fields—and I changed my approach to PD. Eventually I completely flipped my approach. Instead of telling teachers what they should do, I saw myself as a facilitator creating the conditions for dialogue. Instead of seeing myself as an expert, I saw myself as a partner.

I have summarized what I've learned about partnership in seven principles: equality, choice, voice, dialogue, reflection, praxis, and reciprocity. I've found that when I ground presentations in these principles, as opposed to a directive approach, teachers are more likely to be engaged, to learn, to enjoy learning, and to implement what they are learning.

Translating the Principles Into Practice . . .

Those partnership principles are now a central part of the professional development my colleagues and I deliver and describe to educators. But we are finding that knowledge of the partnership principles doesn't inevitably translate into action. Most troubling for me, personally, is that even I fail to act consistently with the principles. Seeing the gap between what I believe and what I do has led me to think more deeply about what it means to truly approach others from the partnership perspective. To help me, and others, translate the partnership principles into action, I have developed questions anyone can ask themselves so that they can move closer to living out these principles.

. . . And Questions That Help

Equality: "Do I interrupt or moralistically judge others?" When we embrace the principle of equality, we recognize the value and dignity of others. One small but important way we live out this principle during conversation is that we let others speak without interrupting them. Speakers usually interrupt to take control, to put themselves in a superior position; interrupting is a power move. If I see others as equals, I need to let them speak.

When we moralistically judge others, we aren't just discerning a clear picture of reality (as we see it), we are implying or stating that others are bad people—"lazy," "selfish," "clueless," and so on. Moralistically judging others violates the principle of equality since judgment, by definition, comes from a place of superiority.

Choice: "Can I let go of control?" Let's stop talking about "buy-in." A partnership conversation is not one where I try to get you to do what I have decided you need to do. A partnership conversation is a free interchange between equals where each person's ideas, thoughts, and beliefs are valued, and where both partners have the courage to be shaped by each other.

Voice: "Do others know I think their opinions are important?" When we act on the principle of voice, others know that they have been heard. Internally, we need to focus on what others say, listening without assumptions. Externally, we need to put away our devices and communicate nonverbally, make eye contact, have an open stance, not complete someone's sentences, and so on, so that others know they have been heard. Honoring the principle of voice means respectfully communicating that we think their ideas are important.

Dialogue: "Do I see others' strengths? Do I want what's best for them and am I open to being shaped by them?" The best writing I've read about creating the conditions for dialogue is in Paulo Freire's *Pedagogy of the Oppressed*. Dialogue, Freire writes, requires humility, faith, and love. By humility, he means that we open ourselves to others' opinions and let go of the need to be right. By faith, he means that we see others' strengths and competencies. By love, he means that we have others' best interests at heart. When these three conditions exist, trust will follow, and trust is necessary for any meaningful partnership.

Reflection: "Do I avoid giving advice?" Generating ideas and solving problems are very pleasurable experiences. Many of us love to do all that thinking, even if we're doing it for other people. We often find it a real struggle not to jump in and tell others exactly what we know is best for them. Unfortunately, when we gift others with our wisdom, we take away their opportunity to solve their own problems, thereby violating their opportunity to think for themselves.

Praxis: "Does our professional development allow sufficient time for necessary adaptations?" The term *praxis*, as I use it, describes learning experiences that involve real-life applications of learning. Professional development grounded in the principle of praxis is designed so that a learner learns new knowledge through applying that knowledge. Real learning happens in real life.

Reciprocity: "Do I want and expect to learn from others?" One of the rewards of the partnership approach is the chance to learn from others. However, to learn from others, we need, first, to believe that others have something to teach us and, second, to embrace the chance to learn from them. In some ways reciprocity is the quintessential partnership principle. When we open ourselves to others, our world gets bigger, and somehow, because we're open to learning, we often have more influence on others as well.

One More Question

In aiming for partnership relationships, we need to ask ourselves, "Am I treating myself like a partner?" We likely won't snap our fingers and completely change the way we interact with others. I haven't—and I've been writing about partnership for decades. The partnership principles provide a vision for interaction; and day to day, reflecting on our beliefs and actions, we will move closer to that vision. But we shouldn't feel devastated when we struggle as a partner. Treat yourself with self-compassion, the way you would treat a friend. If we are going to treat others as partners, we should do the same to ourselves.

The Partnership Principles

Equality: I don't believe any person or group is more valuable than any other. I recognize and honor the dignity of every individual.

Choice: I communicate in a way that acknowledges the professional discretion of others by positioning them as decision makers.

Voice: I want to hear what others have to say, and I communicate that clearly.

Dialogue: I believe conversations should consist of a back-and-forth exchange, with all parties hearing and responding to one another's opinions.

Reflection: I engage in conversations that look back, look at, and look ahead.

Praxis: I structure learning so that it's grounded in real life.

Reciprocity: I enter each conversation open and expecting to learn.

Reflection Questions for "Seven Principles for True Partnership"

1. How can the Partnership Principles shift the way we lead, coach, or facilitate?

2. Which Partnership Principle challenges you the most? Why?

3. Which Partnership Principle is your school/system already implementing/demonstrating? What does this look like in practice?

4. What might need to change in your school/system?

NOTES

Partnership Principles Videos

https://youtu.be/W4ThA4eSUIU
In this video, Jim talks about the principle of equality.

https://youtu.be/TDV3OGiaS3I
Listen in to the power of yes or no, also known as choice, in this video.

https://youtu.be/NQKwt0DWA1c
Jim describes the third principle, Voice.

https://youtu.be/BDRCrQuTAMg
In this video, Jim discusses how to turn contact into connection with dialogue.

https://youtu.be/mZyAGZdGw_8
Listen to Jim describe the importance of reflection.

https://youtu.be/vU5ds3vDYig
Jim explains that we should call off the fidelity police and focus more on praxis.

https://youtu.be/g8IUpSpINO0
In the final principle, Jim shares how reciprocity is the radical learner's approach to reform.

To read a QR code, you must have a smartphone or tablet with a camera. We recommend that you download a QR code reader app that is made specifically for your phone or tablet brand.

TEXT SCRAMBLE ACTIVITY

 Purpose: To discuss a text with a group of people in a meaningful way.

Process:

1. Select a text of focus for a group to read and discuss together.

2. Establish a timekeeper for the group.

3. Before beginning, divide the text into smaller sections. This can be done by grouping paragraphs together or by using subtitles.

4. Have all participants choose a section of the text to read, ensuring that each section of the text has been distributed. If there are more people than there are sections, it is okay for two people to read the same section.

5. Set a timer, and give everyone time to read their section. Encourage them to look for the following things as they read (this can even be a way to take notes as participants read):

   a. What's this section about?

   b. What am I left thinking after reading this?

   c. What would I want to share about this section with others?

   d. What is the bottom line?

6. After everyone has had time to read and jot notes, bring the group back together and go through the text, making space for each person to share about the section(s) they read.

   a. You can modify this protocol for big groups by putting people into smaller groups to do this work and then bringing everyone back together at the end to share their overall thoughts.

7. Once the group has shared their thoughts on each section of the text, offer a few minutes for participants to silently reflect or write about their final thoughts.

<u>Guiding Question:</u> What role should choice and teacher autonomy play in instructional coaching?

<u>Resources:</u> "Why Teacher Autonomy Is Central to Coaching Success" article, Chunk & Chew activity

<u>Activity:</u>

1. Use the Chunk & Chew activity to read the article "Why Teacher Autonomy Is Central to Coaching Success."

2. Wrap up the learning by using the reflection questions that appear after the article.

Why Teacher Autonomy Is Central to Coaching Success

To foster improvement and responsible accountability, instructional coaches must honor teachers' choices and discretion.

Originally published in *Educational Leadership*, 77(3). November 1, 2019.

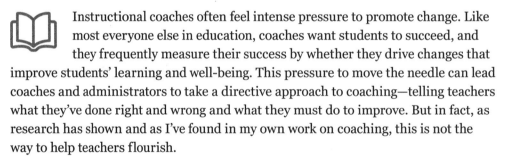 Instructional coaches often feel intense pressure to promote change. Like most everyone else in education, coaches want students to succeed, and they frequently measure their success by whether they drive changes that improve students' learning and well-being. This pressure to move the needle can lead coaches and administrators to take a directive approach to coaching—telling teachers what they've done right and wrong and what they must do to improve. But in fact, as research has shown and as I've found in my own work on coaching, this is not the way to help teachers flourish.

Indeed, after studying coaching for more than 20 years, I have concluded that recognizing and honoring teacher autonomy is an essential and fundamental part of effective coaching.

What Teacher Autonomy Isn't

Before discussing why autonomy is essential, it is important to recognize what autonomy is not. In any organization, there are non-negotiables that must be adhered to—rare is the school where a teacher can say "I'm not much of a morning person; I think I'll start teaching at noon." And choosing to be unprofessional in conduct should not be a choice available to anyone involved in educating our children. No one in a school is free to bully students, be a toxic force on teams, or decide that they no longer need to improve. Fortunately, such unprofessional behavior is rare, but when it exists, it needs to be dealt with directly by administrators. Refraining from upholding professional standards of acceptable teaching is not a matter of honoring autonomy.

But genuine autonomy is a key aspect of coaching work, one that can be complex and challenging for coaches to manage. Indeed, when coaches and leaders recognize the importance of autonomy, they may need to rethink many traditional elements of professional development, including accountability, feedback, and fidelity.

Fostering Self-Determination

An ever-increasing body of research shows that professionals are rarely motivated when they have little autonomy. Researchers have illuminated why autonomy is essential for motivation and why exclusively top-down approaches to change are almost always guaranteed to fail (Amabile et al., 1996; Deci & Ryan, 2000; Pink, 2009; Seligman, 2012).

Edward Deci and Richard Ryan (2000) synthesized their decades of research on motivation into what they referred to as Self-Determination Theory. They proposed that people have three innate human needs—competence, autonomy, and relatedness—that will increase motivation when met and decrease motivation when not met. That is, people will feel motivated when they (a) are competent at what they do, (b) have a large measure of control over their lives, and (c) are engaged in positive relationships. The opposite is also true: When people are controlled and told what to do, aren't in situations where they can increase their competence, and aren't experiencing positive relationships, their motivation will decrease, and they will be "crushed" (p. 68). Research in education has firmly established that this dynamic applies to teachers (Sparks & Malkus, 2015).

Despite evidence of the importance of autonomy, however, research suggests that autonomy is decreasing in schools. One survey-based study found that teachers' perceptions of their autonomy decreased significantly from 2003 to 2012 (Sparks & Malkus, 2015). Close to one in four teachers reported they had no control or only minor control over the books they used, the content they taught, teaching techniques, student evaluation, student discipline, or the amount of homework they gave students.

Coaches must work to change this dynamic. If we want engaged and motivated teachers, we need to ensure that they have significant choices about what they do, including having the right to say no to particular proposals. Choices are the way we define our own humanity—who we are—so stripping away people's right to choose is dehumanizing (Block, 1993).

When professionals are told what to do and given no choice, the best possible outcome is likely compliance—and compliance is not enough to do the complex work needed in our schools. As Daniel Pink (2009) writes in *Drive: The Surprising Truth About What Motivates Us*:

> Living a satisfying life requires more than simply meeting the demands of those in control. Yet in our offices and classrooms, we have way too much compliance and way too little engagement. The former might get you through the day, but only the latter will get you through the night. (p. 112)

Responsible Accountability

One obstacle to honoring teachers' autonomy, in my view, is that school leaders and policymakers often misunderstand the role of accountability. Usually, the term is used to describe how educators are obligated to do something for some external reason. It's common, for example, to hear that teachers' professional learning must be driven by adherence to a mandated instructional program or initiative. Or that teachers must be told what to work on based on school or district priorities.

I refer to such understandings of accountability as irresponsible accountability. This kind of accountability places all the responsibility for decision making outside the teacher. Such an approach is bound to fail. People are rarely motivated by others' goals, and a one-size-fits-all model of change rarely provides helpful solutions for the individual complexities of each unique classroom.

Recently, at a coaching workshop I conducted in Kansas, an instructional coach from Texas painted a vivid picture of what irresponsible accountability can look like in schools. She told us about an interaction that took place when her principal went to talk with a teacher about her students' low test scores. When the principal raised the issue, the teacher pointed out that she was implementing the program the district had told her to implement. "I did everything I was told to do, and I did it with fidelity," she said. "If my students aren't doing well, I'm not the problem—it's your program."

Responsible accountability is different. When educators are responsibly accountable, their professional learning is driven by what they have determined will have an impact on their students' learning. In this way, they are accountable to the improvement process—and to students, parents, other stakeholders, and the profession of teaching. Responsible accountability entails a genuine individual commitment to learning and growth.

An Example of Responsible Accountability

Instructional coaching, done well, should foster responsible accountability. During coaching, teachers should have a great deal of autonomy even though they are learning with a coach. For instance, a coach using the Impact Cycle (Knight, 2018), with stages for identifying, learning, and improving, might video record a lesson and provide the teacher with some suggestions to better interpret what the video reveals.

Following this, the coach and teacher usually have a coaching conversation to identify a goal that the teacher really cares about and that will have an unmistakably positive impact on student learning or well-being. Once a goal is set, they identify a teaching strategy the teacher will implement in an attempt to hit the goal.

During the learning stage, the coach and teacher collaborate to prepare the teacher to implement the new strategy effectively. This often involves the coach explaining the strategy and the teacher modifying it to better meet her students' needs. Often the teacher watches the coach, another teacher, or a video to better understand the strategy before implementing it. Finally, during the improving stage, the teacher, in partnership with the coach, makes adaptations until the goal is met.

Let's look at how this might play out for an individual teacher. Imagine a teacher who views a video recording of her lesson and sees that only 5 of her 31 students responded to the questions she asked. In conversation with her coach, she might decide to set a goal of increasing the number of students responding to questions during each lesson to 20. Once she has set the goal, she and the coach can discuss various strategies she might use to meet it. For example, she might try thinking prompts, effective questions, or a cooperative-learning approach such as think, pair, share (Knight, 2013). She or the coach could videotape her lessons to monitor her progress. As long as she remains committed to her goal, she can keep partnering with the coach to identify strategies or refine what she is implementing until she hits her goal.

This is professional learning that is undeniably accountable—measurable changes will occur that will mean real improvements for students. However, this type of professional learning also involves a high degree of autonomy: The teacher, with support from the coach, observes her own lesson, sets her own goal, adapts the teaching strategies she implements, monitors progress, and determines when she has hit the goal.

The Complexity of Teaching

School leaders and coaches must also understand that teaching is not something that can be boiled down to a set of prescriptive steps. Its complexity requires independent decision making and self-directed growth.

In a groundbreaking study published in 2002, researchers Sholom Glouberman and Brenda Zimmerman broke down the complexity levels of different work tasks. They identified three different types of tasks: simple, complicated, and complex. A simple task, like baking a cake, involves a set of steps that will produce the same results each time when the steps are followed. A complicated task, Glouberman and Zimmerman argued, like putting a person on the moon, involves much more intricate work, but it still involves formulas and steps that should produce predictable outcomes. A complex task, like raising a 3-year old, cannot be broken down into a set of steps because every day and every child is different.

Leadership experts Alexander Grashow, Ronald Heifetz, and Marty Linsky (2009) have described the kinds of challenges presented by simple and complicated tasks as technical challenges. Such challenges "have known solutions that can be implemented by current know-how. They can be resolved through the application of authoritative expertise" (p. 19). By contrast, the kinds of challenges presented by complex tasks are adaptive challenges: "Adaptive challenges can only be addressed through changes in people's priorities, beliefs, habits, and loyalties. Making progress requires going beyond any authoritative expertise to mobilize discovery, shedding certain entrenched ways, tolerating losses, and generating new ideas to thrive anew" (p. 19).

If raising one child is complex, then educating and inspiring a room full of children must be considered dauntingly complex, and certainly anyone who has taught recognizes how many variables are at play in the classroom. Much of teaching, in other words, requires adaptability, meaning that discretion and personal discovery are essential to success, and that one-size-fits-all solutions or external dictates will only hamstring progress.

To be sure, technical solutions are appropriate for simple and complicated classroom tasks like organizing a seating chart or teaching some basic procedures. But much of teaching is complex work, and technical solutions will not suffice. Indeed, Heifetz, Grashow, and Linsky (2009) write that "the most common failure in leadership is produced by treating adaptive challenges as if they were technical problems" (p. 19).

Feedback as Dialogue

When people describe what coaches do, one of the chief tasks they identify is giving feedback. However, as Buckingham and Goodall (2019) recently argued in the *Harvard Business Review*, many people's understanding of feedback is completely backwards. For many of us, feedback "is about telling people what we think of their performance and how they should do it better." But, as Buckingham and Goodall explain, "The research is clear: Telling people what we think of their performance doesn't help them thrive and excel, and telling people how we think they should improve actually *hinders* learning."

Buckingham and Goodall (2009) identify three fundamental flaws in the prevailing understanding of how to provide feedback. First, we are not very good at rating others' performance. Our evaluations of other people, they maintain, have more to do with ourselves than with those we are observing. Second, simply telling others how they fall short actually inhibits, rather than encourages, learning. Buckingham and Goodall present compelling research showing that hearing criticism shifts people into survival mode, thereby "impairing" learning. "Learning," the authors write, "rests on our grasp of what we're doing well, not on what we're doing poorly, and certainly not on someone else's sense of what we're doing poorly." And third, excellence isn't reducible to universal and simple explanations. As Buckingham and Goodall explain:

> Since excellence is idiosyncratic and cannot be learned by studying failure, we can never help another person succeed by holding her performance up against a prefabricated model of excellence, giving her feedback on where she misses the model, and telling her to plug the gaps.

What does this mean in connection with instructional coaching? First, the lesson (again) is that honoring the autonomy of teachers in coaching is essential if feedback is to lead to improved practice. Rather than telling teachers what they like and dislike about a lesson, coaches should structure conversations with teachers as dialogues between two equal partners, where both members of the conversation are heard and where both parties' opinions count.

Second, as education authors like William Sommers, Parker Palmer, and Robert Garmston have pointed out, effective dialogue is often enabled through a third point for conversation that takes the focus off the coach and teacher and directs it toward whatever the two are exploring together. This increases the teacher's role in the feedback process. Two powerful "third points" are student work and video recordings of teachers' lessons.

Third, coaching conversations are more effective when they are nonjudgmental. This doesn't mean that coaches shouldn't share what they think; instead, they should share their thoughts provisionally and with the humility appropriate for any conversation about what happens in a classroom.

Questions of Fidelity

A final argument often given for top-down professional learning is that effective teaching practices must be implemented with fidelity, so coaches need to ensure that teachers are proceeding as prescribed. This point of view is easy to justify in theory. If teachers don't teach evidence-based practices with fidelity, the thinking is, they won't get results. Therefore, coaches need to make sure teachers implement teaching practices the way research says they were meant to be implemented.

Unfortunately, too narrow a focus on fidelity can actually stand in the way of quality instruction. Without question, instructional coaches need to partner with teachers to provide the supports that empower teachers to implement new practices in ways that get results. But it's the results that matter, not the fidelity to process. By results I mean positive changes in student learning and well-being. Fidelity of implementation doesn't mean much if there aren't positive changes for students.

One of the problems with fidelity is that asking teachers to implement exactly what a script says, exactly as the script says, treats teachers like workers on an assembly line rather than professionals. An overemphasis on fidelity could lead to teachers doing every move on a checklist but teaching without passion or engagement, or even teaching in ways that fail to promote student learning.

A second, more important issue is that teaching is too complex to conform to a one-size-fits-all model. A fidelity approach embodies the idea that solutions to instructional challenges are technical—when, in reality, they must be adaptive.

To be sure, instructional coaches need to be deeply versed in the practices they share, and they should be highly skilled at finding precise, easy-to-understand explanations for those practices. However, they need to present information in a way that allows the teacher to do the thinking. When explaining a teaching practice, an effective instructional coach might say, "Here's what the research says. However, do we need to adapt this at all so it will work for you and your students? What do you think about this approach?" When, for the sake of fidelity, coaches tell teachers what to do without honoring their thoughts and opinions, they are crushing motivation and inviting resistance.

Finally, coaching should be a goal-directed process, as opposed to an exercise in micromanagement. Only an effectively executed practice will lead to positive results for students. So rather than telling teachers exactly what to do, instructional coaches should engage teachers in reflective conversations about what they think might work in their classrooms. By treating teachers like professionals, instructional coaches have a much better chance of enabling high-quality teaching and better student learning—and isn't that the whole point?

Real Choices

When school leaders and coaches dismiss the importance of teacher autonomy, they usually do so because they are so concerned about students' needs that they just can't feel at ease giving up control. But as we've seen, a rigid emphasis on accountability and control ultimately hampers teacher development. External mandates and top-down coaching typically fail—because ultimately they are disempowering and dehumanizing and fail to address the complexity of the classroom. A better option is to infuse coaching with autonomy. When teachers have real choices, when they are engaged in coaching that is responsibly accountable, then real student growth is possible.

Reflection Questions for "Why Teacher Autonomy Is Central to Coaching Success"

1. Can you think of a time in your school or district when a "directive approach" to coaching or professional development (PD) had a counterproductive effect on teachers?

2. If so, how could the training have been done differently?

3. Can you describe examples of "responsible accountability" in your school? What conditions helped create them?

4. What could you change in your coaching or supervision to better honor teachers' autonomy? How comfortable are you about making that change?

NOTES

_____

_____

_____

_____

_____

_____

_____

_____

_____

_____

_____

_____

CHUNK AND CHEW ACTIVITY

 Purpose: To engage in reading, reflection, and discussion about a larger text in small chunks.

Process:

1. Select a text of focus for a group to read and discuss together.

2. Establish a timekeeper for the group.

3. Before beginning, gather copies of the text and something to record thinking on for each person (a journal, paper, etc.).

4. The timekeeper will set a 10-minute timer (time can be adjusted to 5 minutes if need be), and each person will begin independently reading the text.

5. When the 10-minute timer goes off, the group will spend 2 minutes independently recording their thinking about what they have just read.

6. At the conclusion of the 2 minutes of independent reflection, the group will turn in and spend 2 minutes (time can be adjusted for bigger groups) discussing what they have read so far and their ideas about that material so far.

7. The group will continue this process of 10-2-2 minute sections until the text has been read in its entirety.

Modifications:

– Adjust the 10 minutes of independent reading time if the group has a short time for the protocol.

– Adjust the 2 minutes of independent reflection if the group wishes to have more time to write or reflect on what they have read.

– Adjust the 2 minutes of group discussion if the group is larger or if the group decides 2 minutes is not long enough to share their thoughts. If the group has a longer chunk of time to gather for this protocol, the recommendation is to extend the group discussion to 4 minutes, making the protocol 10-2-4.

<u>Guiding Question:</u> How can humility contribute to the Partnership Principle of reciprocity?

<u>Resources:</u> "Five Habits of Humility" article, Storytelling activity

<u>Activity:</u>

1. Read through the Storytelling activity to become familiar with the process.

2. Read the article "Five Habits of Humility," and then use the Storytelling activity to discuss humility and reciprocity.

3. Wrap up the learning by using the reflection questions that appear after the article.

Five Habits of Humility

These practices can help coaches achieve the humility they need.

Originally published *in Educational Leadership, 81*(3). November 1, 2023.

 "If we learn to open our hearts, anyone, including the people who drive us crazy, can be our teacher."—Buddhist author and teacher Pema Chödrön

When John Dickson (2011), author of the book *Humilitas*, told a friend he was planning to write about humility, his friend responded snarkily, "Well, John, at least you have the objective distance from the subject!" (p. 12). I feel my friends could make that same comment about me. I'm especially interested in the topic because I recognize a need to foster more humility in myself.

Humility, though, isn't just a personal growth area for me. I want to learn about humility because I have seen ample evidence that it's important in learning, especially in leading and coaching. When I ask coaches and administrators in my workshops to describe leaders who positively shaped their lives, humility is the trait that's always mentioned. Most experts in leadership, positive psychology, self-help, and religion also identify humility as essential. To lead, to persuade, to be a good person, to live a true and beautiful life, they say, we must be humble.

What Is Humility Anyway?

Humility is tricky to define. When I asked people on Twitter to define it, I got a variety of helpful responses. Respondents said humility is putting others ahead of ourselves, listening before talking, caring, and recognizing how small we are within the awesome grandeur of the cosmos. Some defined humility as being a partner, not a controller, or as having the courage to change our views based on what we learn from others. As one respondent, @tech_and_tacos, wrote on Twitter, "Humility involves putting aside pride, position, and ego to connect with others and assist them in reaching their desired goals." Humility is also risky; when we put others' interests ahead of our own, sometimes our interests get overlooked.

We can gain a better understanding of the power of humility when we consider the alternative: arrogance. When we move through the world arrogantly, our pride and self-interest interfere with our ability to learn—after all, if we're sure we're right, what can we learn from others? Arrogance damages relationships and limits our ability to influence people. As John Dickson (2011) noted in *Humilitas*, "It is a simple observational reality that the humble are frequently more persuasive and inspiring than the arrogant" (p. 135).

Understanding what humility is not is just as important as understanding what it is. Humility is not being a doormat. People will be less effective advocates for others if they fail to advocate for themselves. Humility isn't a lack of confidence. Even a humble coach, for example, should be confident about the coaching cycle they're leading and open to learning from their collaborating teacher. Humility also doesn't mean we have low self-efficacy. Consider this quote often attributed to C. S. Lewis: "Humility isn't thinking less of yourself, it is thinking of yourself less."

Yes, We Can Learn Humility

I'm convinced that humility is a learned skill, not just something we're born with (or without). Certainly, our genetic inheritance and environment shape who we are. But the following five "humble habits" should move us down the humble path at least a little.

1. **Listen first.** Letting our partners speak first is a way of demonstrating humility. When we authentically listen, we quiet our minds and prioritize what the other person is saying so we can understand their needs and emotions. When we listen first, we learn what others know before we start sharing what we know. Humble listening isn't a simple technique; it's a way of interacting that communicates that we genuinely value what the other person has to say.

2. **See the good in others.** My working assumption about life is that everyone has goodness in them if you dig deep enough. We can foster our humility by looking for that goodness in others and letting them know we see it. This isn't always easy. Our brains are wired to see the negative first, so we need to be intentional about looking for the good in others. And we need to accept others' imperfections. When we let go of the need to judge and adopt a desire to appreciate, we move closer to being humble.

3. **Be ready to admit you're wrong.** We aren't being humble if we feel we always need to be right. We also aren't learning as much as we could if we're unable to admit when we're wrong. To be a little humbler, we should actively encourage others to help us see our errors, asking questions like, "If someone were to criticize this idea, what would they say?" or "What can you see here that I am missing?"

4. **Get a clear picture of reality.** One of the surest ways to become humbler is to see reality from different perspectives. Having a clear picture of reality gives us perspective on how we fit into the big and complex aspects of life. It can help us be more grateful and more aware of the limits of our own ideas. Usually,

reality will teach us that our suggestions aren't as helpful as we think they are, and people don't want our ideas as much as we think they do. This is why I believe that video is like steroids for learning. Coaches can video record their conversations to see, as my friend Christian van Nieuwerburgh likes to say, "what it feels like to be on the other side of me."

5. **Speak humbly.** If we want to be humbler, we must consider what message our words are communicating. When we say "my school" or "my teachers," for example, we may unintentionally communicate that we have power over others or even that we "own" the teachers. A humbler way of talking is to speak about "our school" or "our community." Additionally, humble communicators often offer ideas provisionally ("Let me just put this on the table for us to discuss" or "You know more about your students than I do") to allow room for others' views. And when people share ideas in a humble way, they often end up being more influential.

Moving Closer

These five habits are only a few ways of practicing humility. What matters most is that we avoid action or ways of communicating that suggest that we think I'm better than this person. We may never achieve purely humble intentions; our actions are always a complex mixture of concern for others and ourselves. But we can move closer to being humbler.

And one other thing to remember: When we think we really are very humble—we probably aren't.

Author's note: Many of the ideas in this column grew out of a conversation I had with my humble friend, Christian van Nieuwerburgh.

Reflection Questions for "Five Habits of Humility"

1. How does humility connect to the Partnership Principle of reciprocity?

2. What are nonexamples of humility? Why do we need to know this, too?

3. What is the most important way we can learn humility?

4. How can humility show up in our coaching?

NOTES

_____

_____

_____

_____

_____

_____

_____

STORYTELLING ACTIVITY

 Purpose: To make meaning by engaging in storytelling with a group on a given topic.

Process:

1. Select a text of focus for a group to read and discuss together.

2. Establish a timekeeper for the group.

3. Give everyone 5 to 10 minutes to read the selected text individually.

4. After reading, share that each person will use the ideas from the text to generate a story that they can call to mind based on an idea from the text, the topic of the text, or anything else that it brings up for them.

5. Give everyone 2 to 3 minutes to come up with (and possibly write down) their story.

6. Decide how stories will be shared:

    a. In pairs

    b. Whole group

    c. In small groups

7. Be sure to establish agreements for how the group will be during each story. For example, will everyone sit quietly? Will people ask questions? Will the speaker stand or sit? Ensure psychological safety is in place, so each person feels ready to share their stories, if they want to.

Modifications:

– Adjust the timing to fit the text and group size.

Storytelling can also be done before reading a text to share what people are already thinking about a topic and then built upon after reading to see what might have changed after engaging in the reading.

Learning Path #4 Resources
What Are the Components of
the Partnership Principle of Dialogue?

Guiding Question: What are the components of the Partnership Principle of dialogue?

Resources: "Dialogue & Trust" article, In Closing activity

Activity:

1. Read through the In Closing activity to become familiar with the process.

2. Read the article, and then participate in the In Closing activity to share what stood out about the elements of dialogue.

3. Wrap up the learning by using the reflection questions that appear after the article.

Dialogue & Trust

Originally published in *Principal Connections, 23*(3). Summer 2020.

When I was an undergraduate student at Wilfrid Laurier University, I stumbled into a philosophy of education course taught by Dr. Robert Litke, which ultimately changed my life. I left the course very interested in education and deeply affected by Paulo Freire's (2017) *Pedagogy of the Oppressed*. Freire's book challenged me then, and it still does today. I find the book to be wise, provocative and humanizing, and, among many other things, it offers a concise summary of some of the necessary conditions for dialogue, and ultimately trust to flourish. Dialogue, Freire says, requires love, humility, and faith.

Love

"Love," Freire (2017) writes," is . . . an act of courage, not of fear . . . [a] commitment to other people" (p. 78). Dialogue, Freire writes, "cannot exist . . . in the absence of a profound love for the world and for [people]" (p. 77). This sounds wonderful, but what does Freire mean by the word love?

Margaret Atwood has famously written, "The Eskimos have 52 words for snow because it is so special to them; there ought to be as many for love." Apparently, Atwood may be wrong about the number of words for snow in the Inuktitut, but she is right that we need many different definitions for love. Few words in English have been more trivialized than that word, and too often it seems like a vague empty term. However, thanks to writers such as Freire, I have come to see love in very specific ways. My definition is shaped by my reading of Dallas Willard, a former philosophy professor at University of Southern California. Willard defined love as "engaging your will for the good of another," genuinely wanting what is best for those around us, or truly having an attitude of benevolence for others. Simply put, when two people engage their wills for the good of each other, the opportunity for dialogue presents itself, and the foundation for trust is put in place. For this reason, love is a necessary prerequisite for dialogue.

The opposite is also true. If we go into a conversation using dialogue as a method to get buy-in, or to manipulate someone into buying what we are selling, a strategy, idea or advice, we aren't going to have a dialogue. The heart of a dialogue is each conversation partner's mutual desire for what is best for each other, or simply put, love.

Humility

"Dialogue," Freire (2017) writes, "cannot exist without humility" (p. 78). Since dialogue is a back and forth form of conversation, we need to go into the conversation, open to, perhaps even expecting to, change our opinions if we want to engage in dialogue. People who are sure they are right, and who aren't interested in learning from others, won't experience dialogue.

To be humble doesn't mean we choose to have low self-efficacy, or worse that we pretend to have low self-efficacy. We can, and should, believe in our ideas and be open to learning, and willing to be wrong. When we approach others with a desire to hear what they have to say, rather than with a desire to put them in their place, then we are moving toward a more dialogical way of being.

Faith

"Faith in [people]," Freire (2017) writes, "is an a priori requirement for dialogue; the dialogical [person] believes in other [people] even before he meets them face to face" (p. 79). Simply put, if we are going to have dialogue with someone else, we need to believe in them. If we dismiss people as having nothing to teach us, then dialogue is pretty much impossible. What does it mean to believe in other people? It means we believe they can and want to do good. It means that we believe they can teach us something. We approach them as learners not as judgers, expecting that they can and will teach us something.

One way to understand what it means to believe in people is to consider thinking about what it looks like when we don't believe in others. This lack of belief can show up in many different behaviors. First off, if we see a conversation as a one-way kind of conversation, where our goal is to give advice, to tell people what they've done right and wrong, to tell people what their next steps should be, we won't experience dialogue. A school where the professional development is designed to tell teachers what to do is often a school where teachers eventually stop thinking for themselves and tell the coach, "Just tell me what to do, and I'll do it."

Trust

When we approach others with love, faith and humility, trust should be the natural outcome. Freire (2017) writes, "it would be a contradiction in terms if dialogue— loving, humble and full of faith—did not produce this climate of mutual trust" (p. 80). Trust is established by dialogue, but it will be diminished or destroyed if love, faith and humility are not there. "False love, false humility, and feeble faith in [people] cannot inspire trust" (p. 80).

I have found Freire's (2017) simple descriptions of the conditions for dialogue and trust to be very helpful. If we sense people are hesitating to trust us, for example, we can reflect on whether we truly are engaging our wills for their good, communicating that we believe in them, and approaching them with humility. When our words and actions embody love, faith and humility, others will trust us, and when trust occurs, we may find ourselves swept up in important, life-changing conversations.

Reflection Questions for "Dialogue & Trust"

1. How can we practice the concept of love in coaching?

2. What might humble conversations look, sound, or feel like?

3. How can we communicate or demonstrate faith in our conversation partners?

4. What impact would it have on trust if humility, faith, or love was missing?

NOTES

IN CLOSING ACTIVITY

 Purpose: to share final thoughts about a text and to build on those ideas by hearing diverse perspectives.

Process:

1. Select a text for this protocol, and have all participants read the text.

2. Once everyone is done reading, give them time to go back through the text and find three big ideas that resonated with them.

3. On a piece of paper or sticky note, have participants write those three big ideas down.

4. Then, invite participants to reread all three of the big ideas and come up with one sentence that captures the essence of those big ideas. In other words, summarize what stood out to them the most with one sentence.

5. Once everyone has their summary sentence, the rounds begin. Here are the three steps for each round:

    a. To begin, one person (the speaker) will read aloud their summary sentence.

    b. Then, the rest of the group will take turns sharing what that person's summary sentence means to them by building on their ideas.

    c. Once anyone who is interested has shared their ideas about the speaker's summary sentence, it is the speaker's turn again. At this time, the speaker will say, "In closing . . . " and share the final thought they have after hearing from the group.

6. The rounds continue for each person in the group to share their summary sentence and follow the three steps listed in the previous step.

    a. This can be modified for large groups by creating smaller groups to ensure efficient use of time and increased voice equity.

<u>Guiding Question:</u> How can the equality Partnership Principle help us avoid moralistic judgment when working with teachers?

<u>Resources:</u> "When Times Are Tough, Show Compassion" article, Principle of Coaching video: Moralistic Judgment

<u>Activity:</u>

1. Watch the video about moralistic judgment. After the video, discuss or think about how this might align with the Partnership Principle of equality.

2. Then, engage in reading about compassion with the article.

3. Wrap up the learning by using the reflection questions that appear after the article.

When Times Are Tough, Show Compassion

Originally published in *The Learning Professional: The Learning Forward Journal, 42(6)*. December 2021.

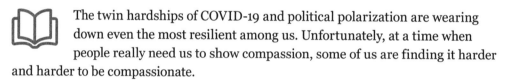 The twin hardships of COVID-19 and political polarization are wearing down even the most resilient among us. Unfortunately, at a time when people really need us to show compassion, some of us are finding it harder and harder to be compassionate.

Compassion, as Sara Schairer (2019) has explained, is different from both sympathy and empathy. "Sympathy," Schairer writes, "means you can understand what the person is feeling," whereas empathy means "you feel what a person is feeling." Finally, compassion means that you are "willing to relieve the suffering of another." In short,

- Sympathy = understanding.

- Empathy = understanding + feeling.

- Compassion = understanding + feeling + action.

As I've reflected on Schairer's definitions and my own attempts to be more compassionate during these challenging times, I've come up with two things I can do to try to be more compassionate.

Choose Affirmation Over Moralistic Judgment

One thing that can interfere with the ability to be compassionate is moralistic judgment. As Margaret Wheatley (2009) has written, "It's not our differences that divide us. It's our judgment about each other that do" (p. 47). When we moralistically judge others, we move beyond simply looking at reality and add negative thoughts or words about others' character or competence. Moralistic judgment, at its core, means expressing contempt ("I can't believe they talk, teach, parent, or simply act like that!"). Not surprisingly, it is difficult to feel contempt and be compassionate at the same time.

The opposite of moralistic judgment is affirmation, noticing the good in others as opposed to noticing the bad. When we affirm others, we see their strengths and, at the same time, hold up a mirror for them so they can also see their strengths. I can start to be less judgmental by considering what I truly believe: Do I want to separate myself from others (as being judgmental always does), or do I want to connect with others? If I believe in our common humanity, I want to connect with others and, therefore, need to try my best to affirm rather than moralistically judge others.

Choose Gratitude Over Resentment

Feelings of resentment also make it hard to be compassionate. We resent others when we think they are getting more or are being treated better than we are. Feelings of resentment are especially common when resources are limited or times are uncertain, as is the case today. I learned about overcoming resentment some time ago when my wife, Jenny, had a terrible case of food poisoning. After I rushed her to the hospital and watched the medical team give her intensive emergency treatment, I started to worry that the poison in her system was so toxic that it could be fatal.

In that moment, when I thought I might lose my life partner, all the petty resentments I'd ever felt toward her disappeared instantaneously. All I felt was gratitude for her and an overwhelming awareness that I didn't want to lose her. For me, this awareness of gratitude is the way to reduce resentment. Gratitude helps me see the resentments that are superficial. Resentment, after all, is believing I didn't get what I deserved. Gratitude, on the other hand, is noticing the many great gifts I receive from the people I know. As such, gratitude is the antidote to resentment.

In conclusion, let me add three final points. First, seeing the good in others can reduce moralistic judgment, and being grateful can reduce resentment, but that doesn't mean we should ignore unjust actions or abuse. For example, we need to fight against (not affirm) systemic racism, sexism, and all forms of dehumanizing action by people and systems, and we need to confront (not excuse) those who dehumanize us.

Second, showing compassion for others is difficult if we don't feel compassion for ourselves. As Kristin Neff (2012) has explained, we are often harder on ourselves than we would ever be on anyone else. To be compassionate toward others, we need to start with ourselves. That is, we should "treat ourselves," Neff writes, "with the same kindness, caring, and compassion we would show to a good friend" (p. 6).

Third, deep change takes deep work. Becoming more grateful and more affirmative is a lifetime journey. I know this from personal experience. I won't become a new person overnight, but I can take one small step toward being more affirmative and more grateful, one step closer to being the compassionate person my friends, colleagues, and loved ones need.

PARTNERSHIP
PRINCIPLES

Taking that one step won't completely change me, but it might help me be more compassionate, and, on any given day, that might be all that someone needs.

Reflection Questions for "When Times Are Tough, Show Compassion"

1. What did you used to think of compassion? What do you think now?

2. What holds us back from compassion? Why?

3. What role does gratitude play in compassion?

4. What do you most agree with from the article?

NOTES

Principles of Coaching Video

Moralistic Judgment

https://youtu.be/ZHr0XVkVyw4
Watch this video to hear about how we should avoid moralistic judgment so we can remain true partners.

<u>Guiding Question:</u> What role does the Partnership Principle of praxis play in coaching?

<u>Resources:</u> Praxis scenarios

<u>Activity:</u>

1. Use the praxis scenarios to learn, discuss, and reflect.

2. Wrap up the learning by discussing how praxis will play a role in your coaching.

PRAXIS SCENARIOS

 Purpose: To consider and reflect on how the Partnership Principle of praxis can be used in coaching situations.

Scenario 1

Nichole is coaching Julie whom she has known "forever." Julie tells Nichole she wants to work on "higher levels of student engagement" and tells Nichole she would love her to bring her some strategies because she is "at a loss with these kids." Nichole is excited Julie has asked for coaching support—even if it is just to find strategies. That said, she knows Julie would love the Impact Cycle and seeing her students meet goals if she could just get her started on the process. Nichole has found several engagement strategies to share. Her coaching meeting with Julie is next week, and she is worried Julie will just take the strategies, vent, and not want to set a student-focused goal.

Reflect

As Nichole's coach, outline next steps to help her move from "good intentions to action" with Julie. How could she enroll her in an Impact Cycle? Be as detailed as possible when describing her next steps to move Nichole into the Identify Phase and setting a PEERS goal.

NOTES

Scenario 2

Rhonda is coaching Matt. He is new to the school this year. Matt tells her he wants to work on classroom management. Matt says he already knows what he wants for a goal and wonders if Rhonda could bring him some strategies and come in and coach him for the next few classes, just until he "gets the curriculum down." Rhonda comes to you, her Coach Lead, seeking advice. She was truly hoping to begin an Impact Cycle with Matt and feels he would be willing but doesn't have a clear understanding of Instructional Coaching as he is new to the district.

Reflect

Describe in as much detail as possible what your coaching conversation with Rhonda would sound like. What kinds of questions would you ask her? What resources might you use? How would you help her partner with Matt to help him set a student-focused goal and commit to starting the Impact Cycle coaching process?

NOTES

_____

_____

_____

_____

_____

_____

_____

_____

_____

_____

_____

_____

_____

_____

_____

_____

_____

Learning Path #7 Resources
How Can I Reflect on My Use of the Partnership Principles?

Guiding Question: How can I reflect on my use of the Partnership Principles?

Resources: Video Reflection: Partnership Principles

Activity:

1. Use the Partnership Principles Video activity to reflect on your practice.

2. Wrap up the learning path by discussing how video can continue to inform your coaching.

VIDEO REFLECTION: PARTNERSHIP PRINCIPLES

 Purpose: To reflect on how we embody Partnership Principles in our conversations with others.

Materials: In this activity, participants will be recording themselves during a conversation. Cell phones make great tools for this, and no other tool is needed. Simply find a way to prop up the phone and record the conversations that will happen in pairs. The video will be reviewed by the partnership only, not shared with anyone else or in the group setting.

Process:

1. Invite participants to choose a partner for this activity.

2. Once all participants have a partner, explain that they will be audio or video recording conversations with each other to reflect on the Partnership Principles. Recording yourself can be uncomfortable, so let them know that they have a choice: They can choose to only *audio* record themselves, or they can *video* record themselves. They can choose their preference when it comes time to record. Consider, too, choosing a space for this learning opportunity that has room for pairs to spread out and not be close to each other during the recording process. An invitation to leave the room and meet back after they record their conversations might also be an option, to ensure the learners feel safe using video.

3. The first step will be for each set of partners to review the Seven Partnership Principles and talk about what they mean to them as coaches.

   a. Optional resources to use for reference: The Principles of Coaching videos or the "Seven Principles for True Partnership" article.

4. Once the partnerships have reviewed the principles and shared their ideas about what they mean for coaches, invite them to rejoin their partners and decide who will be "Partner A" and who will be "Partner B."

   a. Partner A will coach first, and Partner B will be the coachee first (coachee = the person being coached).

5. The task will include the partners taking turns coaching one another, while also recording the conversation. For each round, the coach can ask the following kickstart question to begin the conversation. Then, the partnership should continue in the conversation for 3 minutes, recording the entire exchange. The first round will follow the following structure:

   a. Press record on your phone, pointing at the partnership.

   b. Partner A (coach): "What's on your mind today?" (This is the kickstart question.)

   c. Partner B (coachee): responds.

   d. Continue the conversation for 3 minutes.

6. Once Round 1 is complete, Round 2 will begin, and the partners will rotate roles. Partner B will coach, and Partner A will be coached. Remember to record!

7. Once both rounds are complete, everyone will rewatch the video of themselves coaching and use the questions below to reflect:

   a. Which Partnership Principles do I observe in my coaching?

   b. Which Partnership Principles come naturally to me?

   c. Which Partnership Principles were not observed in my coaching?

   d. What are my next actions?

8. Once all participants have had time to reflect on their video, they will meet back with their partners and share their noticings with each other.

9. After the partners have time to talk together, invite the whole group to share answers to the reflection questions out loud. *Do not ask to have participants share the video with the whole group.*

10. Once the activity has come to a close, invite them to continue using video as a way to reflect on their practice.

Modifications/Notes:

- Time for each round can be modified to fit the needs of the group.

- Groups of three can be used if it makes it easier to record the coach/coachee conversations.

- Not everyone will be comfortable with using video. Invest in the psychological safety of the learning environment, allow people to choose their groups/partners, and respect the confidentiality of the videos by allowing people to record on their own devices.

- This activity can also be divided up into two rounds. Round 1 can be where coaches reflect on *any* of the Partnership Principles they observe in their conversations. Round 2 can be used for coaches to intentionally look for how they have embodied one or two specific principles. For example, coaches might rewatch/relisten to their recording and see how they embodied the Partnership Principle of dialogue.

END OF CHAPTER REFLECTION

Now that you have explored learning opportunities about the Partnership Principles, take time to reflect on this Success Factor overall. Use the following reflection questions, or reflect in your own way, and fill the lines with your ideas.

REFLECTION QUESTIONS

1. On a scale of 1 to 10, 1 being not at all and 10 being significant, what impact did these Learning Paths have on your practice? What led you to choose the rating you did?

2. What is a major aha you had as you learned about the Partnership Principles?

3. What will you do next with your ideas?

NOTES

NOTES

Chapter 2

//

Communication Skills

*"The more you listen to someone . . . and the more that person listens
to you, the more likely you two will be of like minds."*

~Kate Murphy

Success Factor #2: Communication Skills

Dialogue, one of the Partnership Principles that Jim shares about in *Unmistakable Impact*, *The Impact Cycle*, *Better Conversations*, and *The Definitive Guide to Instructional Coaching*, allows coaches to see the benefit of a healthy back-and-forth conversation: It is life-giving (Knight, 2022, p. 27). Coaches who desire to improve the way they ask questions and listen are thinking deeply about Success Factor #2: Communication Skills. When coaches reflect about how they communicate, they prioritize relationships and commit to continued growth (Knight, 2016, 2022). Communication skills that can help us bring focus to our listening and increase our presence in conversations include listening and questioning.

So Why Should We Be Talking About Communication Within Schools and Systems?

We spend much of our life in conversation. If we invest in improving conversations within schools and systems, that means that the time we are in conversation can be more positive and productive. It means that we can "dramatically improve educator and student learning" as well as create dialogue that leaves everyone "feeling better about life" (Knight, 2016, pp. 2–4). When schools and systems explore these communication skills, they are moving closer to facilitating life-giving conversations for everyone, including students.

Resources Included in This Chapter

ARTICLES	ACTIVITIES	SCENARIO	CHECKLISTS	VIDEOS
"The Conversation Workout"	EVE Video	The Mouthpiece	Listening Effectively	The Principles of Coaching:
"The Beautiful Question"	Expanding Perspectives		Writing Effective Questions	1. Why Conversations Break Down
"Stop Coachsplaining!"	The Listening Fully		Noticing Effectively	2. Effective Listening
	Say In One Sentence			3. Good Questions
"One Habit That Improves Conversation Skills"	Communication Skills Video Reflection			4. Trust
"How Language Helps or Hinders Thinking"	Stir the Room			
	Coaching Trio			

Optional Learning Paths

Learning Path #1

Guiding Question: What do we need to keep in mind as we have conversations?

Resources: Principles of Coaching video: Why Conversations Break Down, EVE Video activity

Activity:

1. Read through the EVE Video activity to become familiar with the process.

2. Use the Principles of Coaching video: Why Conversations Break Down to explore big ideas about successful conversations.

3. Wrap up this learning path by reflecting on one big idea from Jim's video that will inform future conversations.

Learning Path #2

Guiding Question: How do communication skills impact our lives?

Resources: "The Conversation Workout" article, Expanding Perspectives activity

Activity:

1. Read through the Expanding Perspectives activity to become familiar with the process.

2. Facilitate the Expanding Perspectives activity using *The Conversation Workout* article.

3. Wrap up this learning path by using the reflection questions that appear after the article.

Learning Path #3

Guiding Question: What are the components to effective listening?

Resources: Principles of Coaching video: Effective Listening, Listening Effectively checklist, The Listening Fully activity

Activity:

1. First, watch the Effective Listening video. After the video, talk about what you heard (in pairs, small groups, or as a whole group), or journal your ideas about effective listening.

2. Then, explore the Listening Effectively checklist one line at a time, and discuss or reflect using the questions that follow the checklist.

COMMUNICATION SKILLS

3. Finally, engage in The Listening Fully activity, using the reflection questions after the activity to debrief the experience.

4. Wrap up this learning path by going back to the checklist to self-assess/reflect on how effectively you listened during the activity.

Learning Path #4

Guiding Question: What is a "good" question?

Resources: "The Beautiful Question" article, Principles of Coaching video: Good Questions, Writing Effective Questions checklist

Activity:

1. To begin, work in pairs, small groups, or on your own to write a list of ten coaching questions. As you work, discuss or reflect on why these are good coaching questions.

2. Choose to either watch the video or read the article (information is similar in both).

3. After the video or article,

    a. Use the reflection questions that appear after the article to reflect on your learning.

    b. Reflect on the questions you wrote in Step 1 using the information from the video or article. Discuss or reflect on what you are noticing.

4. Using the Writing Effective Questions checklist, choose one or two questions from your list to analyze or revise, or discuss what you have done well in writing coaching questions.

5. Wrap up this learning path with one final reflection question: What does this leave you thinking about coaching questions?

Learning Path #5

Guiding Question: How can coaches avoid overexplaining in conversations?

Resources: "Stop Coachsplaining!" article, Say In One Sentence activity

Activity:

1. Use the Say In One Sentence activity to read "Stop Coachsplaining!" and to answer the article's reflection questions.

2. Wrap up this learning path by answering the guiding question.

Learning Path #6

<u>Guiding Question:</u> What roles do noticing and presence play in coaching conversations?

<u>Resources:</u> "One Habit That Improves Conversation Skills," Noticing Effectively checklist, Communication Skills Video Reflection activity

<u>Activity:</u>

1. To begin, discuss or reflect on everything you already know about noticing and presence when it comes to coaching conversations.

2. Next, read the article and answer the article's reflection questions.

3. Then, discuss or reflect on the Noticing Effectively checklist, and how coaches can use the skill of noticing in conversations.

4. Finally, use the Video Reflection activity to practice noticing during a conversation.

5. Wrap up this learning path by answering the guiding question.

Learning Path #7

<u>Guiding Question:</u> How does the language we use impact our communication?

<u>Resources:</u> "How Language Helps or Hinders Thinking," Give One Get One Move On activity

<u>Activity:</u>

1. Read the article.

2. Use the Stir the Room activity to conduct four rounds of discussion using the reflection questions that go with the article.

3. Wrap up this learning path by answering the guiding question.

Learning Path #8

<u>Guiding Question:</u> What role does trust play in conversations?

<u>Resources:</u> Principles of Coaching video: Trust, The Mouthpiece scenario

<u>Activity:</u>

1. Watch the video, then engage in a discussion about trust and the role it plays in coaching conversations.

2. Next, read through the scenario.

3. Engage in a discussion about the scenario using the reflection questions that follow the scenario.

4. Wrap up this learning path by answering the guiding question.

Learning Path #9

Guiding Question: How can I refine my communication skills as a coach?

Resources: Coaching Trio activity, Principles of Coaching videos: Effective Listening and Good Questions, Listening Effectively checklist, Writing Good Questions checklist

Activity:

1. Read through the Coaching Trio activity to become familiar with the process.

2. Watch both videos, then decide if you want to focus on listening or questioning during this learning path (you choose!).

3. Once you have chosen, browse the checklist that aligns with your focus (either listening or questioning).

4. Complete the activity.

    a. Note: you will practice your selected skill when you are role "B" in the activity. For example, if you are working on listening, you will actively work to listen well as your partner (role "A") talks about whatever they discuss as the presenter.

5. Wrap up this learning path by discussing major takeaways or by answering the guiding question.

Guiding Question: What do we need to keep in mind as we have conversations?

Resources: Principles of Coaching video: Why Conversations Break Down, EVE Video activity

Activity:

1. Read through the EVE Video activity to become familiar with the process.

2. Use the Principles of Coaching video: Why Conversations Break Down to explore big ideas about successful conversations.

3. Wrap up this learning path by reflecting on one big idea from Jim's video that will inform future conversations.

EVE VIDEO ACTIVITY

Purpose: To engage a group in a new approach to Know, Want to Know, Learned (KWL): sharing previous experiences, learning from a video, and writing ideas down for further exploration.

Process:

1. Select a video of focus for a group to watch and discuss together.

2. The facilitator will prepare the video and print handouts with the EVE chart (handouts are optional; participants can also draw the EVE chart on paper).

E WHAT PREVIOUS EXPERIENCES DO YOU HAVE ABOUT THE VIDEO'S TOPIC?	V WHAT ARE YOU LEARNING/HEARING FROM THE VIDEO?	E WHAT WOULD YOU LIKE TO EXPLORE FURTHER AFTER THE DISCUSSION?

3. The facilitator will explain the three columns of EVE:

   a. The first "E" is for participants to write about previous experiences related to the video's topic. For example, if the video is about "building trust," then the participants will write down their previous experiences with building trust.

   b. The "V" is for participants to write everything they can from the video: ideas, questions, thoughts, and so on.

   c. The second "E" is for participants to write ideas they would like to explore. This is for after the discussion.

4. Once the facilitator has explained the columns, they will invite the group to go to the first "E" column and write down previous experiences with the video's topic (let the group know the video's topic, but the facilitator can decide how detailed or vague they are in the description).

5. Now, show the video, and ask participants to write notes in the "V" column.

6. After the video, engage the group in dialogue about their notes in the "V" column.

7. Once the discussion is over, the final "E" column is for the group to reflect individually about any ideas, notes, and so on that they would like to explore after watching the video and hearing from the group.

Modifications:

− The facilitator can choose to group participants by their "what to explore further" ideas and create inquiry groups for further discussion.

Principles of Coaching Video

Why Conversations Break Down

https://youtu.be/eY9vGDrt2mQ
In this video, Jim shares four ideas to keep in mind when having productive conversations.

<u>Guiding Question:</u> How do communication skills impact our lives?

<u>Resources:</u> "The Conversation Workout" article, Expanding Perspectives activity

<u>Activity:</u>

1. Read through the Expanding Perspectives activity to become familiar with the process.

2. Facilitate the Expanding Perspectives activity using "The Conversation Workout" article.

3. Wrap up this learning path by using the reflection questions that appear after the article.

The Conversation Workout

Our schools are only as good as the conversations in them.

Originally published in *Educational Leadership, 79*(3). November 1, 2021.

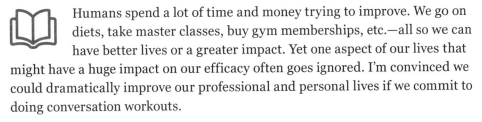 Humans spend a lot of time and money trying to improve. We go on diets, take master classes, buy gym memberships, etc.—all so we can have better lives or a greater impact. Yet one aspect of our lives that might have a huge impact on our efficacy often goes ignored. I'm convinced we could dramatically improve our professional and personal lives if we commit to doing conversation workouts.

Effective communication is essential for our professional success. Whatever people's role in life, our ability to make a difference depends on our ability to make connections. What's more, how people come together in conversation has a significant impact on the learning that happens in our schools—for both children and adults. Learning occurs within relationships. The healthier the relationship, the more learning takes place.

The same can also be said for our lives. Our best days and worst days almost always involve conversations with others. If we can improve our interactions in just a small way, we should experience better conversations with family and friends, and as a result, live better lives.

What's a Conversation Workout?

Just like working out in a gym, a conversation workout involves committing to a plan, learning new skills, and then practicing and getting feedback until we become proficient at those skills. At the gym, people might learn the best way to lift weights or do exercises. In a conversation workout, we learn about beliefs, skills, and habits we can use to have better conversations. Then we keep working until we become proficient in those skills and habits.

I've been studying conversation for decades. To write my book *Better Conversations* (Knight, 2015), I read works by dozens of wise researchers and journalists and learned from more than 100 people who tested the conversational tools I created. Here, based on my research and experience, are four starting points for any conversation workout.

1. ***Ask real questions.*** When we ask a real question, we are genuinely interested in what our conversational partner thinks or feels. Real questions are honest and unassuming. They're not our opinions with a question mark at the end of them. Real questions give power to our conversation partners by inviting reflection, exploration, and clarification.

2. ***Really listen.*** In her book, *You're Not Listening*, Kate Murphy (2020) explains that we struggle to listen because people talking usually speak at a much slower pace compared to how quickly our brains process their words. As a result, our ever-active brains get restless, and we lose track of what's being said. Additionally, we live in a time when interruption is a culturally accepted norm—just watch a political conversation on television—and we are surrounded by digital distractions, beeping at us for our attention.

Despite these challenges, listening remains an essential communication skill. Recently, I asked instructional coaches on Twitter to describe how their life had improved as a result of learning to coach. More than 75 percent of the people who responded said the most important change in their lives was learning to listen.

Really listening means that, at least temporarily, we suspend our desire to be heard, so we can hear what our conversation partner says—and, in fact, notice what sometimes isn't said. To really listen, we stay fully present in the conversation and let go of the need to control it. We communicate that we believe the other person has something to say, and we communicate respect. Our conversation partners can see and feel that we're genuinely interested in them. One benefit of really listening is that often we find ourselves in a conversation where our partner is truly interested in what we have to say.

3. ***Think the best of other people (stop judging).*** No doubt our evolutionary inheritance has wired our brains to be judgmental. We're quick to judge our friends and coworkers. The trouble is, judgment is destructive in so many ways. Most of us don't want to get close to people who make us feel like we're bad people, and it's hard to learn from people who roll their eyes when we talk, whether they do so literally or not. Moralistic judgment kills intimacy, and it kills learning.

I'm not sure that we can ever completely stop judging, but if we understand where our judgments come from, we can limit their destructive impact. In his book *Non-Violent Communication: A Language of Life* (2015), Marshall Rosenberg contends that our moralistic judgements are actually expressions of our own unmet needs. If we can explore what needs are buried in our judgments, we should be better able to regulate our negative evaluations of others, making it easier for people to connect and learn with us.

4. ***Foster trust.*** In *Better Conversations*, I identified five variables that build or damage trust: character, reliability, competence, warmth, and stewardship. We trust people who are honest and transparent, who do what they say they will do when they say they will do it, and who do their work effectively. We trust people who are positive, kind, and respectfully affectionate. We also trust people who demonstrate goodwill toward us. Educators can foster trust by working on any of these variables.

How to "Work Out" With These Ideas

Read with an action mindset. There are many great books about communication, but simply reading the words likely won't change how we think and act. To have better conversations, we must read with the intent to internalize what we read. Then, we need a plan to make those words become our reality.

Start small. When we read new ideas about communication, we may be tempted to try everything at once. To foster trust, for example, we could plan to address all five variables just discussed. That approach likely won't work. Pick one idea and practice it until you become proficient, then move on to something else.

Pay attention. Life comes at us fast, and it's very easy to miss key noticings. To have better conversations, we need to pay attention. I've found it useful to record in a journal what basically happens in my conversations—even for just one day—and how well I succeed or flop at a targeted skill. This practice can help you better understand your triggers and what tends to distract you, so you can better regulate your behavior in conversations.

Use video. Seriously. Record a conversation with an intimate partner or a work colleague you feel trust with, and watch it for insight on your talking tendencies. If we spend thousands of hours working out to improve our bodies, shouldn't we do the same to improve our relationships? Video is an essential part of a conversation workout because most of us don't have a clear picture of how we do what we do. Video reveals us *as we really are*. Sometimes it's a joy to see, sometimes a disappointment. But if we want to get better, we need to see our conversations realistically. That includes seeing, through ongoing videos, that we are improving.

Learnable—and So Worth It

Better beliefs, skills, and habits for interacting are learnable. We can learn to be better communicators in the same way we learn to play a sport or cook a dish. Working out to be a better communicator helps us be better professionals, and in an era when conversations seem harder than ever, better conversations are even one way we can help create a better world. More impact, a better life, a better world; that seems like a workout worth doing.

COMMUNICATION
SKILLS

Reflection Questions for "The Conversation Workout"

1. What happens in effective conversations?

2. How can coaches "warm up" for these conversation workouts?

3. What strengths do you already have for effective conversations?

4. What else would you add to these ideas?

NOTES

_____
_____
_____
_____
_____
_____
_____
_____
_____
_____
_____
_____
_____
_____
_____
_____
_____
_____
_____
_____
_____

EXPANDING PERSPECTIVES ACTIVITY

 Purpose: to hear different perspectives and approaches to the content of a text.

Process:

1. Start by selecting a text for a group discussion.

2. Explain the process:

    a. Participants will be placed in groups of four (modify as needed for small groups or based on the needs of your learners).

    b. Each of the four members will select one "perspective" to hold as they read the article. That means that as participants read, they are reading with that perspective in mind, allowing it to shape how they interact with the text.

    c. Once everyone has read the article, the group will take turns sharing out. As each person shares their perspective, the rest of the group is invited to respond to, add to, or build upon the ideas.

3. Then, have participants choose their perspective:

    a. **Appreciate:** the appreciate perspective reads the article to search for ideas that they appreciate the most out of everything that has been shared.

    b. **New thinking:** the new thinking perspective searches the article for new ideas, content, or skills that can be shared with others.

    c. **Still processing:** the still processing perspective finds and shares ideas that are challenging, concepts that push their thinking, or concepts that they might not completely agree with at this time.

    d. **Take action:** the take action perspective reads to find concepts that inspire them to start, stop, or explore new actions.

4. The group members read the article, holding on to their perspectives.

5. Once the group members have read, they begin sharing out, one perspective at a time. Invite all participants to respond to each perspective to add to or build upon the shared ideas.

6. At the conclusion of the activity, the following reflection question can be used for individual or group reflection: **How have you expanded your perspective today?**

COMMUNICATION SKILLS

<u>Guiding Question:</u> What are the components to effective listening?

<u>Resources:</u> Principles of Coaching video: Effective Listening, Listening Effectively checklist, The Listening Fully activity

<u>Activity:</u>

1. First, watch the Effective Listening video. After the video, talk about what you heard (in pairs, small groups, or as a whole group), or journal your ideas about effective listening.

2. Then, explore the Listening Effectively checklist one line at a time, and discuss or reflect using the questions that follow the checklist.

3. Finally, engage in The Listening Fully activity, using the reflection questions after the activity to debrief the experience.

4. Wrap up this learning path by going back to the checklist to self-assess/reflect on how effectively you listened during the activity.

Principles of Coaching Video
Effective Listening

https://youtu.be/aS0faMljtfM
In this video, Jim discusses two big ideas to consider about the art of listening.

CHECKLIST: LISTENING EFFECTIVELY

TO LISTEN EFFECTIVELY, I . . .	✔
Embrace silence to allow for thinking	
Talk less than my conversation partner	
Don't interrupt (except when it is helpful)	
Prepare to be present by taking care of myself	
Put away distractions	
Listen to understand beliefs, assumptions, and emotions	
Avoid judgments, assumptions, and comparisons	
Avoid completing my conversation partner's sentences	
Maintain an appropriate and comfortable level of eye contact	

Reflection Questions for the Listening Effectively Checklist

Look at each line of the checklist, and discuss/consider the following questions:

1. What does this line mean for coaches?

2. What does this line look or sound like?

NOTES

THE LISTENING FULLY ACTIVITY

 Purpose: to practice deep listening.

Process:

1. Share the overall outcome of the activity: to exchange an opportunity with a partner to be heard without interruptions or distractions.

2. Ask participants to find a partner (adjust for groups with odd numbers).

3. Designate the partners to be Partner A and Partner B.

4. Partner A will go first in the process, and then Partner B will take their turn.

5. In Round 1, Partner A will speak about one of the following prompts for two minutes. Partner B will focus their attention on Partner A, listening to their words, their emotions, and the journey they take while answering the prompt. Partner B will also avoid interruptions and distractions. It is preferrable that there are no phones present during the activity, so that external distractions can be minimized.

6. Once Round 1 is over, both partners will share their experiences as the speaker (Partner A) and the listener (Partner B) for one minute.

7. Then, Round 2 begins. In this round, Partner B will be the speaker (for two minutes), and Partner A will be the listener. Partner A will focus their attention on Partner B, listening to their words, their emotions, and the journey they take while answering the prompt. Partner A will also avoid interruptions and distractions. It is preferrable that there are no phones present during the activity, so that external distractions can be minimized.

8. Once Round 2 is over, both partners will share about their experience as the speaker (Partner B) and the listener (Partner A) for one minute.

9. After the activity has come to a close, the reflection questions listed here can be used to wrap up the experience:

    a. What does this leave you thinking about being present in conversations?

    b. What did you learn when you focused completely on your partner?

    c. What was difficult for you while listening/speaking?

    d. How will this inform your practice?

Prompts for partner discussion:

– What is a favorite childhood memory, and why is it important to you?

– What has been an influential experience for you in your career?

– What hopes do you have for your future?

<u>Guiding Question:</u> What is a "good" question?

<u>Resources:</u> "The Beautiful Question" article, Principles of Coaching video: Good Questions, Writing Effective Questions checklist

<u>Activity:</u>

1. To begin, work in pairs, small groups, or on your own to write a list of 10 coaching questions. As you work, discuss or reflect on why these are good coaching questions.

2. Choose to either watch the video or read the article (information is similar in both).

3. After the video or article,

   a. Use the reflection questions that appear after the article to reflect on your learning.

   b. Reflect on the questions you wrote in Step 1 using the information from the video or article. Discuss or reflect on what you are noticing.

4. Using the Writing Effective Questions checklist, choose one or two questions from your list to analyze or revise, or discuss what you have done well in writing coaching questions.

5. Wrap up this learning path with one final reflection question: What does this leave you thinking about coaching questions?

The Beautiful Question

Asking good questions can be a superpower—in coaching and in life.

Originally published in *Educational Leadership, 80*(4). December 1, 2022.

> *"Always the beautiful answer who asks a more beautiful question."*
>
> —E. E. Cummings, from introduction to *New Poems* (1938)

Years ago, I was on a break during a communications class I was coteaching with a colleague, Francis Gunn. We were drinking coffee and having lunch, and Francis turned to two businessmen who had sponsored the course and asked them a simple question: "You two must have had quite a few experiences together. What were some of your adventures?" That one question opened up the conversation like a key unlocking a treasure box. Our two colleagues told us one hilarious story after another about their exploits around the world. Such is the power of a good question.

COMMUNICATION
SKILLS

What Makes for Good Questions

When I was writing *The Definitive Guide to Instructional Coaching* (Knight, 2022), I looked at more than 50 books with information about asking questions. That research convinced me that asking good questions, as Francis Gunn did, is a life skill, not just a coaching skill. Our lives are lived in conversations, and when we ask better questions we have better conversations. Effective questions are:

Empowering. Good questions give power to the person who is asked the question, not the person asking it. If I ask someone I'm coaching a question like, "On a scale of 1–10, how close was that class to how you wanted it to go?" I'm not asking that teacher to guess what I think, I'm asking them to share their thoughts. Good questions signal that I think you have something worth saying, and I want to hear your opinion. They shine a light on our partner's comments, not on our thinking.

Authentic. Good questions are real questions, ones for which the questioner doesn't already have an answer. When I ask a real question, I ask it because I'm genuinely curious about my partner's answer, not because I am trying to get them to arrive at a conclusion I've already reached. One simple rule to make questions more authentic is to avoid asking questions for which "no" is a possible answer, as such a question is likely fishing for agreement rather than truly asking for another's thoughts, feelings, or opinions. If I ask, "Don't you think the students would be more engaged if you asked more open-ended questions?" I'm not really asking a question. I'm giving you advice and then putting a question mark at the end of it.

Respectful. Well-asked questions communicate our respect for others. One of my favorite questions comes from coaching expert Michael Bungay Stanier, who suggests asking, "I imagine you've thought a lot about this. How have you addressed issues like this in the past?" This question communicates that we know our conversation partner has good ideas and worthwhile thoughts, and we want to hear them.

The opposite of a respectful question is one that communicates criticism or contempt, such as, "Why didn't you give the students more instruction before you had them do the group work?" Respectful questions build connection, while disrespectful questions sow distrust or division.

Invitational. What I refer to as invitational questions are sometimes called probing questions, but I don't like that term. I agree with researcher Irving Seidman, who writes that, with the word probe, "I always think of a sharp instrument pressing on soft flesh. . . . The word also conveys a sense of the powerful interviewer treating the participant as an object" (2013, p. 86). I prefer invitational.

Invitational questions encourage participants to think deeper ("What leads you to believe ____?"), to generate more ideas ("What are some small steps you could take to move closer to your goal?"), or to access thoughts and feelings ("What will it feel like when your students hit their goal?").

A Few of My Favorite Questions

When you pay attention to your questions, over time, you'll discover you have favorite questions, ones you ask often because they generate rich answers. I suggest you keep track of your favorite questions. Then, experiment: Ask different versions of these questions in different settings and notice the impact they have on your conversations. In the accompanying box, I've noted some of the favorite questions of coaches I know or whose work I read. Over time, I've learned that certain questions will move a conversation forward and in each interaction, I draw from my memory and ask some of those questions to open up the discussion.

Good questions are real manifestations of your curiosity and caring. Good questions are like intellectual fireworks, leading to explosions of ideas and more learning for the questioner and the conversation partner. I began this column with a quotation from the poet E. E. cummings, to the effect that beautiful questions lead to beautiful answers. I would say, similarly, that great questions lead to great conversations, which leads me to a final question: What's something you can do to deepen your ability to ask more empowering, authentic, respectful, and invitational questions?

A Few Educators' Favorite Questions

- "You've probably thought a lot about this. What are you thinking you might do?"—Michael Bungay Stanier

- "Given the time we've got today, what's the most important thing we should talk about?"—Susan Scott

- "What do you want to think about?"—Nancy Kline

- "If suddenly a miracle happened and everything was going perfectly in your class, what would it look like? What would be the first thing you'd notice?" —Solution Focused Coaching

- "Which option gives you the most energy?"—John Campbell

And Two Questions Many Coaches Favor

- "What issue, if faced, would make a substantial difference in your class (or your life)?"

- What advice would you give someone else who was in your situation?

Principles of Coaching Video

Good Questions

https://youtu.be/ZdiCXXetWkw

Listen in as Jim talks about using good questions in coaching conversations.

Reflection Questions for "The Beautiful Question"

1. What are the elements of a good question?

2. What happens when a coach asks a good question?

3. What questions would you add to the "favorites" list?

4. What else needs to happen for teachers to have space to think and reflect?

NOTES

_____

_____

_____

_____

_____

_____

_____

CHECKLIST: WRITING EFFECTIVE QUESTIONS

EFFECTIVE QUESTIONS . . .	✔
Are hard enough to be worth answering	
Are easy enough that they can be answered	
Are short	
Are easy to understand	
Are focused on the person answering the question	
Are solution-focused	
Avoid making another person wrong	
Communicate respect	
Increase clarity	
Can be open or closed	
Can be evocative or generative	
Are not leading questions	
Do not have a hidden agenda	
Are questions we don't know the answer to	
Invite others to think more clearly	
Are adapted to be most helpful in each unique conversation	

<u>Guiding Question:</u> How can coaches avoid overexplaining in conversations?

<u>Resources:</u> "Stop Coachsplaining!" article, Say In One Sentence activity

<u>Activity:</u>

1. Use the Say In One Sentence activity to read "Stop Coachsplaining!" and to answer the article's reflection questions.

2. Wrap up this learning path by answering the guiding question.

Stop Coachsplaining!

"Making your case" to a teacher rarely works.

Originally published in *Educational Leadership*, 81(1). September 1, 2023.

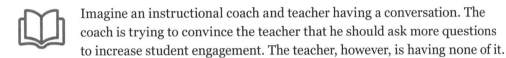 Imagine an instructional coach and teacher having a conversation. The coach is trying to convince the teacher that he should ask more questions to increase student engagement. The teacher, however, is having none of it. From his perspective, too many questions would inhibit reflection, and more questions wouldn't promote the kind of learning he wants to see in his students. The conversation goes back and forth, with each side making their case and no progress being made. The more the coach pushes, the more the teacher digs in, and the more the teacher digs in, the more the coach pushes and keeps giving reasons or research to back up why questioning is a good strategy.

I know about this conversation because it's one that I have experienced—on both sides. I've been the teacher and I've been the coach—and in both cases, there was no real change. When I have coached others, I've often felt that since I have expertise, I should (or must) tell them what to do so they can quickly see improvements. The reality is, however, that just telling people what to do, even with elaborate explanations why, rarely works. I have a word to describe this kind of communication: "coachsplaining."

Coaches engage in coachsplaining when they do most of the talking and the thinking. Coaches coachsplain when they tell teachers what they've done right and wrong, and then deliver a strong message about strategies the teachers should use. When they tell teachers what to do before asking teachers what they think they should do, that's also coachsplaining. A "coachsplainer" probably feels it's their job to solve teachers' problems for them.

Of course, there are times when giving advice can be very helpful. Too often, though, coaches jump to coachsplaining when it's unnecessary, and this actually inhibits professional learning.

Five Reasons to Not Coachsplain

This approach usually fails because:

1. *It doesn't account for complexity.*

   For complex work like teaching, the simple suggestions that come from coachsplaining usually don't help. Complex challenges require solutions that are adapted over time to the unique strengths and needs of students and teachers. One-size-fits-all solutions often make things worse, not better (Heifetz, Grashow, & Linsky, 2009). Real change happens when coaches and teachers collaborate and adapt teaching strategies gradually until a teacher's instructional practice clearly addresses students' needs. For example, a coach and teacher might start out by co-constructing a rubric for student writing. After sharing the rubric with students and reviewing student writing, the teacher might realize that important aspects of writing have been left out of the rubric. Recognizing the rubric needs to change, the teacher might revise it on her own or partner with the coach to make the rubric more effective.

2. *It misplaces the focus.*

   Coachsplaining usually puts the focus on how teachers are teaching. Coaches tell teachers strategies they should use so their students will be more engaged and learn more. But research has found that during coaching, the focus should be on students, not strategies (Hasbrouck & Michel, 2021). This doesn't mean strategies aren't important. But discussion should start with the changes teachers want to see for their students before teacher and coach discuss what the teacher might do to bring those changes about. Teacher goals focused on students strengthening their achievement or behavior provide a way to measure whether strategies are working and monitor progress.

3. *It robs teachers of status.*

   In interactions, most people expect to be treated in ways appropriate for the status they think they deserve—and watch to see if that's happening. If people aren't conferred with the status they expect, they usually check out (Schein, 2009). When coaches coachsplain, it communicates that they see themselves as more important than the teachers with whom they're collaborating. Coaches who put themselves one up in this way, and put teachers one down, shouldn't be surprised when teachers stop listening.

4. *It saps motivation.*

   People are rarely motivated by other people's goals for them. Evidence (and much of our own experience, if we think about it) shows that telling people what their goal is doesn't lead to commitment (Pink, 2009). Real change starts from the inside out.

5. *It thwarts learning.*

   Overexplaining and telling others what to do takes learning opportunities away from them. The implicit message communicated is that we don't think the other person can solve their own problems. To get the schools our students deserve, we need teachers who are professionals—so teachers must be treated like people capable of using their own professional judgment. Doing the thinking for teachers creates dependence, inhibits learning, and deprofessionalizes teaching.

The Power of Humility

Sometimes the temptation to coachsplain can be overwhelming. As professionals dedicated to helping teachers be their best, we see a need, and because we want what's best for students and teachers, we want to tell the teacher what to do. The reality is that most classrooms are so complex that a humble, adaptive approach is more effective. When a coach starts by asking teachers what they think and listening with curiosity rather than speaking to gain control, that coach is more likely to do what's best for students and teachers. And that puts the focus where it should be.

Reflection Questions for "Stop Coachsplaining!"

1. On a scale of 1 to 10, 1 being "all the time" and 10 being "never," how often do you find yourself *coachsplaining*?

2. Should coaches talk more or less than their conversation partner? Why?

3. What happens to the teacher when a coach is coachsplaining?

4. What could coaches do to avoid the coachsplaining temptation?

NOTES

_____

_____

_____

_____

_____

_____

_____

_____

_____

_____

_____

_____

_____

_____

_____

_____

SAY IN ONE SENTENCE ACTIVITY

 Purpose: To support a group in summarizing a text and think about the implications for their work.

Process:

1. Select a text of focus for a group to read and discuss in this activity.

2. Explain that the group will read the entire article and then answer a set of questions *in one sentence* to summarize what they have read.

3. After the group has read the text, give them time to summarize their ideas to answer the reflection questions (in ONE sentence for each question).

4. Then, ask the question one at a time, and go around the group. One at a time, they should say their one sentence out loud with no interruption for discussion.

5. After the entire group has said their answer to the first question, the facilitator can invite them to discuss what they are left thinking.

6. This process will continue for each reflection question.

Modifications:

–   This could also work with a video.

–   Participants can do this in small groups for larger audiences.

–   A final question such as, "What are the implications for your work?" is a way to wrap up the conversation and move the thinking forward.

Learning Path #6 Resources

What Roles Do Noticing and Presence Play in Coaching Conversations?

<u>Guiding Question:</u> What roles do noticing and presence play in coaching conversations?

<u>Resources:</u> "One Habit That Improves Conversation Skills" article, Noticing Effectively checklist, Communication Skills Video Reflection activity

<u>Activity:</u>

1. To begin, discuss or reflect on everything you already know about noticing and presence when it comes to coaching conversations.

2. Next, read the article and answer the article's reflection questions.

3. Then, discuss or reflect on the Noticing Effectively checklist and how coaches can use the skill of noticing in conversations.

4. Finally, use the Video Reflection activity to practice noticing during a conversation.

5. Wrap up this learning path by answering the guiding question.

One Habit That Improves Conversation Skills

This simple act can deepen conversations and connections in schools.

Originally published in *Educational Leadership, 79*(7). April 1, 2022.

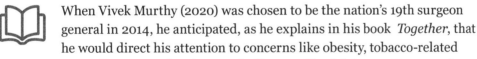 When Vivek Murthy (2020) was chosen to be the nation's 19th surgeon general in 2014, he anticipated, as he explains in his book *Together*, that he would direct his attention to concerns like obesity, tobacco-related diseases, mental illness, or other frequently discussed health issues. To ensure he was addressing the top health concerns, Murthy conducted a listening tour across the country. When he asked people to talk about their health, he repeatedly heard about one topic he hadn't expected. "Loneliness," Murthy writes, "ran like a dark thread through many of the more obvious issues that people brought to my attention, like addiction, violence, anxiety, and depression" (p. xv).

The Loneliness Crisis

In *Together*, Murthy reveals the scale of the loneliness problem by sharing some statistics. In a 2018 study by the Kaiser Family Foundation, 22 percent of U.S. adults said they "often or always feel lonely." An AARP study (Frank, 2018) using UCLA's loneliness scale reported that one out of three American adults over the age of 45 are lonely.

Studies from several other countries show that pervasive loneliness isn't confined to the United States. All these studies were done before the pandemic, but I think we can safely assume that loneliness hasn't gone down since COVID-19 arrived.

What these statistics imply is that the next time you sit in a meeting with a small group of fellow educators, at least three and maybe more of the people gathered feel chronically alone.

One antidote to loneliness is connection through conversation. It's as true for K–12 educators as anyone that a single conversation can help you feel heard and seen, breathe life into your existence, and show you that you aren't alone. That's why I've spent much of my professional life studying and writing about communication, particularly in my book *Better Conversations* (Corwin, 2015).

Conversation is especially important in schools—even more so during the pandemic, which has brought with it so much uncertainty and forced isolation. The quality of the conversations that occur in schools can profoundly affect children and adults. Indeed, the best way to improve what happens in schools, might be to improve the way we talk with both children and adults.

Conversation, Interrupted

But there's a problem: Many of us want to be better communicators, but again and again we fall back into old habits that thwart real communication. We know what we should do, we just don't do it. I often fall into this trap myself.

To better understand how people might persist in changes toward having deeper exchanges, I established the Life-Giving Conversations Project at the Instructional Coaching Group. We study what happens when people try to adopt simple, life-giving communication habits. The project is just starting, but I'm confident we have identified one habit that can radically improve anyone's conversations. What is that habit? Put away your phone.

To realize why this is central, consider what Sherry Turkle (2015), an expert on how technology affects personal relationships and interactions, says in Reclaiming Conversation. Turkle acknowledges that technology has many advantages, but also describes the negative impact addictive use of a smartphone can have:

> We are somehow more lonely than before . . . our children are less empathetic than they should be for their age, and . . . it seems nearly impossible to have an uninterrupted conversation at a family dinner. We catch ourselves not looking into the eyes of our children or taking the time to talk with them just to have a few more hits of our email. (p. 12)

What Happens When We're Phone-Free . . . and Why It's Hard

I've been studying conversations with a small group of dedicated adults who've been putting their phones away on a regular basis just to see what difference it makes. Every day, my research partners and I identify when we will put our phones away. At the end of the day, we write a few notes in a journal to record what went well and what we'll do differently the next day.

Everyone involved is finding that putting away our phones seems to be making a big difference. We're having deeper, better, more joyful and more important conversations. At home or at work, in casual friendships or committed relationships, stepping away from your phone can transform surface interactions into conversations that build authentic connection.

But while putting the phone away is an easy physical task, for many people, it's still not easy to do. Many of us struggle to go five minutes without glancing at our phone. If the phone rings or buzzes, trying to ignore it can feel like sitting beside warm, chocolate chip cookies when we're dieting; it's hard to resist just one look. One look becomes a short check for texts, and then email, and, well, just a few minutes on Instagram—and suddenly our conversation is over.

Fortunately, there are a few simple things you can do to make it easier to adopt this new conversation-enhancing habit:

— Identify specific times when you want to put away your phone (for me that's anytime I have an opportunity for a meaningful conversation).

— Put your phone out of reach or in a different room when you're about to have a conversation.

— Take time in the evening to reflect on the rewards you experienced from putting the phone down that day—or any costs of not doing so.

— Ask those closest to you whether they feel a difference in your conversations when you're phone-free. Positive comments from your partner, child, or friend may be all you need to persist.

No Trivial Step

We'll never completely get rid of our smartphones—and we shouldn't. Having a video communication system; the world's largest library of books, music, and videos; and access to millions of apps and games on a pocket-sized device is a wonder. We'd be silly not to use such devices. However, if administrators, coaches, and teachers just put their phones away during important conversations, they could experience the kind of connection that can help others—and themselves—feel less alone. Given the scale of the loneliness crisis, this habit might seem trivial, but I believe it can transform your relationships. I'm hoping it will transform mine.

Reflection Questions for "One Habit That Improves Conversation Skills"

1. What does this article bring up for you?

2. On a scale of 1 to 10, 1 being never and 10 being all the time, how often do you feel like people are truly present in conversations?

3. What does the loneliness crisis mean for instructional coaches?

4. How might small steps toward presence improve teaching and learning?

_____

_____

_____

_____

NOTES

_____
_____
_____
_____

CHECKLIST: NOTICING EFFECTIVELY

TO NOTICE EFFECTIVELY, I . . .	✔
Recognize when my attention shifts and bring it back	
Notice my own thoughts, feelings, and behaviors	
Notice my conversation partner's thoughts, feelings, and behaviors	
Notice strengths in my conversation partner	
Notice energy levels and shifts during the conversation	
Notice nonverbals: body language, tone, facial expressions	

Reflection Questions for the Noticing Effectively Checklist

Look at each line of the checklist and discuss/consider the following questions:

1. What does this line mean for coaches?

2. What does this line look or sound like?

NOTES

_____
_____
_____
_____
_____
_____
_____
_____

COMMUNICATION SKILLS
VIDEO REFLECTION ACTIVITY

Purpose: To reflect on how we show up as conversation partners.

Materials: In this activity, participants will be recording themselves in a conversation. Cell phones make great tools for this, and no other tool is needed. Simply find a way to prop up the phone and record the conversations that will happen in pairs. The video will be reviewed by the partnership only, not shared with anyone else or in the group setting.

Process:

1. Invite participants to choose a partner for this activity.

2. Once all participants have a partner, explain that today they will be audio or video recording conversations with each other to reflect on their communication skills. Recording yourself can be uncomfortable, so let them know that they have a choice: They can choose to only *audio* record themselves, or they can *video* record themselves. They can choose their preference when it comes time to record. Consider, too, choosing a space for this learning opportunity that has room for pairs to spread out and not be close to each other during the recording process. An invitation to leave the room and meet back after they record themselves in their conversations might also be an option, to ensure the learners feel safe using video.

3. The task will include the partners engaging in casual conversation with each other, while also recording the conversation. Only one person in the partnership needs to set up their phone to record. While video recording is best, because participants will be able to see nonverbals and hear the spoken words, it is still acceptable for partnerships to choose audio recording only.

   a. One partner in the pair will press record on their phone, pointing at the partnership.

   b. Begin a conversation by asking a question such as, "What's on your mind today?"

   c. Partners continue the dialogue, going back-and-forth for 2 to 3 minutes.

4. Once the 2-to-3 minute conversation is complete, the pairs will rewatch the video of themselves talking and use the "Noticing Effectively" checklist to see what they noticed or did not notice during the conversation.

5. After the partners have time to talk together, invite the whole group to share what they noticed about their conversations and the Noticing Effectively checklist. *Do not ask participants to share the video with the whole group.*

6. Once the activity has come to a close, encourage them to continue using video as a way to reflect on their practice.

Modifications:

– Groups of three can be used if it is easier to record the coach/coachee conversations.

– Not everyone will be comfortable with using video. Invest in the psychological safety of the learning environment, allow people to choose their groups/partners, and respect the confidentiality of the videos by allowing people to record on their own devices.

– Another option for approaching this activity is to ask participants to aim to demonstrate the ideas on the Noticing Effectively checklist during their conversations and then to reflect on that one intention after with the video/audio recording.

Guiding Question: How does the language we use impact our communication?

Resources: "How Language Helps or Hinders Thinking" article, Give One Get One Move On activity

Activity:

1. Read the article.

2. Use the Stir the Room activity to conduct four rounds of discussion using the reflection questions that go with the article.

3. Wrap up this learning path by answering the guiding question.

How Language Helps or Hinders Thinking

Used well, words free up educators' thinking and understanding. Used carelessly, they inhibit both.

Originally published in *Educational Leadership, 80*(6). March 1, 2023.

> "We tried to talk it over, but the words got in the way."
>
> —Leon Russell, from "This Masquerade"

In Walker Percy's (1999/1980) novel *The Second Coming*, one of the two main characters, Allie, struggles to reconstruct her world after she loses her memory. As she is rebuilding her life, Allie also decides to rebuild a stove in her new home. But she can't start until she learns the words she needs to fix the stove, so she asks the book's other main character, Will, for help. "'Give me the words' [Allie said]. She took out pad and pencil. He wrote: Creeper. Ten-inch crescent wrench. WD-40. 'Good . . . I know it . . . but not the word.'"

Armed with the words she needs, Allie is ready to begin rebuilding the stove—and her life, as it turns out. Such is the power of language.

The Power of a Shared Vocabulary

A few years ago, I wrote about the importance of a shared vocabulary, noting that words not only let us talk about topics we otherwise would have no way to communicate about, but also help us realize things we wouldn't otherwise be able to see. Several years ago, I wrote in a post for the International Literacy Association's blog, "Words might be humanity's greatest invention. A word is a candle held up in the darkness to help us move forward."

In schools, a shared vocabulary can help us think, plan, and act in ways that benefit children. When teachers have a shared understanding of different meanings for the word *engagement*, for example, they're able to explore strategies that might increase emotional, cognitive, or behavioral engagement. Better conversations, made possible by a shared vocabulary, should lead to better experiences for students.

What Can Go Wrong With Word Power

Recently, I've been noticing something else about words; they can also *inhibit* thought and inquiry. We see this most obviously in political discourse. To use just one example, according to *Merriam Webster*, the word *woke* was originally used in political conversations to describe anyone who is "aware of and actively attentive to important societal facts and issues (especially issues of racial and social justice)." Now the word is more often used pejoratively to silence or stereotype the ideas of anyone who might be considered politically liberal. When someone is labeled "woke," many people begin to automatically judge, dismiss, and even silence that person's ideas. Although words can open up conversation and thinking, certain loaded words also shut those conversations down.

Words can also be used in ways that inhibit thinking in schools. Take, for example, the phrases *research-validated* or *research says*. Of course, understanding the evidence in support of an intervention or teaching strategy is very important. But injecting the word *research* can simply end a fruitful dialogue about what's best for kids. In my experience, "research says" limits thinking more often than it enhances thinking because when people hear those words, they often feel silenced, even though researchers themselves frequently debate findings.

Other words can inhibit thought too, particularly when they are used to stereotype people. Teachers who are exhausted from innovation overload can be labeled "resistant" if they don't embrace a new teaching strategy. Administrators are sometimes given names that diminish or even dehumanize them. I worked with one district where the administrative offices were referred to as "the head shed," and the term wasn't meant to call attention to the good thinking that took place "downtown."

Terms such as *learning disabled* can help us better understand students' unique needs and secure help for them in school. But such a term can also focus attention on the student as a problem—and distract people from considering whether the school is providing adequate instruction and support. Language that stereotypes, dehumanizes, moralistically judges, or silences others always stops inquiry dead in its tracks.

What We Can Do

Fortunately, there is something we can do to counteract this phenomenon. We can ask questions that move a conversation away from the stifling effects of certain words and toward curiosity and more helpful information, especially in schools. When someone says a teaching strategy is *evidence-based* or *research-based*, we can ask about the evidence. What kind of studies were done and when? Do any other studies contradict the findings? Were the studies that support this strategy's effectiveness done with students like those in our school? How confident can we be that the findings will apply in our setting with our unique students?

Ultimately, what matters most is whether a strategy is likely to have an unmistakably positive impact on student learning or well-being. That should be the final deciding factor when choosing strategies.

When we hear labels used that simplistically categorize students, let's ask more about the unique learning needs of the students under discussion. What has worked for a particular student? What does she say she needs? Is the label this student has been given possibly interfering with our ability to truly see the student?

We should also pay attention to our own thinking. We're all human—and for some reason, it sometimes feels good to judge another person or simplify our thinking through stereotypes. We should ask ourselves whether we might be turning to stereotypes in a situation. It's normal to want to use words, including powerful terms or jargon, in ways that persuade others to share our viewpoint. So when we prepare to voice our opinion or offer feedback to a colleague, let's stop and consider, *Am I using words to identify the best solution for children—or to be "right" and win an argument?*

The problems we face today, in our schools, our lives, and even in the world, are so complex that they can only be solved by better thinking. Words can promote or disrupt thinking. So let's use words for better thinking—our lives, our schools, and our children need it.

Reflection Questions for "How Language Helps or Hinders Thinking"

1. How have words had power in your experience?

2. On a scale of 1 to 10, 1 being not at all and 10 being very important, how important is this topic of language for instructional coaches? Why?

3. How can we become more aware when it comes to language?

4. Why is this topic important for our students?

NOTES

_____

_____

_____

_____

_____

_____

STIR THE ROOM ACTIVITY

 Purpose: to share responses to reflection questions after reading a text.

Process:

1. Choose a facilitator and timekeeper for this activity.

2. Distribute an article for a group to read. Provide plenty of time for the participants to read the article in its entirety.

3. Once everyone has had time to read the text, invite them to independently answer the reflection questions that accompany the article.

4. After everyone has finished reading and responding to the reflection questions, request that they stand up to prepare to move around the room.

5. There will be as many rounds to this activity as there are reflection questions. If there are four questions, there will be four rounds. Each round can be anywhere from 3 to 5 minutes, depending on the time available and size of the group.

6. Begin each round of the activity by asking a reflection question and then inviting everyone to "mix and mingle" to find someone in the room to partner with and share their responses to that reflection question. The person calling out the questions may choose to go in order or mix up the questions!

7. Once a timer goes off for Round 1, continue mixing and mingling and answering reflection questions until all questions have been discussed. People should be partnering with someone new for each discussion, if possible.

8. At the end of the final round, ask everyone to return to their seats and write down the most impactful idea they heard or realized during their discussions.

<u>Guiding Question:</u> What role does trust play in conversations?

<u>Resources:</u> Principles of Coaching video: Trust, The Mouthpiece scenario

<u>Activity:</u>

1. Watch the video, then engage in a discussion about trust and the role it plays in coaching conversations.

2. Next, read through the scenario.

3. Engage in a discussion about the scenario using the reflection questions that follow the scenario.

4. Wrap up this learning path by answering the guiding question.

Principles of Coaching Video
Trust

https://youtu.be/z1kckK7GrSE
Listen to Jim's ideas about the role of trust in coaching.

THE MOUTHPIECE SCENARIO

 Instructional coach Lori Smith was dedicated to having a big impact on student achievement at Dewey Middle School, and she had accomplished a great deal. Reading teachers at her school had done a great job of implementing reading strategies from the Project Big Step curriculum, and the teachers had nicely integrated those strategies into the Dewey School Improvement Plan. Most of the other teachers at Dewey were implementing other Big Step interventions, and the school was generally recognized as moving in the right direction. The achievement scores of students at Dewey were going up, and the school was becoming a much more positive place for educators and students.

Lori prided herself on being professional. She was organized, positive, and a hard worker. She did a great job of making sure teachers were well prepared to implement the Big Step curriculum. Everyone also recognized that Lori was a highly skilled and inspirational teacher. Students listened to her when she was leading model lessons, and she managed classroom behavior in a manner that was positive, supportive, and effective. Kids learned when she taught, and teachers learned when they watched her teach.

For the most part, Lori liked the staff at Dewey, and she was well liked by the staff. Lori had been at the school for three years, and some of the teachers had become important friends in her life. Unfortunately, Lori couldn't say that she was friends with or even liked every teacher. In particular, she felt a great deal of animosity toward Mike Keenan, a young teacher who taught special education.

Mike wasn't easy to like. He enjoyed making loud jokes about other teachers at the school. During staff meetings, Mike spoke more than anyone else, and frequently, it appeared Mike hadn't been listening to others during meetings. Teachers frequently rolled their eyes when Mike gave one of his speeches during meetings, and when Mike didn't get his way, he sulked. He made critical personal comments about staff when they didn't agree with him, and on more than one occasion, he told Lori she was just being "pig-headed" and not listening to common sense.

Mike also seemed to be an ineffective instructor. He seemed unprepared for lessons. Frequently, Mike appeared to treat his students more like friends than students, which meant that students were frequently off-task and sometimes uncomfortable. It seemed to Lori that Mike was more concerned about feeling liked by the students than ensuring that the kids were learning. Ironically, of course, students didn't particularly like or respect him. Lori considered Mike to be a loud, immature, and unprofessional teacher. Lori confided to others that she felt "creepy" whenever she talked with him in his classroom.

Not surprisingly, many teachers at the school made fun of Mike behind his back. In fact, making fun of Mike was a popular activity in the staff lounge. At first, Lori tried to stay out of the gossipy conversation, but she wasn't able to keep her feelings to herself. Lori actually came up with a nickname for Mike that most staff started to use for him behind his back: "The Mouthpiece." As time went by, Lori became an eager participant in conversations about "The Mouthpiece." Lori told herself that she needed to blow off steam about Mike, and since many of the staff she gossiped with were actually her friends, it was only natural that she'd talk with them about him.

One afternoon, Lori walked by Mike's classroom, and she could see that he was struggling with both what he was teaching and how he was teaching. "He needs help," she thought. "It would really help him and his students if I showed him how to teach behavioral expectations, but I really don't want to work with The Mouthpiece." That afternoon, Principal Fraser visited Lori in her office. "Lori," she said, "We've got to do something to help Mike. If our SPED kids don't do better, we won't make AYP, and we need to make sure Mike is doing the best for his students. I'm going to be putting pressure on Mike to do better, and I need you to make Mike a priority the rest of this year."

Reflection Questions for The Mouthpiece Scenario

1. What do you think about Lori's actions in the school? Is there anything she should be doing differently?

2. Is it OK for Lori to gossip behind Mike's back? Is it OK to make negative comments about teachers behind their backs? If you think Lori should avoid some gossip, what can she do to avoid getting drawn into talking behind others backs?

3. What should Lori do now? Should she work with Mike? Assuming you think she should work with him, how should she use the partnership approach with him? What should be Lori's next steps?

NOTES

COMMUNICATION SKILLS

<u>Guiding Question:</u> How can I refine my communication skills as a coach?

<u>Resources:</u> Coaching Trio activity, Principles of Coaching videos: Effective Listening and Good Questions, Listening Effectively checklist, Writing Good Questions checklist

<u>Activity:</u>

1. Read through the Coaching Trio activity to become familiar with the process.

2. Watch both videos, then decide if you want to focus on listening or questioning during this learning path (you choose!).

3. Once you have chosen, browse the checklist that aligns with your focus (either listening or questioning).

4. Complete the activity.

   a. Note: you will practice your selected skill when you are role "B" in the activity. For example, if you are working on listening, you will actively work to listen well as your partner (role "A") talks about whatever they discuss as the presenter.

5. Wrap up this learning path by discussing major takeaways or by answering the guiding question.

COACHING TRIO ACTIVITY

 Purpose: this activity is for a group of three to practice, reflect, and gain insights from others.

Process:

1. Explain the three roles to the participants:

    a. The coach is the person who is asking questions.

    b. The coachee is the person who is speaking and reflecting.

    c. The observer is the person who is watching the exchange between the coach and coachee to share insights after the conversation has concluded.

2. Invite participants to form groups of three. Within those groups, have them decide who will hold each of the roles during Round 1 of the activity.

3. For each round, follow these steps:

    a. The observer will also serve as the timekeeper and will start a 3-minute timer before the coach begins.

    b. Then, the coach asks a kickstart question, like, "What is on your mind about our topic?"

    c. The coachee answers the question and uses the conversation to think deeply about the topic at hand.

    d. The coach continues to facilitate the coachee's thinking by using questions, by listening fully, and by holding the focus on the coachee.

    e. At the end of the 3 minutes, the observer calls "time" and asks the coachee to finish their last thought.

    f. The observer will set a 2-minute timer and allow the coach and coachee to reflect on the conversation. Then, the observer will share what they noticed from the exchange.

4. There will be three rounds during this activity. In each round, the participants will change roles so that each person has the opportunity to serve in each role.

5. Once the activity has come to a close, bring all participants back together to reflect using these questions:

    a. What stood out to you as you participated in a coaching trio?

    b. How will your experience influence your practice?

Principles of Coaching Videos
Effective Listening and Good Questions

https://youtu.be/aS0faMIjtfM
In this video, you will hear Jim talk about effective listening.

https://youtu.be/ZdiCXXetWkw
Here are Jim's ideas on asking good questions.

CHECKLIST: LISTENING EFFECTIVELY

TO LISTEN EFFECTIVELY, I . . .	✔
Embrace silence to allow for thinking	
Talk less than my conversation partner	
Don't interrupt (except when it is helpful)	
Prepare to be present by taking care of myself	
Put away distractions	
Listen to understand beliefs, assumptions, and emotions	
Avoid judgments, assumptions, and comparisons	
Avoid completing my conversation partner's sentences	
Maintain an appropriate and comfortable level of eye contact	

CHECKLIST: WRITING EFFECTIVE QUESTIONS

EFFECTIVE QUESTIONS . . .	✓
Are hard enough to be worth answering	
Are easy enough that they can be answered	
Are short	
Are easy to understand	
Are focused on the person answering the question	
Are solution-focused	
Avoid making another person wrong	
Communicate respect	
Increase clarity	
Can be open or closed	
Can be evocative or generative	
Are not leading questions	
Do not have a hidden agenda	
Are questions we don't know the answer to	
Invite others to think more clearly	
Are adapted to be most helpful in each unique conversation	

END OF CHAPTER REFLECTION

Now that you have explored learning opportunities about Communication Skills, take time to reflect on this Success Factor overall. Use the following reflection questions, or reflect in your own way, and fill the lines with your ideas.

REFLECTION QUESTIONS

1. On a scale of 1 to 10, 1 being not at all and 10 being significant, what impact did these learning paths have on your practice? What led you to choose the rating you did?

2. What idea has had the greatest impact on the way you communicate?

3. How will you continue to refine your communication skills?

NOTES

Chapter 3

Coaches as Leaders

*"I define a leader as anyone who takes responsibility for
finding the potential in people and processes, and who has
the courage to develop that potential."*

~Dr. Brené Brown

Success Factor #3: Coaches as Leaders

Instructional coaches lead as they move about their daily work of doing what's best in their system for students. As a leader, coaches must first lead themselves through knowing their purpose, developing a personalized plan to managing their time, building habits, and practicing self-care (Knight, 2022). Once coaches lead themselves, they are far more likely to successfully lead others by balancing humility with ambition, being a multiplier, creating alignment, and making good decisions (Knight, 2022).

So Why Should We Be Talking About Coaches as Leaders Within Schools and Systems?

When coaches lead, they are seen as trustworthy and reliable. This is built through actions that show all they do is in service of students. Their beliefs and habits can be replicated by others within their system so processes can be identified that work to show improvement for students across all elements.

Resources Included in This Chapter

ARTICLES	ACTIVITIES	SCENARIOS	VIDEOS
"What Is the Measure of a Life?"	Listening Dyads	Leading Others Scenarios	The Measure of My Life
"To Live an Undivided Life"	Exchange of Views		How Coaches Can Foster Hope
"How to Foster Hope in Tough Times"	Modified Literature Circle		Empathy
"How Not to Hit Land Mines in Coaching Conversations"	Four *Is* Protocol		Understanding Change
"What I've Learned From a Traumatic Accident"	In Closing		
"5 Simple Reflection Practices"	Exploring Viewpoints		
"The Moral Universe Won't Budge Unless We Move It"	Discuss and Observe		
"Take Time for Self-Care"			
"To Change, Start Where You Really Are"			

Optional Learning Paths

Learning Path #1

Guiding Question: How might you determine your purpose when leading yourself?

Resources: "What Is The Measure of a Life" article or "To Live an Undivided Life" article, The Measure of My Life video, Listening Fully activity

Activity:

1. Use the Dyad activity to read about and watch videos on leading yourself.

    a. Read either article, and watch Jim's video.

    b. Use the Dyad activity to discuss your purpose and how you live an "undivided life" as a leader.

2. You could use the reflection questions that appear after each article or come up with your own to guide the Dyad activity.

3. Debrief Dyad activity using the questions provided.

Learning Path #2

Guiding Question: How can I foster hope as a coach?

Resources: "How to Foster Hope in Tough Times" article, How Coaches Can Provide Hope video, Exchange of Views activity

Activity:

1. Use the Exchange of Views activity to read about and watch videos on fostering hope

    a. Read the article, and watch Jim's video.

    b. Use the Exchange of Views activity to identify dilemmas where hope might be missing and find ways to foster hope.

2. You could use the reflection questions that appear after each article, if needed.

Learning Path #3

Guiding Question: How can I ensure I am giving choice and voice and consider identity when I lead and coach?

Resources: "How Not to Hit Land Mines in Coaching Conversations" article, Four *I*s Protocol activity

Activity:

1. Use the Four *Is* Protocol to discuss thoughts on the article.

   a. Read the article.

   b. Use the Four *Is* Protocol after reading.

2. You could use the reflection questions that appear after the article, if you choose.

3. Debrief Four *Is* Protocol and text interaction if you choose.

Learning Path #4

Guiding Question: How can I be a more reflective practitioner?

Resources: "What I've Learned From a Traumatic Accident" article and "5 Simple Reflection Practices" article, Modified Literature Circle activity

Activity:

1. Use the Appreciative Inquiry activity to read about and discuss the articles on reflective practices.

   a. Read both articles.

   b. Use the Modified Literature Circle activity to discuss the articles. Adapt as necessary.

2. Use the reflection questions that appear after each article, if you choose.

3. Debrief Literature Circle activity if you choose.

Learning Path #5

Guiding Question: How can coaches help move their systems toward justice and equity?

Resources: "The Moral Universe Won't Budge Unless We Move It" article, The In Closing activity

Activity:

1. Use the In Closing activity to discuss thoughts on the article.

   a. Read the article.

   b. Use the In Closing activity after reading.

2. You could use the reflection questions that appear after the article, if you choose.

3. Debrief In Closing activity.

Learning Path #6

<u>Guiding Question:</u> How can coaches be sure they are taking time for self-care?

<u>Resources:</u> "Take Time for Self-Care" article, Empathy video

<u>Activity:</u>

1. Read the article, and watch the video.

2. Use the reflection questions that appear after each article to discuss the article and accompanying video.

3. Debrief ways to continue self-care as well as encourage it for those you coach.

Learning Path #7

<u>Guiding Question:</u> How can coaches model and encourage getting a clear picture of reality in order to change for good?

<u>Resources:</u> "To Change, Start Where You Really Are" article, Understanding Change video

<u>Activity:</u>

1. Read the article, and watch the video.

2. Use the reflection questions that appear after each article to discuss the article and accompanying video.

3. Brainstorm ways to partner with teachers to confront reality.

Learning Path #8

<u>Guiding Question:</u> How can I look at others to understand how I lead?

<u>Resources:</u> Leading Others Scenarios, Exploring Viewpoints Activity

<u>Activity:</u>

1. Use the Leading Others scenarios document to read about the scenarios and discuss the reflection questions.

2. For a more formal activity, use the Exploring Viewpoints Activity to work through scenarios.

Learning Path #9

<u>Guiding Question:</u> How can I use my colleagues to receive feedback and improve my coaching skills?

<u>Resources:</u> Videos of coaching conversations, Discuss and Observe Activity, Listening and Questioning Checklist

<u>Activity:</u>

1. Bring videos of any coaching conversation to watch and discuss. These can be short snippets of any coaching conversation (5 minutes or less) where the coach wants to get feedback on what they've said and done. When videoing, make sure both the coach and the teachers' faces show.

2. Use Discuss and Observe activity to discuss videos. You can use the Listening and Questioning Checklist provided as a guide for what to watch and listen for when watching the video. The coach whose video is being observed might also have specific look-fors and/or questions they'd like to pose to the group for feedback.

3. This can also be done live in a role-play situation.

<u>Guiding Question:</u> How might you determine your purpose when leading yourself?

<u>Resources:</u> "What Is The Measure of a Life" article or "To Live an Undivided Life" article, The Measure of My Life video, Listening Fully

<u>Activity:</u>

1. Use the Dyad activity to read about and watch videos on leading yourself.

    a. Read either article, and watch Jim's video.

    b. Use the Dyad activity to discuss your purpose and how you live an "undivided life" as a leader.

2. You could use the reflection questions that appear after each article or come up with your own to guide the Dyad activity.

3. Debrief Dyad activity using the questions provided.

What Is the Measure of a Life?

Originally published in *Educational Leadership, 80*(5). February 1, 2023.

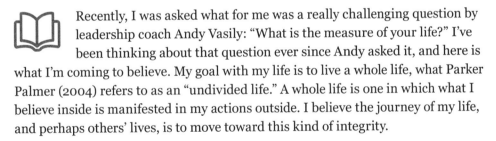 Recently, I was asked what for me was a really challenging question by leadership coach Andy Vasily: "What is the measure of your life?" I've been thinking about that question ever since Andy asked it, and here is what I'm coming to believe. My goal with my life is to live a whole life, what Parker Palmer (2004) refers to as an "undivided life." A whole life is one in which what I believe inside is manifested in my actions outside. I believe the journey of my life, and perhaps others' lives, is to move toward this kind of integrity.

Inside, my beliefs are increasingly clear: I want to focus my energy on what is good for others and not only myself. I want to approach others with humility, giving others the credit they deserve and downplaying any credit to myself. I want to believe in others, to be their ally, to start from the belief that people are doing their best given what they are dealing with. I want to be a voice for those whose voices are silenced. I want to be honest, generous, forgiving, and grateful even in the most difficult times.

Do my actions always reflect my beliefs? Am I living a perfectly undivided life? Of course not. I fall short every day. Much too often, I let my own personal concerns walk all over the concerns of others. I am too distracted, too rushed. Too often I'm so focused on getting what I want that I forget to be grateful for what I've already been given.

The Need for Self-Compassion

When I talk about this struggle for wholeness with people I meet, they tell me they too think their actions fall short of their beliefs. And in this post-pandemic time, when many have suffered truly heart-breaking losses, and almost all of us feel emotionally exhausted, we shouldn't be surprised that it's so difficult to be the person we desire to be. This challenge is especially difficult for educators, who feel the urgency of the moral purpose behind their work. "To teach," I often say, "is to feel guilty." Teaching is such complex, emotional work that it would be impossible for every lesson or coaching conversation to be flawless.

What makes our struggle even more difficult is the fact that, as researchers like Kristin Neff have shown, most of us are way more critical of ourselves than we would ever dream of being about others. We want to live with integrity, but far too often we feel like we've failed—and we're not afraid to criticize ourselves for our failures. We can feel demoralized by our failures, by all the times our self-centeredness, lack of self-control, or fear have led us to act in ways we regret. But I don't think our failures should define us. What if we allowed ourselves to be defined not by our failures, but by those days when we listen, when we're grateful, when we're loving? My friend Charlotte Ostermann says that "The truest thing about us is the highest thing about us—not the worst thing—and we should live into that goodness." Coaches, leaders, teachers and all other colleagues in schools can do a great service if they remind people of this truth.

Defined by Who We Are Now

The past is gone—and it doesn't define us. Others who criticize us often don't really know us, and their opinions shouldn't define us. The future hasn't come yet, so it can't define us. Who we are is how we live out each new moment; we're defined by what we do in the present. And the great journey of life is to have more moments that are whole, where our outside actions reflect our internal beliefs, where we're trying to be the truest version of ourselves.

Believing that each moment is alive with the potential for wholeness gives me hope and keeps me going even when I know I haven't been my best. When I consider Andy's question, I see the measure of my life being how I respond in each minute, each interaction, each day. My next moment is another opportunity to live an undivided life, and in the moment that's all that really matters to me. Imagine what it might do for teachers' morale and energy if they began to feel this way, too.

Reflection Questions for "What Is the Measure of a Life?"

1. What are my own beliefs about how I lead?

2. How do I show myself self-compassion?

3. What's on my mind after I read this article?

4. What might need to change in my school/system?

_____

_____

_____

_____

_____

_____

_____

_____

To Live an Undivided Life

Originally published in *Principal Connections*. December 2010.

"How do I know who I am until I see what I do?"

—E.M. Forster as paraphrased by Adam Grant

A few years ago, Jenny, my life-partner, attended a workshop about how to live a meaningful life. When she entered the session's room, she saw a tape measure had been placed on each participant's chair. After the audience was seated, the presenter asked the workshop members to grab their tape measures and rip off the front part of their tape up to the number of years they've been alive. Then, he asked people to estimate how long they expected to live and rip off a section of the tape measure after that number. Finally, he said "Hold up your tape measure and look at it. This is your life. What do you want to do with it?"

My guess is that many of the people in that room answered they wanted to live a life of service. When asked such a question, most of us say we want to do more for our family, our friends, our colleagues and the greater community. We want to give more and take less. We want to be remembered as people who cared about other people, not just ourselves. In his book summarizing the benefits of service, *Give and Take* (2014), Adam Grant writes, "most people rate giving [his term for acts of service] as their single most important value. They report caring more about giving than about power, achievement, excitement, freedom, tradition, conformity, security and pleasure (p. 21)."

We believe in service and talk about its importance. But there is often a large gap between what we say and what we do. And what we do often sheds light on our true beliefs. We may say we want to act in service of other people, but if it always conforms to what is best for us, our actions reveal that our beliefs are much more self-centred than service-centred.

One way to live a life in which our actions reflect our beliefs is to work out these beliefs in our day-to-day lives. Because we don't just embrace a new belief about service and then automatically become a new service-centred person. We must first get clear on who we want to be and then work towards becoming that person. Life, as people like Parker Palmer and Thomas Merton have said, is about a movement towards an undivided life—a life where what we do outside of ourselves is the same as what happens inside of us.

How then do we move towards having an undivided life? I'm sure there are many roads that people can take to that kind of life. After having studied coaching and behaviour change for more than two decades, I'd like to suggest a few things people could try out, recognizing that everyone's journey will be unique.

First, there is great value in getting clear on what it is you believe. Writing a statement that describes what we are trying to accomplish in life, how we want to interact with other people and how we want to act, can be very helpful. For example, we might write, "I want to breathe life into other people in every conversation," or, "I want my actions to show clearly that my will is dedicated to doing good for other people." Our statements about purpose can be refined over time, but getting clear on who we want to be, and writing it down, can be an important first step towards an undivided life.

Our next step might be to do what Nir Eyal (2019) refers to as time blocking. To do things for other people, we need to build time into our calendar. Because if we don't, many big actions are not going to happen. To live an undivided life, we have a limited number of choices: we can talk about our beliefs, or we can change our day-to-day life to make room for the acts of service. Not all acts of service require intentional time. Many small actions, which we could call micro-actions, happen in an instant. For example, in a flash, we can encourage or discourage someone around us. So, a second way in which we can move from talk to action is to reflect on each day and ask ourselves how well we lived out our service statement describing who we are and how we want to serve.

This form of reflection could involve some simple questions such as those included in the After-Action Review developed by the US Army—What was supposed to happen? What really happened? What accounts for the difference? What should I do next time? Or it can involve a more spiritual reflection process such as the Daily Examen, first described by Ignatius Loyola. Another option is to conduct what I call an interaction analysis—to look back over our whole day at the end of the day and consider each interaction.

One way or another, to truly live an undivided life, most of us need to (a) get clear on what we believe, (b) make time for it, and (c) reflect frequently on how well we live out those beliefs so we can try to do better next day. If we do these three things, perhaps at the end our lives, when we've used up all the days on our own tape measures, we will feel that peace that comes from knowing we were the person we said we were, and the satisfaction that comes from knowing our actions will have great potential to be a benefit to others every day.

Reflection Questions for "To Live an Undivided Life"

1. If I were to write a statement about my beliefs, what would it say?

2. Do my beliefs match my actions? How do I know?

3. What's on my mind after I read this article?

4. What might need to change in my school/system?

NOTES

_____

_____

_____

_____

_____

_____

_____

_____

_____

_____

_____

_____

_____

_____

_____

_____

_____

_____

COACHES AS LEADERS

THE LISTENING FULLY ACTIVITY

 Purpose: to practice deep listening.

Process:

1. Share the overall outcome of the activity: to exchange an opportunity with a partner to be heard without interruptions or distractions.

2. Ask participants to find a partner (adjust for groups with odd numbers).

3. Designate the partners to be Partner A and Partner B.

4. Partner A will go first in the process, and then Partner B will take their turn.

5. In Round 1, Partner A will speak about one of the following prompts for 2 minutes. Partner B will focus their attention on Partner A, listening to their words, their emotions, and the journey they take while answering the prompt. Partner B will also avoid interruptions and distractions. It is preferable that there are no phones present during the activity so that external distractions can be minimized.

6. Once Round 1 is over, both partners will share about their experience as the speaker (Partner A) and the listener (Partner B) for 1 minute.

7. Then, Round 2 begins. In this round, Partner B will be the speaker (for 2 minutes), and Partner A will be the listener. Partner A will focus their attention on Partner B, listening to their words, their emotions, and the journey they take while answering the prompt. Partner A will also avoid interruptions and distractions. It is preferrable that there are no phones present during the activity so that external distractions can be minimized.

8. Once Round 2 is over, both partners will share about their experience as the speaker (Partner B) and the listener (Partner A) for 1 minute.

9. After the activity has come to a close, the following reflection questions can be used to wrap up the experience:

   a. What does this leave you thinking about being present in conversations?

   b. What did you learn when you focused completely on your partner?

   c. What was difficult for you while listening/speaking?

   d. How will this inform your practice?

The following are prompts for partner discussion:

- What is a favorite childhood memory, and why is it important to you?
- What has been an influential experience for you in your career?
- What hopes do you have for your future?

 Measure of a Life Video

 https://youtu.be/ffHN0YeGAzot
In this video, Jim talks about living consistently with your principles, getting clear on what matters, and living an undivided life.

Guiding Question: How can I foster hope as a coach?

Resources: "How to Foster Hope in Tough Times" article, How Coaches Can Provide Hope video, Exchange of Views activity

Activity:

1. Use the Exchange of Views activity to read about and watch videos on fostering hope

    a. Read the article, and watch Jim's video.

    b. Use the Exchange of Views activity to identify dilemmas where hope might be missing and find ways to foster hope.

2. You could use the reflection questions that appear after each article, if needed.

How to Foster Hope in Tough Times

Originally published in *The Learning Professional: The Learning Forward Journal, 42*(1). February 2021.

 Hope requires that we believe we can get to our goal by taking the necessary steps along the path. The clearer the path, the more agency and confidence we'll have.

At the beginning of every new year, I create a playlist for my friends filled with music that brings me joy. I call it my happy list. This year, as I chose my songs, I realized that a theme was emerging: new beginnings. As Nina Simone sings, "It's a new dawn, it's a new day, it's a new life for me, and I'm feeling good" (Bricusse & Newley, 1965).

This year's playlist gives voice to my deep desire to turn the corner on the tough times we've all experienced this past year. I know I'm not alone in wanting a new beginning. For many, 2020 was the hardest year of their lives.

In times like this, we can feel tempted to give up whatever fight we are fighting. Coaches and other professional developers and leaders may feel doubly frustrated as they struggle to help others feel hope while they struggle to keep the faith themselves. I urge you to keep moving forward and support your friends and colleagues as they move forward. We are learning more and more about hope, and while the research isn't a guaranteed road map to success, it does identify several tangible actions we can take to remain hopeful.

1. FACE REALITY.

There are many excellent reasons to avoid reality. At times, almost all of us need the emotional protective bubble wrap of defense mechanisms just to negotiate the emotional terrain of everyday life.

The trouble is, as Miller and Rollnick (2013) explain, the motivation to move forward almost always comes from a discrepancy between where we are and where we want to be. So while turning our eyes away from the world may bring us some relief in the moment, it leads to avoiding learning, growth, movement, and, eventually, hope.

One way coaches can help others see reality more clearly is by offering to record them in action. The camera doesn't lie, which is why I like to say video is like rocket fuel for learning. But not everything can be recorded, so it's useful to identify friends and colleagues who are willing to tell us the truth about what they see. A coach, friend, or mentor may even help us see that we are being overly critical of ourselves and offer a more balanced view.

2. SET GOALS.

Hope researchers Snyder (1994) and Lopez (2013) describe hope as a process with three elements: goals, pathways, and agency. Goals are, in essence, our hoped-for future, and there is a mountain of research that tells us goals are important for motivation (see Halvorson, 2012).

Coaches can awaken others (and themselves) to their goals by asking powerful questions, like the famous question from solution-focused coaching (Jackson & McKergow, 2002): If you woke up tomorrow and a miracle had happened, and your class (or something else) was everything you hoped it would be, what would be different? What would be the first thing you would see that would show you that things have changed?

Goals must matter to the person being coached. That means people must choose the goals themselves.

3. IDENTIFY PATHWAYS.

We also need to see one or more pathways to the goal we have set so that we have a clear picture of how to reach it. When coaches partner with others to identify strategies for reaching goals, they foster hope. Sometimes this involves asking questions, such as: What advice would you give someone else with your goal? What have you done in the past to successfully meet challenges like this? (Campbell & van Nieuwerburgh, 2018).

When necessary, coaches can suggest strategies teachers might try. However, how they share that knowledge is a complex communication challenge. If they direct teachers or act like know-it-alls, coaches take away ownership of the goal and, ultimately, take away hope.

4. TAKE ACTION.

Hope also requires that we believe we can get to our goal by taking the necessary steps along the path. The clearer the path, the more agency and confidence we'll have.

Coaches can make the pathway easier to follow by helping teachers plan implementation of a strategy, explaining and modeling teaching strategies, and gathering data so that teachers can see their progress. Seeing our progress makes us more likely to believe that achieving the goal is possible.

In most cases, the best way to build momentum and deepen our agency is to take tiny steps forward and see the positive results. Coaches can help in this process by sharing specific, concrete, positive feedback. One true, specific observation delivered at the right time in the right way can stay with a person for a lifetime.

BE BRAVE

These are tough times, and that makes it all the more important to foster hope in others—and in ourselves. All of the strategies I've shared here can and should be applied by coaches and other professional learning leaders as well as teachers. It takes bravery to persevere. But when we find the courage to look at reality, set goals, identify pathways, and build agency, we can foster hope. As educators, we need to feel hope, because there is a lot worth doing.

Reflection Questions for "How to Foster Hope in Tough Times"

1. Am I asking the teacher to use video? How is that going?

2. Am I also using video as I coach and talking about it?

3. What's on my mind after I read this article?

4. What might need to change in my school/system?

NOTES

THE EXCHANGE OF VIEWS ACTIVITY

 Purpose: the purpose of this activity is for everyone to call to mind a professional challenge, or dilemma, they are working through and consider how they might expand on their thinking by consulting a group.

Process:

1. Write it out—Invite everyone to think deeply about situations that are currently challenging them professionally. These challenges can be anything: relationships with colleagues, tasks that require a lot of work, a project, or something else. Ask participants to write down as many ideas for dilemmas as possible. The facilitator should allow 3 to 4 minutes for this step.

2. Top 2—Now that participants have a list, invite them to review it and choose their top two greatest challenges at work.

3. Details matter—With the top two greatest challenges, ask participants to consider the following questions to generate more specific details about their dilemmas.

   a. Why is this a challenge for you?

   b. If you were someone else observing this dilemma, how might you describe it?

   c. What do you hope changes to make this easier or more manageable?

   d. What stories have you created about this challenge or dilemma?

4. Make a choice and focus up—Now that participants have dug deeply into their top two, it's time to choose one of those to take further into the activity. Have them select one and then develop a question that captures the essence of their dilemma or challenge in question form.

   a. Examples: (1) I am having a hard time getting along with a colleague from a different department. What can I do to build a better working relationship with this person so that we can get our job done? (2) My team and I are on different pages with how we should teach the upcoming unit to our students. What conditions can we put into place to hear each other's ideas and have a productive conversation about this unit?

5. Group discussion—Now, invite participants to form small groups of four to six people.

   a. Share conditions for psychologically safe conversations, such as honor confidentiality, offer one idea at a time, assume positive intent from the speaker, and provide helpful suggestions, not judgments.

   b. Instruct the group to choose who will share their dilemma first. For each speaker, the group will follow this process:

      i. The speaker shares the dilemma/question (1 minute).

      ii. The group shares ideas about how to support the speaker in their dilemma or asks questions to allow the speaker to think more deeply (3 minutes).

      iii. The speaker shares new thinking they have now that the group has shared their insight (1 minute).

c. The process will be repeated until all group members have had a chance to share and receive insights from their group.

6. Reflect—Once the activity has come to a close, bring the group back together and answer the two reflection questions:

a. How did this process support you? (share as a whole group)

b. What is your next step? (individual reflection)

How Coaches Can Bring Hope Video

https://youtu.be/blM1-zQpUTI

In this video, Jim talks about the three components of hope and how coaches use those components to bring hope to their partners.

<u>Guiding Question:</u> How can I ensure I am giving choice and voice and consider identity when I lead and coach?

<u>Resources:</u> "How Not to Hit Land Mines in Coaching Conversations" article, Four *Is* Protocol

<u>Activity:</u>

1. Use the Four *Is* Protocol to discuss thoughts on the article

    a. Read the article.

    b. Use the Four *Is* Protocol after reading.

2. Use the reflection questions that appear after the article, if you choose.

3. Debrief Four *Is* Protocol and text interaction.

How Not to Hit Land Mines in Coaching Conversations

Originally published in *Educational Leadership*, 80(3). November 1, 2022.

 Commenting on a teacher's practice can trigger identity fears. Tread carefully.

I sometimes share a thought experiment in presentations: Imagine that you have a sister who has a daughter. You love your niece almost as much as if she were your own child. Now imagine you see your sister making mistakes as a parent, and you feel you need to talk with her about how she parents. You need to tell her she is, in some way, raising your niece incorrectly. How easy would that conversation be?

Most people tell me they think the conversation would be so emotionally complex that they might be unwilling to have it even though they love their niece and are sure they have good advice to share. When you criticize how someone parents, you seem to criticize who they are as a person, their identity. And when you talk about something that touches another's identity, you walk on dangerous ground.

Teaching, for many educators, is as personal as parenting. Teaching matters a lot, and when you criticize how someone teaches, that teacher's identity is often at play. For this reason, understanding the ingredients of identity, and how to work with them, can help anyone have better conversations in schools, at home, or anywhere else. In working with educators and coaches over the past 25 years, I've found that there are four especially important ingredients of identity connected to a person's inner dialogue about themselves. When you're aware of these ingredients, especially when coaching someone, you should be able to have more productive, life-giving conversations.

Four Parts of Identity to Handle With Care

1. I'm a Good Person

Every person I've ever met either believes—or wants to believe—that they are a morally good person. As a result, conversations break down when people perceive they are being told they aren't acting in a morally correct manner (even if you haven't directly said this). The topic at hand gets forgotten.

One way to keep conversations from becoming overly personal is to provide opportunities for teachers to watch videos of their lessons and draw their own conclusions. What professionals discover for themselves about their practice is often more valuable than the comments of an external observer watching one lesson.

Stanford researchers David Bradford and Carole Robin (2021) also offer a helpful suggestion for avoiding appearing to make a moral judgment. All feedback conversations, they explain, involve three realities: (a) what the other person intended, (b) what the other person did, and (c) what we noticed about the impact of the other person's actions. When we talk about complex topics such as teaching, Bradford and Robin suggest we focus on action and impact and avoid talking about intent: We might say, for example, "I noticed that students got involved in the classroom discussion when you asked open-ended, opinion questions." When we start to talk about intent, people start to feel hurt or defensive.

2. I'm Doing a Good Job

Most of us believe or want to believe that we're at least competent at what we do, and we want others to see us that way. For this reason, we need to look for the good in others and communicate that we see others' strengths whenever we *do* see them. Positive comments are most effective when we avoid broad general statements, like "You're such a patient teacher," and instead describe evidence that proves the overall positive sentiment you want to express ("When you waited for Katrina to answer, and then you praised her, she lit up like a Christmas tree"). When we just tell someone they have a general trait, they often quickly deflect that affirmation by thinking of all the times they *didn't* exhibit that characteristic ("You think I'm patient, you should have seen me getting my son ready for school this morning"). When we describe a single, specific action someone took that embodies a positive characteristic, that comment is much more difficult to deny and more likely to land ("You know, I *did* do that").

3. I Want to Be Accepted

People want to be accepted, or loved, or at least not rejected. Conversations can be poisoned if people perceive we are rejecting them, even if that rejection—temporary and probably more connected to our own emotions—is revealed in a flash through a frown, sigh, or other nonverbal communication.

One form of rejection is moralistic judgment, any communication implying the other is bad in a moral sense. As psychologist Marshall Rosenberg (2015) asserts, moralistic judgment includes verbal communication that signals such judgment—such as blaming, put-downs, labels, and criticism—and also nonverbal communication that implies judgment. Moralistic judgment such as this interrupts learning and extinguishes intimacy. We don't seek help from someone who rolls their eyes when we talk.

4. I Want to Control My Life

Our identity is defined in large part by our ability to make choices. This is definitely so for most people working in education. As a result, when we feel we don't have a choice, we often resist. So when discussing concerns about a teacher's behavior with them, let go of trying to control their actions or choices if you want to have a meaningful conversation and fuel learning.

We can address this identity ingredient by structuring conversations so the person we're talking to can make choices—or at least be invited to do so. A fruitful question is one that coaching expert Michael Bungay Stanier shared with me: "You've probably thought a lot about this. What are you thinking that you might do?" By asking that question, we communicate our assumption that others have valuable ideas. We give control of the conversation to our conversation partner. Even when people really need or solicit advice, it's best to always talk in terms of choices ("Here are three possible ideas that come to mind; which one do you feel most confident implementing as a teacher?")

Speaking So Others Can Hear

Understanding identity this way helps us speak the truth in ways that can be heard. When we find ourselves in potentially complex, personal conversations, we typically respond either by stopping the conversation or pushing on even though we see that our comments are causing our conversation partner to feel upset or defensive. Neither approach leads to a positive outcome. Understanding the ingredients of identity provides a third way. When we separate issues from identity, communicate that we see others' strengths, avoid moralistic judgment, and let go of control, we create conditions where real conversation about real issues can happen.

Reflection Questions for "How Not to Hit Land Mines in Coaching Conversations"

1. How am I communicating with others in ways that respect their identity?

2. How am I offering up choice and voice in coaching conversations?

3. How do these "land mines" show up for me as a coach and leader?

4. What else is on my mind after reading this article?

NOTES

_____

_____

_____

_____

_____

_____

_____

FOUR *IS* PROTOCOL

 Purpose: To think deeply about your responses to a text.

Process:

1. Begin by selecting a text and giving everyone time to read the text in its entirety.

2. Afterward, invite the participants to review the reading and find parts of the text that fit these four ideas:

   a. What from the text is *interesting* to you?

   b. What part of the text would you say is the most *important* idea?

   c. If you were to disagree with part of the text, what would you say *instead* of what was presented?

   d. What *inspired* you from this reading?

3. Once the participants have had time to gather their ideas for the Four *Is*, conduct a group discussion. This can happen in several small groups or in one large group, depending on the number of participants.

4. To wrap up this activity, invite the participants to individually complete this sentence: "<u>I</u> am left thinking. . . ."

<u>Guiding Question:</u> How can I be a more reflective practitioner?

<u>Resources:</u> "What I've Learned From a Traumatic Accident" article and "5 Simple Reflection Practices" article, Modified Literature Circle activity

<u>Activity:</u>

1. Use the Appreciative Inquiry activity to read about and discuss the articles on reflective practices.

   a. Read both articles.

   b. Use the Modified Literature Circle activity to discuss the articles. Adapt as necessary.

2. Use the reflection questions that appear after each article, if you choose.

3. Debrief Literature Circle activity if you choose.

What I've Learned From a Traumatic Accident

Originally published in *The Learning Professional: The Learning Forward Journal, 42*(5). October 2021.

The Morning of July 4: A Life-Altering Bike Ride

 The morning of July 4, I went for an early morning bike ride on my usual loop around my hometown. Just after starting, I hit a slippery patch on the trail, causing my wheels to go out from under me, and I crashed, shattering several bones in my hip and pelvis. I had to have extensive surgery, and I spent three weeks in two different hospitals recovering. In a flash, on that bicycle path, my life was turned upside down.

From the moment that I was lifted into the ambulance, I recognized that I was about to learn a lot. When everything about your life gets disrupted, you can always expect to start learning.

Lessons Learned Through Recovery

The change I experienced tangibly and quickly taught me the obvious lesson that each day, each experience, each person is precious, and we need to value all of it because everything can change in a moment. But there are a few other lessons I have been taught as I've recovered.

Be Patient—Progress Takes Time

For the first eight weeks of my recovery, I saw very little progress. I was discouraged, and I worried that I might never get better. However, as I write this,

I am getting ready to walk without crutches, and each day, I am taking tiny steps forward. Progress, I've learned, especially at the start, can be hard to see. Wise people stop doing things that aren't working, but they also need to guard against recklessly giving up before seeing results. Our obsession with quick fixes can keep us from seeing real fixes.

Disrupt Your Routines to Find New Inspiration

Like most people, I have a long list of tasks I need to complete, and each day I put my head down and try to do them all. After my crash, I couldn't do any of my scheduled tasks. Suddenly, I had time to think, and that led to an explosion of ideas like I've never experienced before. Sometimes doing nothing might be the best work we can do.

Plan to Be Inclusive

My injury helped me see how easy it is to unintentionally exclude people we want to include. I often had experiences that were designed for everyone, but which I couldn't enjoy. For example, I read a short column on self-care, and every suggestion involved walking, something that was impossible for me. As I move forward, I hope that I will think more carefully about how to include everyone. A simple act, such as using a microphone to ensure that everyone hears, can make a huge difference.

Look for Beauty

When I got home from the hospital, I decided to fill my days with the music of J. S. Bach, listening to different compositions each day as I went about the dull, slow work of healing. My daily music ritual has done more than distract me—it has fed my soul. Whether we experience beauty in the still, quiet of the morning, or in Captain America comics, or in the laughter of a 2-year-old, beauty breathes life into us. Especially when times are tough, we need to make time for beauty because beauty will get us through.

Remember That People Are Good

One of the hardest parts of my injury was that I couldn't do the tasks I had planned to do. It's hard to give a Zoom workshop when you're in a hospital bed taking painkillers. Within hours, my colleagues selflessly volunteered to do my work, adding more to their plates to take everything off my plate. They told me, "Don't worry, we've got this. Just get better."

Recognizing the fundamental goodness of other people might be my most important lesson. Throughout my injury, family, friends, coworkers, and complete strangers have put down what they are doing to help me do what I need to do. This was important for me to see.

I've seen so much hatred, division, and fear in our world that I had begun to wonder whether human compassion no longer existed. But since my crash, I have no doubt that people care deeply for each other. Caring is our default mode. That's a lesson I hope I never forget.

Reflection Questions for "What I've Learned From a Traumatic Accident"

1. What have I learned from life's challenges recently?

2. How can I encourage the teachers I coach to learn from the challenging work of teaching?

3. How do I communicate empathy in my coaching conversations?

4. What happens when I don't show up in a coaching conversation with empathy?

NOTES

_____

_____

_____

_____

_____

_____

_____

_____

5 Simple Reflection Practices

Reflecting daily is a habit worth forming.

Originally published in *Educational Leadership, 81*(5). February 1, 2024.

One morning a few months ago, I finished my morning breakfast routine, and my thoughts jumped to, What's next? As I do every morning, I started to plan the meetings, tasks, and other things I needed to do. On this day, though, for no particular reason, it struck me that tackling one task right after another might help me get things done, but it didn't tell me if I was doing the right things.

That morning, I recognized that I needed to start disrupting my pattern of nonstop tasking. I realized I needed to develop a regular habit of reflecting, looking back and looking ahead in terms of what's happening in my life to consider whether I'm doing the right task, not just the next task. Since that morning "wake up," I've deepened my commitment to making reflection a daily habit. Here are five of my favorite reflection practices I've tried over the years.

1. **After-Action Review (AAR).** The U.S. Army (2004) has developed a simple conversational framework people can use after taking any action. Team members who use the AAR process together look back on how an activity went and look ahead to identify what to do better next time by asking four questions: What was supposed to happen? What really happened? What accounts for the difference? What should we do differently next time?

When I first started studying instructional coaching more than 20 years ago, my coaching team used these questions each Friday to reflect on how effectively we had each coached "our" teachers that week and what we could do to improve. Since then, I've used these questions often to reflect after completing an activity (say, a coaching conversation or presentation) or at the day's end to think over the events of the previous few hours.

2. **PERMA Review.** In his book *Flourish* (2011), Martin Seligman identified five essential elements needed for lasting happiness and wellbeing: positive emotions, engagement, relationships, meaning, and accomplishment (PERMA). At different stages of my life, I've used this PERMA acronym to reflect on my own well-being. Daily, I would rank on a scale of 1–5 how well I had experienced each element. This helped me see what factors were enhancing or inhibiting my happiness and consider what I might change to boost my well-being. Each element of the PERMA model pointed me to helpful insights at different times, particularly related to work choices I could make to be more engaged and communication choices I could make to improve my relationships with those closest to me.

3. **Life-Giving Review.** Considering several elements of well-being at the start or end of every day may seem overwhelming. One alternative is to simply consider whether each day's events were more "life-giving" or "life-taking." Life-giving experiences are positive, affirming experiences that give you energy, like engaging in a beloved hobby. Life-taking experiences are the opposite.

To do a life-giving review, look back on the events of your day and reflect on the life-giving or life-taking aspects of each experience. Then, identify what you might do differently moving ahead to have more life-giving experiences.

4. **One-Sentence Review.** Researchers who study habits, such as Wendy Wood (2019), suggest that people are more likely to sustain change when we develop habits, as opposed to relying on executive control or willpower. For this reason, if you want to make reflection a regular part of your life, it might help to begin with a small practice you can easily repeat until it becomes a daily habit. A simple way to build a reflective habit is to write one sentence at the end or start of each day. The sentence might describe one thing you can do to improve your life, something for which you're grateful, or a highlight of the day. Over time, this list of daily sentences will become pages you can periodically look over to identify patterns in your experiences; for instance, you might realize that most of the "highlights" you record happened outside, or with certain people. Of course, once the one-sentence review becomes a habit, you may wish to try deeper reflective practices.

5. **Serious Nothing.** I recently told my friend Jan about my morning epiphany that I was always doing the next thing but not asking if it was the right thing. Jan shared an idea she learned from her mentor, Dallas Willard—to disrupt my day by doing "serious nothing." That means turning off all my devices, putting down my task list, and just pausing to . . . do nothing. Serious nothing could be a quiet time in the morning, a walk, or even sitting in the Starbucks parking lot for five minutes. As Jan explained, people's deepest insights often come at those times

when they aren't thinking about anything in particular: in the shower, while driving across town, etc. Jan now builds into her day a few minutes where she simply does nothing. Those moments often help her gain insight she might not have gotten if she was focused on efficiently doing her daily tasks.

I do have one warning about this practice, though. I've found when I turn everything off and just pause for a few minutes, my serious nothing can turn into a serious nap! But then, I'm pretty certain those naps are another powerful way of increasing my well-being.

COACHES AS LEADERS

Reflection Questions for "5 Simple Reflection Practices"

1. What might work for teachers when reviewing their teaching and students' learning?

2. How might I stop and reflect on my coaching?

3. How do I work reflective practices into the work of my school or system?

4. How might I make reflection sustainable?

NOTES

MODIFIED LITERATURE CIRCLE ACTIVITY

1. Participants group into triads (3) and read the text (in this case, two articles by Jim Knight).

2. Each person takes on a discussion role:

   a. Summarizer (How might you summarize these articles succinctly?)

   b. Questioner (What was an aha you had? What made you think more deeply about your own reflective practices? How might this be helpful information as a coach?)

   c. Connector (Did you make any personal connections? Did you make any professional connections? Have you read something like this before? Where?)

3. Each person uses their role and has 5 to 15 minutes to ask their question(s) and hear responses from each of the readers.

4. When each person is done, the group adds any additional thoughts and reflections they might have about the article.

<u>Guiding Question</u>: How can coaches help move their systems toward justice and equity?

<u>Resources:</u> "The Moral Universe Won't Budge Unless We Move It" article, The In Closing Activity

<u>Activity:</u>

1. Use the In Closing activity to discuss thoughts on the article.

   a. Read the article.

   b. Use the In Closing activity after reading.

2. Use the reflection questions that appear after the article, if you choose.

3. Debrief In Closing activity.

The Moral Universe Won't Budge Unless We Move It

Originally published in *The Learning Professional: The Learning Forward Journal, 42*(3). June 2021.

Introduction

> *"[T]he arc of the moral universe is long but it bends toward justice."*
>
> —Martin Luther King Jr.

Discussion

Do you agree with King's often-quoted statement? In light of the heartbreaking and racist events I see in the news almost daily, I can't say I'm sure. What I do believe, however, is that the moral universe will not budge unless people act in ways that move it toward justice—people like you and me, people like instructional coaches.

As change leaders, instructional coaches are perfectly positioned to move their organizations forward. Coaches, like everyone in our educational organizations, can and should analyze their schools for evidence of structural racism and then fight for change until the system changes.

Coaches can raise awareness of prejudice by first learning about their own biases (Eberhardt, 2019; Project Implicit, 2011) and then partnering with others in coaching cycles that surface implicit bias. Also, coaches can advocate for justice by distinguishing between two kinds of power: power over and power with.

Power over is coercive power used to keep students in line. Teachers with a power over orientation communicate to students that they must do what they are told because they do not have power. In contrast, power with is authentic power that grows out of real relationships with students. Teachers who have a power with orientation demonstrate empathy, build connections, and respect their students (Knight, 2013).

Microaggressions are an especially pernicious form of power over (Sue, 2010). Microaggressions are brief, intentional or unintentional, common forms of abuse directed at groups or individuals. In the classroom, microaggressions can include "calling on and validating one gender, class, race of students while ignoring other students, singling students out in class because of their background, or setting low expectations for particular groups" (Portman et al., n.d.).

The "micro" morpheme might lead people to think that microaggressions are trivial. Nothing could be further from the truth. As Ibram X. Kendi writes, a "persistent daily low hum of racist abuse is not minor. . . . Abuse accurately describes the action and its effects on people: distress, anger, worry, depression, anxiety, pain, fatigue, and suicide" (Kendi, 2019, p. 47).

Coaches can promote power with by partnering with teachers to help them replace microaggressions with what I refer to as microaffirmations. These are actions and words that communicate that we see the dignity, value, and humanity of others. Microaffirmations include giving someone our full attention, authentic affirmative words, and paraphrasing what others say in ways that communicate that we have deeply heard what they have said.

Conclusion

Will the arc of the moral universe bend toward justice? I hope so. Today, though, we can do many things to make it much more likely that King's predictions will come true in our schools. By partnering with teachers to promote power with, we can make a difference. Maybe we won't change the whole universe. But we can change ourselves, and, in so doing, we can change others. If enough of us do that, our universe will move toward justice.

COACHES AS LEADERS

Reflection Questions for "The Moral Universe Won't Budge Unless We Move It"

1. Do you believe instructional coaches can "move their organizations forward"? Why, or why not?

2. How might instructional coaches move the "moral universe . . . toward justice"?

3. What's on your mind after reading this article?

4. What needs to change in your school or system, and what might your role be in making those changes?

COACHES AS LEADERS

NOTES

THE IN CLOSING ACTIVITY

 Purpose: To share final thoughts about a text and to build on those ideas by hearing diverse perspectives.

Process:

1. Select a text for this protocol, and have all participants read the text.

2. Once everyone is done reading, give them time to go back through the text and find three big ideas that resonated with them.

3. On a piece of paper or sticky note, have participants write those three big ideas.

4. Then, invite participants to reread all three of the big ideas and come up with one sentence that captures the essence of those big ideas. In other words, summarize what stood out to you the most with one sentence.

5. Once everyone has their summary sentence, the rounds begin. Here are the three steps for each round:

    a. To begin, one person (the speaker) will read aloud their summary sentence.

    b. Then, the rest of the group will take turns sharing what that person's summary sentence means to them by building on their ideas.

    c. Once anyone who is interested has shared their ideas about the speaker's summary sentence, it is the speaker's turn again. At this time, the speaker will say, "In closing . . . " and share the final thought they have after hearing from the group.

6. The rounds continue for each person in the group to share their summary sentence and follow the three steps.

    a. This can be modified for large groups by creating smaller groups to ensure efficient use of time and increased voice equity.

<u>Guiding Question:</u> How can coaches be sure they are taking time for self-care?

<u>Resources:</u> "Take Time for Self-Care" article, Empathy video

<u>Activity:</u>

1. Read the article, and watch the video.

2. Use the reflection questions that appear after each article to discuss the article and accompanying video.

3. Debrief ways to continue self-care as well as encourage it for those you coach.

Take Time for Self-Care

Originally published in *The Learning Professional: The Learning Forward Journal*, 41(5). October 2020.

 We are experiencing at least five major disruptions simultaneously: a global pandemic, fears about the economy, a national reckoning about racism, divisive rhetoric from Washington, and, if we work in schools, a deep uncertainty about what it is that we actually do as professionals and how, as schools navigate between remote, hybrid, and face-to-face instruction.

All of these changes, whether they have potential for good or not, involve the stress inherent to change. That is why now, more than at any time in our lives, educators must do something that doesn't come naturally to us: We must take the time needed to take care of ourselves. Three simple things can help us to have better self-care: purpose, healthy habits, and compassion (for others and, perhaps more importantly, ourselves).

Purpose

Sometimes, the most important thing we can do in challenging times is just to remind ourselves of the purpose that brought us to school in the first place. Remembering that purpose can help us persevere when the situation is stressful like it is now.

Richard Leider, a life coach and author, has interviewed hundreds of people over the age of 65, asking them to look back and identify what they wish they had done differently in their lives. During those interviews, Leider (1997) heard so much about purpose that he wrote a book about the topic, *The Power of Purpose*.

What Leider learned is that, "without purpose, we eventually lose our way. We live without the true joy in life and work. Until we make peace with our purpose, we will never discover fulfillment in our work or contentment with what we have" (1997, p. 4).

One way we can reflect on our purpose is to consider the four questions at the heart of the Japanese concept of "ikigai," which can be understood as "the reason we get up in the morning" (García & Miralles, 2016, p. 9): What do I love to do? What does the world need? What can I get paid for? What am I good at? I have found it to be very worthwhile to take time to reflect on these questions and journal my answers until I get clearer and clearer on my purpose.

In education, aligning our work with our purpose is often less about discovering and more about remembering. The day-to-day rush of urgent tasks that must be done can keep us so busy that we forget why education matters and what difference we make.

Purpose is particularly important right now when educators face challenges they've never experienced before, like learning a host of new technological tools and instructional approaches and navigating health concerns. Purpose can get us through.

Healthy Habits

We have all thought about healthy habits. We make resolutions and take initial steps, but eventually fall back into our old patterns of behavior. We blame ourselves for not changing and then feel even worse. Research shows that we fail to change not because of a lack of discipline, but because we lack a structure for our behavior change. Willpower by itself does not get the job done. What we need is a habit.

What distinguishes our habits is that, once they are established, we pretty much do them without thinking. Each of us has habits, good and bad.

We brush our teeth, get ready in the morning, and drink our morning coffee, all without thinking. Some habits are good, like working out after school, and some are bad, like drinking a bottle of Sauvignon Blanc every night while reading the news on Twitter.

To take care of ourselves, we need to harness the structure of habits to entrench the behaviors that lead to healthier lives. We need to develop a simple routine that we can easily repeat, ideally doing the exact same actions every day at the same time.

We should alter our context as best as we can to ensure it supports our new habit. If we stick with our habit long enough, perhaps 90 days or more, we can develop something that sticks (Wood, 2019), especially if those behaviors are small and simple (Fogg, 2020).

One good place to start is getting enough sleep. Lack of sleep makes us less intelligent, grumpier, less productive, and more likely to gain weight (Stevenson, 2016). Unfortunately, when you are worried about your family's health, or your economic well-being, or whether structural racism puts your child at risk, or the upcoming election, sleep doesn't always come easily.

Luckily, there are a few simple hacks anyone can do to improve the quality of sleep, including keeping your smartphone outside your bedroom, spending time in the sunshine every day, avoiding caffeine in the afternoon, exercising, and going to bed at the same time every night. Better sleep leads to a better life and a better capacity for taking on the specific unique challenges of this time.

Compassion

The challenges, opportunities, and uncertainties of this particular time in history zap our personal resilience, and this means many of us are not at our best. People are upset because their partner has just lost his or her job, or worried about their mother's health, or angered by the latest offensive political tweet. These exceptional times will lead to exceptional, and not always positive, behavior.

To support others, we need to be compassionate, understanding the emotions and needs of others, moving through our own mental barriers so we can demonstrate empathy, and acting on our understanding of others. That includes understanding that when people lash out because of frustration or fear, it's often not personal.

Of course, you are likely already extending a lot of compassion to others. But you might not be treating yourself with compassion. Self-criticism can lead us to say horrible things about ourselves (often silently to ourselves) that we would never say to someone else (Neff, 2011). If we are committed to effectively taking care of others, we need to start by taking care of ourselves.

To overcome self-criticism, we first need to recognize it, and then start to extend to ourselves the compassion we extend to others. This may involve letting go of the need to compete with others, being kind to ourselves, being mindful, and setting reasonable expectations for what we can accomplish right now.

I don't want to suggest that taking care of yourself is just a matter of adopting a happy frame of mind. Many people are suffering today because they cannot pay for the health care they need or because they are experiencing racist or gender-based systems designed to hold them back. Part of self-care involves working to create systems that are safer, healthier, and more humane. That should be a challenge we all take on.

Today, as we face all of these challenges, I am comforted by the knowledge that people are resilient. We will get through this together. But three simple things can make our getting through easier—reminding ourselves of our purpose, developing healthy habits, and being compassionate toward others and ourselves.

Reflection Questions for "Take Time for Self-Care"

1. What is your purpose? Jot down some thoughts about what keeps you going.

2. How do you show yourself compassion? Is there anything that needs to change?

3. How does self-care show up when you are coaching teachers?

4. What do you most agree with from the article?

NOTES

_____

_____

_____

_____

_____

_____

_____

 Empathy Video

 https://youtu.be/W9044okvlq4

In this video, Jim breaks down sympathy, empathy, and compassion and provides a way to distinguish the three so we can be more effective and more humane in our interactions.

Learning Path #7 Resources
How Can Coaches Model and Encourage Getting a Clear Picture
of Reality in Order to Change for Good?

<u>Guiding Question:</u> How can coaches model and encourage getting a clear picture of reality in order to change for good?

<u>Resources:</u> "To Change, Start Where You (Really) Are" article, Understanding Change video

<u>Activity:</u>

1. Read the article, and watch the video.

2. Use the reflection questions that appear after each article to discuss the article and accompanying video.

3. Brainstorm ways to partner with teachers to confront reality.

To Change, Start Where You (Really) Are

To improve equity, educators must work to get a clearer view of their practice.

Originally published in *Educational Leadership*, *79*(5). February 1, 2022.

 Much of my life, personally and professionally, has been dedicated to answering one question: What does it take to really change? Over the years, through my research and that of others, I've identified several important strategies for bringing about real and lasting change. For example, real change doesn't happen until we apply new ideas in real life. Real change is usually propelled forward by an emotionally compelling goal (Heath & Heath, 2010), and people are more likely to stay motivated to change if they monitor their progress (Amabile & Kramer, 2011).

But before we can implement any of these change strategies, there's one prerequisite: *If we want to make changes that make a difference and last, we must start by getting a clear picture of reality.*

Seeing the present reality clearly helps us identify the highest-leverage changes we should make, the actions we should take to achieve our goals. Perhaps more important, having a clear picture—including of our strengths and shortcomings in teaching practice—is essential to even *want* to bring about change. People usually aren't motivated to change unless they see a gap between where they are and where they want to be.

That Ubiquitous Avoidance

But while a clear picture of reality helps us clarify what we need to do and why, avoiding reality is a near-universal human tendency. Most of us avoid reality at least some of the time because we want to believe that we are competent, good people. Seeing life in its naked brutality can just be too difficult. This is especially true with actions regarding equity because buried within our defense mechanisms is the fear that we might not be as good of a person as we think; we may treat one group of kids less fairly or tune out injustices. So, we often use defense mechanisms to protect ourselves, justifying our behaviors by rationalizing, avoiding unpleasant data by denial and minimization, and shirking accepting responsibility by blaming others.

Often such defense mechanisms are actually helpful and healthy. Change experts Prochaska, DiClemente, and Norcross explain that "without the protection of these 'mental shields' we would be bombarded constantly by undesirable feelings and external threats, both real and imagined. Defensive reactions allow us to avoid, temporarily at least, what we cannot confront, and let us get on with our lives" (Prochaska, Norcross, & DiClemente, 1994, p. 82). So, defense mechanisms protect our emotional state. Unfortunately, if we never address them, they can make it hard for us to change.

Most of us also struggle to see reality clearly because our view of reality is obscured by perceptual errors like confirmation bias and habituation. Confirmation bias is our tendency to seek out data that confirm our preconceived notions. Habituation involves getting so used to whatever we're experiencing that we stop noticing or wondering about key aspects of that experience, like why kids from certain groups are so often in certain classes. The combined impact of defensiveness and perceptual errors is that most of us don't really know what it looks like when we do what we do as educators. This is a huge barrier to change! Fortunately, we can take actions to determine what's really unfolding.

Getting to Reality

Record Yourself

There's a reason why almost every middle and high school football team in the United States watches game film: it shows them what they're really doing on the field. Likewise, a video recording of yourself delivering a lesson, talking with a child, etc. cuts through defense mechanisms and perceptual errors. It shows your tone, how much time you spend with various kids, and so on—and consequently helps identify what you need to change. I highly recommend educators take and watch video of themselves in all kinds of contexts, including in the classroom, presenting, coaching, or during meetings to see how you lead and collaborate.

In schools, video can be an especially important tool for creating equitable classrooms. Video reveals how you interact with each student and may clue you in to subtle biases in your actions or how your classroom is set up.

Ask Those You Interact With

Asking those you interact with as an educator to describe their experiences in class/at school helps you get a clearer picture of your own behavior and its effects. Teachers and coaches learn a lot when they ask students to describe their learning, how engaged they feel in class, or the connection or lack thereof they feel with their school. Administrators and coaches benefit from meeting one-to-one with others in the school to seek feedback.

Instructional coaches can help with feedback seeking. For example, Bill Sommers—a former principal and now a coach for administrators who I've worked with—has adapted Marshall Goldsmith's Stakeholder Coaching method. Sommers begins his coaching by interviewing people who are affected by an administrator's actions (often those a leader notes that he or she has the most contact with), then synthesizes this interview data and shares the results with the administrator. A focus for coaching often surfaces.

Listen to Understand

It's easy to listen to people when they share positive information about us— ("Please, tell me more!"). It's a lot harder to listen when they share negative information. Our defensiveness can keep us from hearing important information that could help us see what's truly happening and move closer to our goals. I know I've damaged relationships that would have remained sounder if I'd done a better job of putting my defensiveness aside and just listened. We don't have to agree with what others say, but we should at least hear them out before we start to disagree.

When we *really* listen, we communicate to others that we value their opinions and expertise. For leaders, this is crucial. The teams where the most learning occurs are those where everyone feels free to share their ideas—whether positive or critical. This atmosphere won't exist when leaders silence people before they have a chance to share their ideas.

The Story of Our Lives

Getting a clear picture of reality, then, is an essential strategy for us professionally, and I think also personally. A life well-lived is a changing, growing life. I will never be the perfect version of myself. But I can be a little bit better—a better husband, parent, grandparent, and a better coach, leader, professional developer, or teacher. Learning, adapting, and setting goals is a big part of writing the story of my life. To write that story, I need a clear picture of reality.

COACHES AS
LEADERS

Reflection Questions for "To Change, Start Where You (Really) Are"

1. How difficult is it for you to see current reality? Why?

2. How are you currently getting feedback on your role as a coach? Does anything need to change?

3. How willing are the teachers you coach to get a clear picture of reality?

4. What's on your mind after you read this article?

NOTES

COACHES AS LEADERS

Change Video

https://youtu.be/KI1AAttTEc4
Real change happens from the inside out: In this video, Jim explains the difference between outside-in and inside-out change and how coaching is designed for inside-out change

Guiding Question: How can I look at others to understand how I lead?

Resources: Leading Others scenarios, Exploring Viewpoints activity

Activity:

1. Use the Leading Others scenarios document to read about the scenarios and discuss the reflection questions.

2. For a more formal activity, use the Exploring Viewpoints activity to work through scenarios.

LEADING OTHERS SCENARIOS

 Purpose: To consider and reflect on how we can lead others. Use the following scenarios and the reflection questions to think deeply about leading others.

Scenario 1:

Daniel is a second-grade teacher who has chosen to work with you after setting a goal for improvement in classroom management. He has taught second grade for thirty-two years, and the first time you met, he expressed disdain for coaching and "outsiders who think they know it all." You have seen Daniel in the hallway since he has set his goal, and he set a time with you and told you he wanted to work on setting up stations because his kids are "out of control." He smiled and said "thank you" as he walked away. After three visits to Daniel's classroom, you notice that the materials at his centers are very organized, and he has spent a lot of time focusing on grouping students intentionally. Daniel has mapped out units and planned differentiated opportunities for students. In conversation after the lesson, Daniel tells you he loves the planning but just can't stand having to "babysit and parent these kids." He admits he is feeling "burnt out" and feels like parents and administrators don't care about him or his hard work.

Reflect:

What are the strengths you notice that you can pull out and "hold up"?

What kinds of questions could you ask to put Daniel in the driver's seat and "open up" the conversation to create a dialogue?

What comes up for you here in your "internal dimension" as listener?

What might your next steps be?

Scenario 2:

Amani is new to your school and is a third-year teacher. She teaches seventh-grade social studies. You have a buildingwide initiative around incorporating "reading in the content areas" into units. After observing Amani three times, you notice she is not using any of the materials shared for this purpose. She shares with you that she finds those texts overwhelming and prefers to stick to the material she knows and that "she is not a reading teacher." In your observations, you notice the classroom environment is engaging and positive, and students are on task. There are many classroom discussions that are lively, and written work is being completed but mostly involves responding to a video or images. Amani is organized and passionate about history. Amani has mentioned she would like the students reading more but is concerned about where to begin.

Reflect:

What are the strengths you notice that you can pull out and "hold up"?

What kinds of questions could you ask to put Amani in the driver's seat and "open up" the conversation to create a dialogue?

What comes up for you here in your "internal dimension" as listener?

What might your next steps be?

EXPLORING VIEWPOINTS ACTIVITY

 Purpose: To enrich conversations and make learning more powerful through examining diverse perspectives.

Process:

1. Participants are encouraged (and helped) to select identifying perspectives according to the group's purpose. Clearly this involves judgment, but no one's self-selected perspective should be argued with; however, all should be willing to negotiate. It must be noted that we all have multiple ways we could describe ourselves and, for this activity, we will settle on one or two. For example, "I am an administrator who is committed to the 10 Common Principles" or "I am a new teacher in my first year." This process may take about 7 minutes. (You could also have people consider and decide on perspectives in advance of this conversation.)

2. Next, a question is presented that has emerged from the work of the group or that has emerged as an important one to the group. For example, "What is engagement, actually?"

3. All participants write their first thoughts in response to the question. This part of the process could take 5 minutes.

4. After this time, each participant gives their preliminary thinking on the question, prefaced with their point of view: For example, "From the point of view of an administrator, I think . . . " This part of the process could take about 10 minutes.

5. During the second round, each person gives their thinking building on what they heard from the other participants: "Having heard each of your perspectives, I now think . . . " (10 minutes)

6. The final round allows you to reflect on the quality of the responses: "I noticed that my/our responses . . . " This part of the activity could take 15 minutes.

<u>Guiding Question:</u> How can I use my colleagues to receive feedback and improve my coaching skills?

<u>Resources:</u> Videos of coaching conversations, Discuss and Observe activity, Listening and Questioning Checklist

<u>Activity:</u>

1. Bring videos of any coaching conversation to watch and discuss. These can be short snippets of any coaching conversation (5 minutes or less) where the coach wants to get feedback on what they've said and done. When videoing, make sure both the coach and the teachers' faces show.

2. Use the Discuss and Observe activity to discuss videos. You can use the Listening and Questioning Checklist provided as a guide for what to watch and listen for when watching the video. The coach whose video is being observed might also have specific look-fors and/or questions they'd like to pose to the group for feedback.

3. This can also be done live in a role-play situation.

DISCUSS AND OBSERVE ACTIVITY

 Purpose: This is an activity in which some participants are in an outer circle and one or more are in the center. During discuss and observe activities, both those in the inner and those in the outer circles have roles to fulfill. Those in the center model a particular practice or strategy. The outer circle acts as observers and may assess the interaction of the center group.

Process:

1. Arrange seating to accommodate two concentric circles. The inner circle may be only a small group or partners.

2. Explain the activity to your participants, and ensure that they understand the roles they will play. You may either inform those who will be on the inside ahead of time, so they can be prepared, or just tell them as the activity begins.

3. The group in the inner circle interacts using a discussion protocol.

4. Those in the outer circle are silent but are given a list of specific actions to observe and note.

5. One idea is to have each participant in the outer circle observe a specific participant in the inner circle (you may have to double, triple, or quadruple up.)

6. Another way is to give each participant in the outer circle a list of aspects of group interaction they should observe and comment on—for example, whether the group members use names to address each other, take turns, or let everyone's voice be heard.

7. You could also consider planning for all participants to have turns being in the inside and the outside circles, though they don't all have to be in both every time you do this activity.

8. Debrief: Have inner circle members share how it felt to be inside. Outer circle members should respectfully share observations and insights. Discuss how the experience could improve all group interactions and discussions.

Modification:

– Each person in the outside circle can have one opportunity during the activity to freeze or stop the inside participants. This person can then ask a question or share an insight.

LISTENING AND QUESTIONING EFFECTIVELY CHECKLIST

TO LISTEN AND QUESTION EFFECTIVELY, I . . .	✔
Make sure my conversation partner does most of the talking	
Pause and affirm before I start talking	
Don't interrupt (except when it is very helpful)	
Ask one question at a time	
Ask for clarification when I'm not certain what is being said	
Ask, "And what else?"	
Assume people are doing their best	
Am nonjudgmental	
Avoid leading questions	
Avoid giving advice disguised as a question	

END OF CHAPTER REFLECTION

Now that you have explored learning opportunities about Coaches as Leaders, take time to reflect on this Success Factor overall. Use the following reflection questions, or reflect in your own way, and fill the lines with your ideas.

REFLECTION QUESTIONS

1. On a scale of 1 to 10, 1 being not at all and 10 being significant, what impact did these learning paths have on your practice? What led you to choose the rating you did?

2. What is a major aha you had as you learned about Coaches as Leaders as a Success Factor?

3. What will you do next with your ideas?

NOTES

_____

_____

_____

_____

_____

_____

_____

_____

_____

_____

_____

_____

_____

_____

_____

_____

_____

_____

The Impact Cycle

"Success means having the courage, the determination, and the will to become the person you believe you were meant to be."

~George Sheehan

Success Factor #4: The Impact Cycle

Instructional coaches partner with teachers to make a difference in students' lives and well-being. In Success Factor #4: The Impact Cycle, coaches can learn *how* to lead that change. This three-stage process is a simple yet powerful structure for coaches to use to facilitate learning for teachers. It is what coaches do and how we keep kids first (Knight, 2018, 2022).

So Why Should We Be Talking About the Impact Cycle Within Schools and Systems?

School and system leaders care deeply about the achievement of students. One way to invest in student-focused programs for teachers is to invest in instructional coaching. The Impact Cycle aids coaches and coaching programs in finding a process that is easy to understand and implement and that leads to positive change for teachers and students (Knight, 2022).

Resources Included in This Chapter

ARTICLES	ACTIVITIES	SCENARIO/ CASE STUDY	CHECKLISTS	VIDEOS
"3 Steps to Great Coaching"	Give One Get One Move On	PEERS Scenarios	The Impact Cycle	The Principles of Coaching:
"In Coaching, 'One Size Fits One'"	Windowpanes	Case Study: Learn and Improve		1. What's a Good Goal
"Real Learning Happens in Real Life"	Gallery Walk			
"Record, Replay, Reflect"	Chalk Talk			
"What You Learn When You See Yourself Teach"	Circle, Square, Triangle Reflection			
"PEERS Goals"	Empathy Anchor			
"4 Steps for Focusing Coaching Sessions"	The Impact Cycle Video Reflection			
"Escape From the Zero-Learning Zone"	Enrolling Teachers			
"Strategies for Enrolling Teachers in a Coaching Cycle"				

THE IMPACT CYCLE

CHAPTER 4. THE IMPACT CYCLE

Optional Learning Paths

Learning Path #1

Guiding Question: What are the stages of the Impact Cycle?

Resources: "3 Steps to Great Coaching" article, Give One Get One Move On (GOGOMO) activity

Activity:

1. Read through the Give One Get One Move On (GOGOMO) activity to become familiar with the process.

   a. Modification option: Instead of creating a two-column T-chart as the activity calls for, the participants can choose to create a three-column T-chart to capture ideas about each of the three stages of the Impact Cycle. Participants can continue to add to their columns as they rotate through the activity rounds.

2. Read through the article, annotating as you learn about the three stages (identify, learn, and improve).

3. Use the GOGOMO activity to discuss the article.

4. Wrap up this learning path by using the reflection questions that appear after the article.

Learning Path #2

Guiding Question: What are the important concepts for coaches to know when partnering with teachers in the Impact Cycle?

Resources: "Real Learning Happens in Real Life" article, "In Coaching, 'One Size Fits One'" article, Windowpanes activity, Gallery Walk activity

Activity:

1. Read through the Windowpanes activity to become familiar with the process.

   a. Gather materials.

2. Engage in the Windowpanes activity with the two articles in this learning path.

3. Conduct a Gallery Walk so everyone can see the posters up close.

4. Wrap up this learning path by using the reflection questions that appear after the articles.

Learning Path #3

<u>Guiding Question:</u> How can video be used with teachers and coaches?

<u>Resources:</u> "Record, Replay, Reflect" article, "What You Learn When You See Yourself Teach" article, Chalk Talk activity

<u>Activity:</u>

1. Read through the Chalk Talk activity to become familiar with the process.

    a. Gather materials.

2. Use the Chalk Talk activity to read the articles and engage in the activity. Questions that could be used for this activity include the following:

    a. Why are cameras important learning tools?

    b. How can video be used for instructional coaches?

    c. How can video be used for teachers?

    d. How can video be used for teams?

    e. What conditions ensure the use of video is successful?

3. Wrap up this learning path by using the reflection questions that appear after the articles.

Learning Path #4

<u>Guiding Question:</u> What do goals look like in instructional coaching?

<u>Resources:</u> "PEERS Goals" article, Principles of Coaching video: What's a Good Goal, PEERS scenarios, Circle, Square, Triangle Reflection activity

<u>Activity:</u>

1. Begin by reading about goals in instructional coaching with the "PEERS Goals" article.

2. Reflect on the reading by using the reflection questions that appear after the article.

3. Afterward, layer on the Principles of Coaching video: What's a Good Goal, and then continue reflecting by using the questions that follow the video.

4. Use the PEERS scenarios sheet to continue thinking about PEERS goals.

5. Wrap up this learning path by completing the Circle, Square, Triangle Reflection activity that appears after the PEERS Scenarios.

Learning Path #5

<u>Guiding Question:</u> What is important about the learn and improve stages of the Impact Cycle?

<u>Resources:</u> "4 Steps for Focusing Coaching Sessions" article, Case Study: Learn and Improve

<u>Activity:</u>

1. Read the article "4 Steps for Focusing Coaching Sessions."

2. Use the reflection questions that appear after the article to reflect and discuss.

3. Next, read through the case study.

4. Wrap up this learning path by answering the reflection questions that appear after the case study.

Learning Path #6

<u>Guiding Question:</u> What are the potential challenges with learning, and how can we overcome them?

<u>Resources:</u> "Escape From the Zero-Learning Zone" article, Empathy Anchor activity

<u>Activity:</u>

1. Read through the Empathy Anchor activity to become familiar with the process.

2. Engage in the Empathy Anchor activity using the article in this learning path.

3. Wrap up this learning path by using the reflection questions that appear after the article.

Learning Path #7

<u>Guiding Question:</u> What is the Impact Cycle, and how do I share about this process with others?

<u>Resources:</u> The Impact Cycle checklist, the Impact Cycle Video Reflection activity

<u>Activity:</u>

1. Read through the Impact Cycle Video Reflection activity to become familiar with the process.

2. Read the Impact Cycle Checklist. Reflect on or discuss each line on the checklist to ensure clarity of the stages and steps in the Impact Cycle.

THE IMPACT CYCLE

3. Engage in the Impact Cycle Video Reflection activity.

4. Wrap up this learning path by using the reflection questions that appear after the video reflection activity.

Learning Path #8

<u>Guiding Question:</u> How can I enroll teachers into coaching cycles?

<u>Resources:</u> "Strategies for Enrolling Teachers in a Coaching Cycle" article, Enrolling Teachers activity

<u>Activity:</u>

1. Read through the article, and answer the reflection questions.

2. Partner up, and complete the activity.

3. Wrap up the learning path by using the reflection questions that appear after the activity.

Guiding Question: What are the stages of the Impact Cycle?

Resources: "3 Steps to Great Coaching" article, Give One Get One Move On (GOGOMO) activity

Activity:

1. Read through the Give One Get One Move On (GOGOMO) activity to become familiar with the process.

    a. Modification option: Instead of creating a two-column T-chart as the activity calls for, the participants can choose to create a three-column T-chart to capture ideas about each of the three stages of the Impact Cycle. Participants can continue to add to their columns as they rotate through the activity rounds.

2. Read through the article, annotating as you learn about the three stages (identify, learn, and improve).

3. Use the GOGOMO activity to discuss the article.

4. Wrap up this learning path by using the reflection questions that appear after the article.

3 Steps to Great Coaching

Jim Knight, Marti Elford, Michael Hock, Devona Dunekack, Barbara Bradley, Donald D. Deshler, and David Knight

Originally published in *The Learning Professional: The Learning Forward Journal*, *36*(1). February 2015.

> *"Coaching done well may be the most effective intervention designed for human performance."*
>
> —Atul Gawande (2011)

 Atul Gawande's comment is often used to justify coaching. What people overlook in his comment, however, are the words "done well." Coaching "done well" can and should dramatically improve human performance. However, coaching done poorly can be, and often is, ineffective, wasteful, and sometimes even destructive.

What, then, is coaching done well? For the past five years, researchers at the Kansas Coaching Project at the University of Kansas Center for Research on Learning and at the Instructional Coaching Group in Lawrence, Kansas, have been trying to answer that question by studying what coaches do. The result of that research is an instructional coaching cycle that fosters the kind of improvement Gawande describes.

THE IMPACT CYCLE

One coach who uses the instructional coaching cycle is Jackie Jewell from Othello School District in Washington. A participant in one of our research projects, Jewell used the coaching cycle when collaborating with Melanie Foster, a new elementary teacher in her district. Foster had sought out Jewell for coaching because she felt she needed to improve the way she gave positive attention to students. While Jewell would happily have focused on increasing Foster's positivity ratio, instead she suggested that it might be worth confirming that encouragement was the right goal.

To start, Jewell recorded one of Foster's lessons using her iPad and shared the video with her. After watching the video separately, both agreed that Foster was effective at encouraging students. But Foster saw something else she wanted to work on: student engagement. Her students were not staying focused during small-group activities. Armed with this new insight, she set a goal that students would be on task at least 90% of the time during small-group activities.

Jewell recorded another lesson, which revealed that students were on task about 65% of the time. It also showed that students didn't fully understand the expectations for their activities. In other words, students were off task because they didn't know what to do. Agreeing that Foster needed to set more explicit expectations for small groups, Jewell and Foster created a checklist describing the expectations, and Jewell modeled how to teach them. Foster also decided that she and her learning assistant would talk to each small group at the start of activities to make sure groups were clear about what they were to do. Once students understood their tasks, they hit the goal quickly after only a few modifications. Eventually, students were consistently on task 90% or higher, and this showed up in their test scores as well. Before coaching, students received scores on quizzes that were on average about 20%. After coaching, their scores averaged above 70%. Coaching helped Foster teach more effectively, and her improved instruction led to better student learning.

HOW WE STUDY WHAT COACHES DO

Kansas Coaching Project and Instructional Coaching Group researchers have studied instructional coaching since 1996, focusing in the past five years on the steps coaches move through to help teachers set and hit goals.

In the process, we experimented with a research methodology that we used to identify a process to be studied, assess what works and doesn't work when the practice is implemented, and refine the process based on what is learned during implementation.

To study instructional coaching, Kansas Coaching Project researchers worked with coaches from Beaverton, Oregon, and Othello, Washington. In addition, Instructional Coaching Group researchers conducted more than 50 interviews with coaches around the country. In large part, the instructional coaching cycle is the result of what was learned from these studies and interviews.

Researchers followed these steps:

1. Instructional coaches implement the coaching process.

2. They video record their coaching interactions and their teachers' implementation of the teaching practices.

3. They monitor progress toward their goals.

4. Researchers interview coaches and teachers to monitor progress as they move through the coaching cycle.

5. Researchers meet with coaches two or three times a year (at the end of each coaching cycle) to discuss how the coaching process can be refined or improved.

6. Refinements are made, and the revised coaching model and research process is repeated.

Researchers have moved through this cycle eight times in Beaverton and Othello. Over time, moving through increasingly effective coaching cycles, we have come up with a simple but powerful way to conduct instructional coaching.

THE INSTRUCTIONAL COACHING CYCLE

The coaching cycle that Jewell used involved many steps embedded in three components.

1. **Identify:** Jewell and Foster got a clear picture of reality (by video recording the class), identified a goal (90% time on task), and identified a teaching strategy that would help them hit the goal (teaching expectations).

2. **Learn:** Jewell used a checklist and modeling to make sure Foster understood how to use the identified strategy.

3. **Improve:** Jewell and Foster monitored progress toward the goal and made modifications to the way the strategy was used until the goal was hit. Here is how the cycle works.

Identify

The coach and teacher collaborate to set a goal and select a teaching strategy to try to meet the goal.

This involves several steps. First, the coach helps the teacher get a clear picture of reality, often by video recording the teacher's class. Then the coach and teacher identify a change the teacher would like to see in student behavior, achievement, or attitude.

Next, they identify a measurable student goal that will show that the hoped-for change has occurred. For example, a coach and teacher in Othello set the goal of reducing transition time from a four-minute average to a 20-second average. Since there were four transitions per period, hitting the goal added 15 minutes of instructional time to each 50-minute period—giving students 40 more hours of learning over the course of the year.

Other data besides video that might be gathered include student work, observation, and formal and informal evaluation results. Video, however, is quick, cheap, and powerful, and, if teachers only look at student work, they may miss some important aspect of their teaching.

Teachers frequently have an imprecise understanding of what their teaching looks like until they see a video recording of their class. When video is used within coaching, it is best if teacher and coach watch the video separately (Knight, 2014).

THE IMPACT CYCLE

After data have been gathered, the coach and teacher meet to identify next steps. Coaches can use these questions to guide teachers to set powerful goals:

1. On a scale of 1 to 10, how close was the lesson to your ideal?

2. What would have to change to make the class closer to a 10?

3. What would your students be doing?

4. What would that look like?

5. How would we measure that?

6. Do you want that to be your goal?

7. Would it really matter to you if you hit that goal?

8. What teaching strategy will you try to hit that goal?

Once a measurable goal has been established, the instructional coach and teacher choose a teaching strategy that the teacher would like to implement in an attempt to hit the goal. To support teachers during this step, coaches need to have a deep knowledge of a small number of high-yield teaching strategies that address many of the concerns teachers identify. Coaches in Beaverton and Othello learned the teaching strategies in *High-Impact Instruction: A Framework for Great Teaching* (Knight, 2013).

Goals that make the biggest difference for students are powerful, easy, emotionally compelling, reachable, and student-focused.

Powerful. The most effective goals address important aspects of student learning. Also, powerful goals address ongoing issues in the classroom rather than single events.

Easy. Not every goal is easy to reach, and goals are not improved if they are watered down or made less than powerful. However, given the choice between two equally powerful goals, take the one that is easier to reach. An easy-to-achieve goal leads more quickly to meaningful change for students, reinforces teachers' and students' efforts sooner, and frees up time for other tasks, such as setting other improvement goals.

Emotionally compelling. If teachers are going to invest a lot of time in changing their teaching to reach important goals, they have to choose goals that matter to them.

Reachable. Reachable goals have two characteristics: They are measurable, and they are ones teachers can reach because they have strategies to do so.

Student-focused. Usually these are goals that address student achievement, behavior, or attitude. The power of a student-focused goal is that it is objective and, therefore, holds coach and teacher accountable until meaningful improvements are made in students' lives.

Learn

Once teacher and coach set a goal and choose a teaching strategy, the teacher must learn how to implement the strategy. For the coach, this means explaining and modeling teaching strategies.

When instructional coaches explain teaching strategies, they need to give precise and clear explanations. Coaches are clearer when they use checklists. This doesn't mean coaches prompt teachers to mindlessly implement every step on a checklist. However, before teachers make adaptations, coaches need to be certain teachers know what they are modifying.

Coaches need to be precise and provisional when they explain teaching practices. They should clearly explain the items on a checklist while also asking teachers how they might want to modify the checklist to best meet students' needs or take advantage of their own strengths as teachers.

One benefit of establishing objective goals as a part of instructional coaching is that goals provide a way to assess whether teachers' modifications improve or damage the teaching strategies they use. If teachers modify strategies and hit their goals, their modifications didn't decrease effectiveness and may have helped students hit their goal. However, if the goal is not met, the coach and teacher can revisit the checklist to see if the strategy needs to be taught differently.

Coaches who explain strategies in precise and provisional ways foster high-quality implementation yet give teachers the freedom to use their professional discretion to modify teaching strategies to better meet students' needs.

The next step is modeling. To understand how to implement teaching strategies, teachers need to see them being implemented by someone else. The coaches from Beaverton, Oregon, found that modeling can occur in at least five ways.

> **In the classroom.** Teachers report that they prefer that coaches only model the targeted practice, rather than the whole lesson. While coaches model, collaborating teachers complete checklists as they watch the demonstration. Coaches may ask someone to video record the model so that coach and teacher can review it later.

> **In the classroom with no students.** Some teachers prefer that coaches model teaching strategies without students present.

> **Co-teaching.** In some cases, such as when a lesson involves content unfamiliar to the coach, coach and teacher co-teach.

> **Visiting other teachers' classrooms.** When teachers are learning new procedures or management techniques, they may choose to visit other teachers' classrooms to see how they implement them.

> **Watching video.** Teachers can also see a model of a teaching strategy by watching a video, either from a video sharing website or provided by the coach.

Improve

Instructional coaches monitor how teachers implement the chosen teaching strategy and whether students meet the goal.

Coaches can accomplish this by video recording classes and sharing the video with collaborating teachers so they can assess for themselves how they implemented the new teaching strategies and whether students have hit the identified goals.

Many goals cannot be seen by looking at video, so coaches may have to gather observation data, or teachers and coaches may have to review assessment data or student work.

Next, coach and teacher get together to talk about how the strategy was implemented, and especially whether students hit the goal. This conversation usually involves these questions:

1. What are you pleased about?

2. Did you hit the goal?

3. If you hit the goal, do you want to identify another goal, take a break, or keep refining the current new practice?

4. If you did not hit the goal, do you want to stick with the chosen practice or try a new one?

5. If you stick with the chosen practice, how will you modify it to increase its impact? (Revisit the checklist.)

6. If you choose another practice, what will it be?

7. What are your next actions?

When teacher and coach meet, they should use these questions to focus their conversation. Many coaches begin by asking teachers what they think went well. Following that, they discuss whether they met the goal. When teachers reach their goals, coaches ask whether they want to set and pursue other goals or take a break from coaching. When teachers don't reach their goals, they identify changes that need to be made.

Teachers and coaches keep moving forward by modifying the way they use the identified teaching strategies, trying another strategy, or sticking with an identified teaching strategy until they reach the goal.

Improvement Questions

DID YOU HIT THE GOAL?	
YES	NO
Do you want to:	Do you want to:
A. continue to refine your use of the practice?	A. Revisit how you teach the new practice?
B. Choose a new goal?	B. Choose a new practice?
C. Take a break?	C. Stick with the practice as it is?

MEASURE OF EFFECTIVENESS

The instructional coaching cycle is only one element of effective coaching programs. Effective coaches also need professional learning that ensures they understand how to navigate the complexities of helping adults, have a deep understanding of a comprehensive, focused set of teaching practices, communicate effectively, lead effectively, and work in systems that foster meaningful professional learning (Knight, 2007, 2011, 2013).

However, as important as those factors are, it may be most important that coaches understand how to move through the components of an effective coaching cycle that leads to improvements in student learning.

Instructional coaches who use a proven coaching cycle can partner with teachers to set and reach improvement goals that have an unmistakable, positive impact on students' lives. And that should be the measure of the effectiveness of any coaching program.

Checklist: Impact Cycle

IDENTIFY:	✓
Teacher gets a clear picture of current reality by watching a video of their lesson or by reviewing observation data, student interviews, or student work.	
Coach asks the identify questions with the teacher to identify a goal.	
Teacher identifies a student-focused goal.	
Teacher identifies a teaching strategy to use to hit the goal.	
LEARN:	✓
Coach shares a checklist for the chosen teaching strategy.	
Coach prompts the teacher to modify the practice if the teacher wishes.	
Teacher chooses an approach to modeling that they would like to observe and identifies a time to watch modeling.	
Coach provides modeling in one or more formats.	
Teacher sets a time to implement the practice.	
IMPROVE:	✓
Teacher implements the practice.	
Data is gathered (by teacher or coach in class or while viewing video) on student progress toward the goal.	
Data is gathered (by teacher or coach in class or while viewing video) on teacher's implementation of the practice (usually on the previously viewed checklist).	
Coach and teacher meet to confirm direction and monitor progress.	
Coach and teacher make adaptations and plan next actions until the goal is met.	

THE IMPACT CYCLE

Reflection Questions for "3 Steps to Great Coaching"

1. What do coaches and teachers accomplish in the identify stage?

2. What are ways coaches and teachers can engage in learning together?

3. What role does data play in the improve stage?

4. How can coaches be successful in instructional coaching cycles?

THE IMPACT CYCLE

NOTES

GIVE ONE GET ONE MOVE ON ACTIVITY (GOGOMO)

 Purpose: To share ideas gathered from a video, text, case study, observation, or experience.

Process:

1. Select a focus of inquiry (video, text, case study, observation, or experience).

2. Designate a facilitator of the protocol and a timekeeper.

3. Have each member of the group create a T-chart on a piece of paper, in their journal, or hand out copies of a T-chart graphic organizer. One column of the T-chart will be labeled "My ideas," and the other column will be labeled "Learned from others."

4. Set a timer for 5 minutes, and have each person write down as many ideas from the focus of inquiry as they can on the "My ideas" side of the T-chart.

5. After the 5 minutes, the group will stand up with their graphic organizer and a pen/pencil.

6. The protocol will include moving around the room to meet with someone else and "give and get" an idea from each partnership.

    a. To begin, the facilitator will say "GOGOMO," and the group will partner up.

    b. The timekeeper will set a 2-minute timer.

    c. In the partnership, people will share one idea from their "My ideas" column and then listen as their partner shares one, too.

    d. People will record the ideas collected from their partners in the "Learned from others" column of their T-chart.

    e. Partners will continue sharing until the end of the 2-minute round.

    f. When the timer goes off, the facilitator will say, "GOGOMO," and the group will mix and mingle again, meeting with new partners to continue exchanging ideas and learning from one another.

    g. Ideally, there will be three or four rounds of GOGOMO, each lasting 2 minutes.

7. At the conclusion of the three or four rounds, everyone returns to their seats.

8. Individuals will spend 2 minutes rereading what they have learned from both sides of the T-chart and select two ideas that resonate with them the most.

9. At the end of the 2 minutes of rereading, the group will share out their ideas together.

Modifications:

– The facilitator and timekeeper can be the same person, if the group is small.

– Each round of GOGOMO lasts 2 minutes, but that time can be adjusted based on the needs of the group.

– There are three or four rounds of GOGOMO, but that can be adjusted for groups who have less or more time to gather.

– The protocol ends with a whole-group share out, but this can also be an individual reflection for groups who prefer not to wrap up the discussion in that way.

<u>Guiding Question:</u> What are the important concepts for coaches to know when partnering with teachers in the Impact Cycle?

<u>Resources:</u> "Real Learning Happens in Real Life" article, "In Coaching, 'One Size Fits One'" article, Windowpanes activity, Gallery Walk activity

<u>Activity:</u>

1. Read through the Windowpanes activity to become familiar with the process.

    a. Gather materials.

2. Engage in the Windowpanes activity with the two articles in this learning path.

3. Conduct a Gallery Walk so everyone can see the posters up close.

4. Wrap up this learning path by using the reflection questions that appear after the articles.

Real Learning Happens in Real Life

Originally published in The Learning Professional: The Learning Forward Journal, 42(2). April 2021.

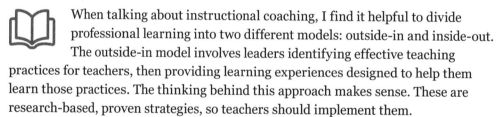

When talking about instructional coaching, I find it helpful to divide professional learning into two different models: outside-in and inside-out. The outside-in model involves leaders identifying effective teaching practices for teachers, then providing learning experiences designed to help them learn those practices. The thinking behind this approach makes sense. These are research-based, proven strategies, so teachers should implement them.

Unfortunately, the outside-in model frequently encounters problems. Teachers can find it difficult to fit the new strategy into their existing way of teaching, but they are expected to implement it even if they don't like it. If teachers explain that they don't think a strategy is appropriate for their students, or that it is a bad fit for their approach to teaching, they often are labeled as resistant.

The argument goes that the strategy is proven, so teachers need to implement it whether they like it or not. Not surprisingly, the outside-in model often has little impact on what really happens in classrooms.

Research suggests that the inside-out model is more likely to lead to real change (see, for example, Ibarra, 2015). For this model, teachers identify students' needs, then identify a strategy to address those needs. Following this, teachers learn the strategy and adapt it until students' needs are met.

Teachers still implement proven teaching strategies, but rather than trying to implement a strategy they didn't choose and might not value, they implement a strategy they chose to address important student needs. Simply put, with the inside-out model, real learning happens in real life.

With this model, instructional coaches help make the learning real. Coaches empower teachers to see the reality of their classroom by video recording teachers' lessons, interviewing their students, reviewing student work with teachers, or gathering observation data. Then they help teachers identify clearly defined, achievable, student-focused goals that are deeply important to teachers and will have an unmistakably positive impact on student learning or well-being.

Coaches also draw on a deep understanding of effective teaching practices to help teachers pick the teaching strategies they will use to try to hit those goals. Finally, coaches partner with teachers to adapt those strategies so that they are most effective.

Theoretically, teachers could do inside-out professional learning on their own. They could get their own clear picture of reality and identify their own goals, do the research to identify and learn teaching strategies, and make adaptations to those strategies until the goals are achieved. But, in reality, this is too much without the support of an expert partner whose job is to think through these steps.

Teaching in and of itself makes significant cognitive demands, and there are few teachers who can do all of the knowledge work that teaching entails plus the complex work involved in learning and implementing new strategies. To do the work of the inside-out model, teachers need a partner: an instructional coach.

Reflection Questions for "Real Learning Happens in Real Life"

1. Is outside-in or inside-out more effective for learning? Why?

2. What is the meaning behind "real learning happens in real life"?

3. How can coaches use the lesson in this article?

4. What experience do you have with "real learning in real life"?

THE IMPACT CYCLE

NOTES

In Coaching, "One Size Fits One"

Coaching is "adaptive" work, but it needs structure to be impactful.

Originally published in *Educational Leadership*, 79(4). March 1, 2022.

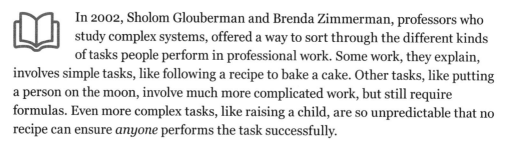 In 2002, Sholom Glouberman and Brenda Zimmerman, professors who study complex systems, offered a way to sort through the different kinds of tasks people perform in professional work. Some work, they explain, involves simple tasks, like following a recipe to bake a cake. Other tasks, like putting a person on the moon, involve much more complicated work, but still require formulas. Even more complex tasks, like raising a child, are so unpredictable that no recipe can ensure *anyone* performs the task successfully.

Glouberman and Zimmerman (2002) explain that for complex work like parenting or inventing a new machine—challenges known as *adaptive*, as opposed to *technical* ones, for which clear steps exists—cookie-cutter solutions don't work. That's because we can't predict what will happen. "Because every child is unique and must be understood as an individual . . . there is always some uncertainty of the outcome" (p. vi), they assert.

Teaching is an adaptive challenge. If raising one child is complex work, think how much more complex it is to teach 30 or more students in the same room, all with unique needs and abilities—and during a pandemic. As Eric Liu (2006) says in *Guiding Lights*, his book about transformative mentors, "Teaching is not one-size-fits-all; it's one-size-fits-one."

Since teaching is adaptive, it follows that coaching to support teachers must also be adaptive—but it's not always treated as such. In their classic work *The Practice of Adaptive Leadership* (2009), Heifetz, Linsky, and Grashow say, "The most common failure in leadership is produced by treating adaptive challenges as if they were technical problems" (p. 14). I'd paraphrase that to say that the most common failure in coaching may be to tackle complex work using the one-size-fits-all strategies we would use for simple or even complicated work.

Freedom Within Form

But what does adaptive coaching look like in the day-to-day work of coaches? Although coaching can't be done in rote fashion, I believe we make a big mistake if we assume that being adaptive involves simply making up what we're doing as we go.

One concept that helps me understand adaptive coaching is the idea of freedom within form. Yes, coaching is adaptive, but "adaptive coaching" is made possible by powerful underlying structures. While it may sound counterintuitive, effective structures actually increase freedom. An example of such a structure is the talking stick used by many elementary school teachers around the world. The idea is simple: Whoever holds the stick gets to talk as long as they wish while everyone else listens without interrupting. Generally, all kids get a turn using the stick, and no one gets a second turn until all have had their chance to speak. That simple structure increases freedom for most students because if students just spoke whenever they wanted to, some students' voices, possibly only a small group, would dominate, while others would never be heard. The talking stick structure (or form) enhances overall freedom by ensuring every student can say what they want to say.

The talking stick structure is so helpful that in 2018, U.S. Senator Susan Collins (R-Maine) used it, with mixed success, with her Senate colleagues during budget discussions to end a government shutdown. One senator said it was a highly entertaining meeting. However, as two CNN reporters described:

> on one occasion, one of the . . . senators was speaking while another asked a question and then turned with another quick, longer, louder question. The member . . . holding the stick "forcefully delivered" the stick across the room—but it missed its mark and caused damage to a shelf in Collins' office. (Fox & Diaz, 2018)

Apparently, kindergartners use the talking stick more effectively than U.S. senators.

Structures That Give Coaching Power

Just like teachers or senators using the talking stick, good coaches use structures to create conditions that help enable teachers to make effective, adaptive decisions. (Crucially, however, it's the teachers who make the final decisions.) Instructional coaching, as I describe it, involves many powerful forms that give coaches freedom.

First, it usually involves a coaching cycle or conversational framework. Effective instructional coaches often use what I refer to as an Impact Cycle consisting of three stages: (1) *Identify*, during which the teacher identifies a clear picture of reality, a goal, and a strategy they will use to hit that goal; (2) *Learn*, during which the teacher learns whatever approaches, techniques, or skills they need to learn so that they'll be able to implement the new strategy as they pursue the goal; and (3) *Improve*, during which the teacher makes adaptations to the way they use the strategy (sometimes even changing the strategy or possibly the goal) until the goal is met.

During the Identify stage, the coach draws from a memorized list of questions to invite the teacher to think deeper about their students and their teaching. Powerful questions (such as, "What would you like to have happening that's not happening now?") artfully shared can be like intellectual fireworks leading to an explosion of beautiful ideas. But the questions must be used authentically, adapted to each unique situation. People tend to tune out when they sense someone is moving through a standardized list of queries.

During the Learn stage, a coach might use a checklist to explain a strategy—but again, the checklist is simply the point of departure for an adaptive dialogue with the collaborating teacher. The coach uses the checklist to describe the nuances of a strategy, but also asks the teacher how *they* want to adapt the strategy so it will be most effective for their students and teaching style. So, this stage, too, is decidedly not one-size-fits-all.

Finally, in the Improve stage, the coach and teacher explore adaptations the teacher will make so that the teacher and their students will meet the goal. Sometimes this means tweaking a strategy—such as modifying a rubric or having students practice listening skills before collaborating—or switching to a different one. It could mean adapting how progress toward the goal is measured, or even simply waiting for the strategy to work. Adaptations are almost always necessary before the teacher hits her chosen target.

Coaching, as a one-to-one form of communication, is an ideal format for making such individualized changes. Nevertheless, adaptive change requires structures that allow for efficient progress toward goals. Who knows—maybe using structures like those undergirding coaching could, with practice, even lead to more productive conversations on the Senate floor?

Reflection Questions for "In Coaching, 'One Size Fits One'"

1. What is the challenge with "one size fits all"?

2. What structures already exist in your school's or system's coaching?

3. How might freedom, within the structures, be incorporated?

4. How is the Impact Cycle model an example of freedom within form?

THE IMPACT CYCLE

NOTES

WINDOWPANES ACTIVITY

 Purpose: To synthesize ideas about a text and collaborate with others on new learning.

Process:

1. Select two or three texts to use for this activity.

2. Designate a facilitator of the activity and a timekeeper.

3. Ask participants to get into groups of two or three (based on the number of texts being used). For example, if there are three texts being used, groups will have three members. This is called the Original Group.

   a. Once in an Original Group, have the groups decide who will read each of the texts. For example, if there are three texts (Text A, Text B, and Text C), which group member will read Text A? Text B? Text C? Each group member should select a different text, ensuring that each group has all selected texts assigned to be read.

4. Give ample time for everyone to read their selected text individually and annotate their thoughts as they read.

5. After the time for individual reading has passed, have all participants in the room who read Text A come together to form a new group: a group of people who read Text A. Form another group for Text B, and so on for the number of texts that are being used. These are called the Poster Groups.

6. With the Poster Groups who have read the same text, ask the groups to create a collaborative poster using the "Windowpanes Guidelines" visual. Each Poster Group will generate a poster to synthesize their ideas from their text onto the poster. Allow ample time for all groups to complete the task.

7. Once all posters are complete, have participants take a picture of the poster with their devices. Participants will take these pictures back to their Original Group to use for sharing.

8. Send everyone back to their Original Group from Step 3.

9. Once in their Original Groups, participants will take turns sharing about their text by sharing the poster picture they have brought with them.

Modifications:

- If the group is small enough, facilitators can skip taking pictures of the posters and do a Gallery Walk, group share out, or Poster Group presentations.

- The number of texts used is up to the facilitators of the activity.

- Windowpane topics may be changed based on the facilitator's discretion.

WINDOWPANES GUIDELINES	
What is the main idea of your text?	What is a phrase from the text that is important and what does it mean?
How does this inform our coaching practice?	What image, diagram, or chart could you create to visually represent the ideas from your text?

THE IMPACT CYCLE

GALLERY WALK ACTIVITY

 Purpose: To invite participants to view posters, presentations, or other types of work from other groups of learners.

Process:

1. Select an activity for participants to complete in groups.

2. Give directions for the activity and time for groups to complete the task.

3. At the conclusion of the activity, make time for a Gallery Walk: a structured rotation of groups to allow everyone to view each other's work.

4. Structure:

   a. Ask all participants to travel around the space with the group with whom they completed the task.

   b. Decide how much time each group will have to observe each group's work. For example, if conducting Gallery Walk in a 20-minute time period and there are four group's work to view, then each group can have 5 minutes to view each group's work/product.

   c. Establish a timekeeper to tell the groups when to rotate.

   d. Groups will rotate to view each other's work.

      i. While at each rotation, the group should have a focus for their observation. For example, at each group's work, the observing group might leave positive comments, they might take notes, they might compare and contrast their ideas with the other group's ideas, and so on. Share this focus with the groups before they begin rotating.

5. At the conclusion of the rotations, have groups turn in and share what they noticed overall from their Gallery Walk.

Modifications:

– Adjust the protocol for the amount of time allotted for the Gallery Walk.

– A silent walk can be conducted where people move around freely and on their own. The purpose of this is to allow individuals to explore other groups' work in a way that works best for them.

Guiding Question: How can video be used with teachers and coaches?

Resources: "Record, Replay, Reflect" article, "What You Learn When You See Yourself Teach" article, Chalk Talk activity

Activity:

1. Read through the Chalk Talk activity to become familiar with the process.

   a. Gather materials.

2. Use the Chalk Talk activity to read the articles and engage in the activity. Questions that could be used for this activity include the following:

   a. Why are cameras important learning tools?

   b. How can video be used for instructional coaches?

   c. How can video be used for teachers?

   d. How can video be used for teams?

   e. What conditions ensure the use of video is successful?

3. Wrap up this learning path by using the reflection questions that appear after the articles.

Record, Replay, Reflect

Videotaped lessons accelerate learning for teachers and coaches.

Jim Knight, Barbara A. Bradley, Michael Hock, Thomas M. Skrtic, David Knight, Irma Brasseur-Hock, Jean Clark, Marilyn Ruggles, and Carol Hatton

Originally published in *The Learning Professional: The Learning Forward Journal*, *33*(2). April 2012.

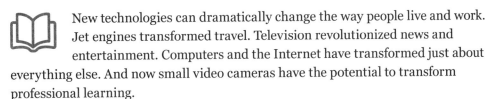 New technologies can dramatically change the way people live and work. Jet engines transformed travel. Television revolutionized news and entertainment. Computers and the Internet have transformed just about everything else. And now small video cameras have the potential to transform professional learning.

While teachers have used video to review their lessons for decades, cameras were, until recently, complicated to use and so large and cumbersome that they interrupted the learning taking place in the classroom. Now, cameras are tiny—half the size of a deck of cards—and easy to use, often controlled by the push of a single button.

Recognizing the potential of this new technology, researchers at the Kansas Coaching Project at the University of Kansas Center for Research on Learning conducted a three-year study to analyze what happens when coaches and teachers watch themselves on video. The results of this study show why these cameras are important and how they can be used by instructional coaches, individual learners, and teachers in the classroom and in study groups.

Why cameras are important

Cameras serve four important functions within professional learning:

1. Cameras help educators (teachers, coaches, administrators, and others) obtain an objective, accurate view of themselves at work. In analyzing teachers watching themselves on tape, researchers found that teachers are often surprised by what they see. Research conducted by change expert Prochaska and his colleagues (Prochaska, Norcross, & DiClemente, 1994) demonstrates that people are often unaware of the true nature of their professional practice. According to these researchers, people are often unaware of their need to improve. Video gives educators an honest picture of their professional practice.

2. Video recordings propel educators forward into change. After watching themselves on video, many teachers feel compelled to improve learning in their classrooms almost immediately. Stacy Cohen, an instructional coach for a Kansas Coaching Project study, reported that the night one of her collaborating teachers first saw a video of her lesson, the teacher stayed up until 2 a.m. reworking her lesson plans because "she couldn't stand to see how bored her students looked."

3. Video recordings are important for goal setting within coaching. Because the information recorded on video provides a rich picture of reality, educators who review video of their lessons are more inclined to write learning goals that matter to them. Coaching, as Hargrove (2008) explained, is often more successful when it is pulled forward by the goals of the person being coached (what he calls "pull coaching") as opposed to when it is pushed forward by the coach's goals ("push coaching").

4. Because video recorded on small cameras is easy to gather and of high quality, it provides a picture of reality that can be used to measure progress toward a goal. Real improvement requires what Colvin (2008) referred to as "deliberate practice" and precise feedback. Video is an easy and effective way for teachers working with coaches, on their own, or in teams to get the feedback they need to move forward as learners. As one coach commented, "I am thankful to have the video that documented all of our conversations so I can see the progress that we made. I know that you have to go out of your comfort zone in order for good learning to happen, and this has been my experience."

How cameras can be used

Instructional coaches

Researchers analyzed hundreds of hours of video recordings of instructional coaches and held three-day focus groups with coaches three times during each year of the three-year study. One result: All coaches in the study believe that cameras are essential tools for instructional coaches.

Instructional coach Susan Leyden is typical of the participating coaches when she comments, "The video is key to everything." Leyden says video is essential to identify an instructional challenge, set a goal, watch students, and have an objective record. Leyden notes that because video is objective, it makes coaching less personal. "The video is huge because it takes me out of it," she says.

When coaches use cameras with teachers, the video recordings they produce become central to the coaching process. Thus, instructional coaches in the research project embedded video into the entire instructional coaching process (Knight, 2007), using video recordings with teachers to gather data on classroom reality, set goals, identify the coaching focus, and monitor progress.

To get the most out of using video recordings, the coaches employed the following practices:

- To alleviate the awkwardness many people feel watching themselves on video, coach and teacher should play with the camera a while before recording a lesson.

- Before recording, coach and teacher should decide whether it is more important to see students or the teacher and then position the camera appropriately.

- After recording, coach and teacher should first watch the video recording separately. This allows the teacher to experience the video in his or her own way, and it allows the coach time to prepare questions for an exploratory coaching conversation.

- Coaches should prepare teachers carefully for watching the video. Coaches in the study gave teachers a document explaining how to get the most out of watching the video and surveys that teachers could use to focus attention on either their own practice or students' performance or behavior.

- Before the coaching conversation and while watching the video separately, teachers and coaches should identify two or three video clips where they think learning is proceeding well and two or three other clips where the learning was not proceeding as well and that they would like to discuss further.

- During discussion of the video, coaches should either watch the video or talk about it. The study showed that when coaches and teachers tried to watch and talk simultaneously, the conversations were ineffective. What is good for teachers is also good for instructional coaches. Coaches in the Kansas Coaching Project study found watching themselves on tape valuable. In fact, when coaches in the study were asked to identify the best form of professional learning for coaching, they unanimously said watching oneself on tape. One coach's comments are typical: "I am probably learning more than they are."

HOW TO GET THE MOST OUT OF WATCHING VIDEO		
GOAL	**PREPARATION**	**WATCHING THE VIDEO**
Identify two sections of the lesson that work and one or two sections that need improvement.	Watching oneself on video is one of the most powerful strategies teachers and coaches can use to improve their practice. However, it can take some time to become comfortable with the process. Here are some preparation tips:	• Plan to watch the entire video at one sitting.
	• Find a place to watch where there are no distractions.	• Take notes on anything that is interesting.
	• Read through teacher and student surveys or other material to determine what to watch for.	• Be sure to include the time from the video beside any note.
		• Watch for positive elements as well as areas needing improvement.
	• Set aside a block of time to watch the video uninterrupted.	• After watching the video, review the notes and circle items to discuss with the coach.
	• Have pen and paper ready to take notes.	

Individual learning

In 2009, one researcher conducted an informal study that asked more than 300 people from around the world to coach themselves on important communication skills such as listening, finding common ground, and building emotional connections. In most cases, participants coached themselves by video, recording selected conversations with colleagues, friends, students, and family, then watching to see what they could learn from the video.

Those who watched video of their conversations reported that they gained insight into such aspects of their communication skills as their facial expressions ("I thought I was attentive, but my facial expressions showed otherwise"), areas where they could improve ("In watching myself on video, I confirmed to myself that I monopolize conversations"), and areas where they improved ("I know this time I gave more eye contact . . . and tried to make sure my conversation partner really saw I was interested. I leaned in and nodded as well as gave some comments that showed my interest in the conversation").

One participant wrote, "The video and listening tapes made a huge difference. Thinking about how you listen is not enough. When you see yourself and/or listen to yourself, it makes the process real. It made me focus and really pay attention to what I was doing."

Teachers in the classroom

Video recording provides a way for teachers to review and reflect on their teaching practices. Teachers can get a rich record of how students are performing or how they are teaching by setting up a camera in the classroom. For example, teachers can use video to record such aspects of teaching as the level, type, or kind of questions they ask, how frequently they praise students compared to how frequently they criticize them, clarity of instruction, pacing, and animation. Teachers can watch the video to assess their facial expressions and other nonverbal communication, to see if they are ignoring some parts of the room, or to note if bias toward particular students or groups of students has crept into their practice.

Video can also help teachers get a second look at students. Teachers can assess whether students are authentically engaged or which activities or teaching practices seem to most effectively increase student engagement. Video can also provide insight into each class's culture, giving teachers a window into what students' actions suggest about their assumptions about the purpose of learning, the boundaries of respectful communication, and the connection between effort and success.

Finally, video helps teachers see actions or expressions that foster or inhibit emotional connections. Rolling the eyes, making sarcastic comments, talking down to students, or looking uninterested can destroy connections. Video also shows actions that encourage connection, such as praise, smiles, or words of encouragement.

Learning teams

Teachers can learn a great deal about their practice when using video recordings during collaborative learning. Jean Clark, an educational leader from Cecil County, Md., created a process that brought teachers together to watch and discuss video recordings of themselves teaching. All teachers in the video study groups were implementing the same teaching practice, and the video study group was a way for everyone to deepen their understanding of how to teach it.

Before each meeting, one teacher volunteered to prepare and share a video for the next session. To prepare the video, the volunteer recorded himself or herself using the teaching routine in the classroom. After recording the class, the teacher used video editing software to identify aspects of the lesson that went well and a section of the lesson that needed improvement. Editing the film caused teachers to watch their lessons many times, and those repeated viewings led them to see details of their lessons that wouldn't have been obvious after watching just once.

At the next video study group meeting, the teacher shared his or her video with the group, showing each section and asking for comments. Clark guided team members to collaborate and identify values they would work from while discussing each other's video. Thus, comments about lessons were positive, honest, constructive, and useful.

Usually, the volunteer shared two positive clips first. After showing each one, he or she commented on the lesson and asked colleagues for feedback. Each teacher in the video study group went through this process.

Clark reported four benefits to the video study groups:

1. Teachers learn a great deal by watching themselves teach, especially after they have watched themselves several times.

2. Video study groups are good follow-up to professional learning by increasing the likelihood and quality of implementation after training.

3. The dialogue that occurs during video study groups deepens group members' understanding of how to teach the targeted practice and often introduces them to other teaching practices while watching others teach and listening to team members' comments.

4. When teachers come together for such conversation, they often form a meaningful bond because the structure of a video study group compels everyone to stand vulnerably in front of their peers and engage in constructive, supportive, and appreciative conversations with colleagues. Those bonds may ultimately be more important than all of the other learning that occurs since they create supportive, positive relationships among peers.

A clear picture of performance

Better teaching equals better learning. However, improvement of any sort is usually fleeting at best without a clear picture of current performance and an accurate and powerful way of measuring progress. While the video camera is only one part of any effective approach to professional learning, teachers and coaches can benefit from turning the camera on themselves to see how well they are performing.

FIGURE 4.1

Watch Your Students

Date _____.

After watching the video of today's class, please rate how close your students' behavior is to your goal for an ideal class in the following areas:

	Not close						Right on
Students are engaged in learning (90% engagement is recommended).	1	2	3	4	5	6	7
Students interact respectfully.	1	2	3	4	5	6	7
Students clearly understand how they are supposed to behave.	1	2	3	4	5	6	7
Students rarely interrupt each other.	1	2	3	4	5	6	7
Students engage in high-level conversation.	1	2	3	4	5	6	7
Students clearly understand how well they are progressing (or not).	1	2	3	4	5	6	7
Students are interested in learning activities in the class.	1	2	3	4	5	6	7
Comments							

FIGURE 4.2

Watch Yourself

Date _____.

After watching the video of today's class, please rate how close your instruction is to your ideal in the following areas:

	Not close					Right on	
My praise-to-correction ratio is at least 3-to-1.	1	2	3	4	5	6	7
I clearly explain expectations prior to each activity.	1	2	3	4	5	6	7
My corrections are calm, consistent, immediate, and planned in advance.	1	2	3	4	5	6	7
My questions are at the appropriate level (know, understand, do).	1	2	3	4	5	6	7
My learning structures (stories, cooperative learning, thinking devices, experiential learning) are effective.	1	2	3	4	5	6	7
I use a variety of learning structures effectively.	1	2	3	4	5	6	7
I clearly understand what my students know and don't know.	1	2	3	4	5	6	7
Comments							

Reflection Questions for "Record, Replay, Reflect"

1. On a scale of 1 to 10 (1 being not at all and 10 being extremely important), how important are cameras as learning tools for reflection?

2. How can video be used for instructional coaches?

3. How can video be used for teachers or teams?

4. What conditions ensure the use of video is successful?

THE IMPACT CYCLE

NOTES

_____
_____
_____
_____
_____
_____
_____
_____

What You Learn When You See Yourself Teach

Using video cameras in a way that recognizes teachers' professionalism can have a dramatic effect on teaching and learning.

Originally published in *Educational Leadership, 71*(8). May 1, 2014.

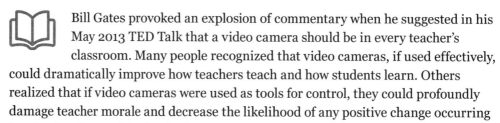 Bill Gates provoked an explosion of commentary when he suggested in his May 2013 TED Talk that a video camera should be in every teacher's classroom. Many people recognized that video cameras, if used effectively, could dramatically improve how teachers teach and how students learn. Others realized that if video cameras were used as tools for control, they could profoundly damage teacher morale and decrease the likelihood of any positive change occurring in schools. The truth is that both sides are right.

For the past five years, I've been studying how educators can use video cameras. At the Kansas Coaching Project at the University of Kansas Center for Research on Learning, I've been involved in two research projects (Bradley et al., 2013) that explore how coaches and teachers can effectively use video as part of the instructional coaching process. At the Instructional Coaching Group, my colleague Marilyn Ruggles and I have conducted more than 50 interviews with teachers, instructional coaches, and principals who are using video every day to improve teaching.

Our biggest finding? Video cameras, when used in a manner that respects the professionalism of teachers, can have a positive effect on teaching and learning, as the following examples illustrate.

How It Can Work Using Video With Coaching

When reading specialist Jody Johnson from Beaverton, Oregon, agreed to collaborate with instructional coach Lea Molzcan, Jody knew which class she wanted to target, but she wasn't sure what she wanted to work on. Lea started the coaching process by video recording Jody's 8th grade class, then she and Jody watched the video separately, meeting afterward to discuss what they saw.

Jody saw a lot. Students took a full 10 minutes to settle down before the reading lesson could actually begin. Ten minutes each day for a whole school year was an awful lot of wasted time. However, the video also showed Jody that students were very engaged during guided reading. In fact, both Lea and Jody saw that the students

THE IMPACT CYCLE

genuinely loved reading such books as those in Lincoln Peirce's Big Nate series or in Jeff Kinney's Diary of a Wimpy Kid series. The video, then, was both encouraging and discouraging. The students could be engaged and embrace reading, but it took a long time to get them there. When Jody and Lea met, Jody decided her goal was to get students ready to learn within three minutes of the start of class. They identified two things Jody could do. First, she would move guided reading to the beginning of the period and tell students that they'd only get 10 minutes to read, starting when the bell rang, and that class would only start when everyone was settled and ready to learn. Second, she would explicitly teach her expectations for how students were to behave at the start of the class.

After Jody initiated these changes, the students blew away the goal. Class began to start in less than two minutes, which added eight minutes of instruction to every class. The orderly beginning also positively affected what happened during the rest of the class. Because of these two small changes that the coach and teacher identified when they discussed the video, the students became actively engaged throughout the class, and, most important, they were learning. Lea told me that although none of the students had ever before achieved proficiency on the state reading test, almost all students in Jody's class were proficient at the end of that year.

Using Video With Teacher Evaluation

In spring 2013, when Chad Harnisch, a principal at Rice Lake High School in Wisconsin, considered the 60 teacher evaluations he had to complete, he wasn't happy. Chad had found that conversations during teacher evaluations rarely led to meaningful dialogue about teaching. "The conversation," Chad said, "always has an element of confrontation because the teacher is remembering what she thinks happened from her perspective, and I'm remembering what I think happened from my perspective, and there can be a disconnect between those two remembrances."

Chad decided to try to improve these conversations by integrating video into his teacher evaluation process. He asked Amy Pelle, an accomplished English teacher at Rice Lake, if she would be interested in volunteering. They met to ensure they both agreed on how to use the evaluation tool—which happened to be about Domain 3, Instruction, in Charlotte Danielson's Framework for Teaching (Danielson, 2007). Chad video recorded a lesson, and he and Amy met twice, first to talk about the lesson as seen through the filter of the evaluation and a second time to talk about Amy's goals.

Chad was incredibly impressed by Amy's class. Had he done a traditional evaluation, he said, they wouldn't have had much to talk about. He would have simply written down on the evaluation form, "distinguished, distinguished, distinguished." But after watching the video, they were able to have a real conversation about how Amy might engage one student who concerned her.

The principal and the teacher didn't spend their time talking about their various memories of the classroom—they spent their time talking about teaching. According to Chad, "the video allowed us to have a more professionally rich conversation." He plans to offer this option to all his teachers.

THE IMPACT CYCLE

Using Video With Teams

Principal Cyrus Weinberger and clinical professor Rychie Rhodes at Red Hawk Elementary School in Erie, Colorado, were convinced that video could accelerate professional learning in their school, so they established teams of teachers who volunteered to participate. Before each team meeting, Rychie recorded a teacher teaching his or her lesson, edited the recording down to about 15 minutes, and copied this video clip to a DVD. She then sent a copy to every teacher on the team. Team members watched the DVD before the next learning team meeting.

To prepare for the team discussion, each team member took notes while watching the video, using a template the principal had developed. The template focused everyone's attention on (1) the learning activity, (2) what the teacher was doing, (3) what students were doing, and (4) the feedback they wanted to provide. The use of video and the template led to practical, deep dialogue. Said Rychie, "It's amazing how much more objective and richer the dialogue is after teachers have had time to think about the video."

During team meetings, the person who was video recorded usually started the conversation by answering the first question on the template ("What is the learning activity?"), followed by other team members who talked about what they had seen. The group worked through the questions on the template, and Rychie took notes that she shared afterward by e-mail. At the end of the discussion, the person who was video recorded summarized what he or she had learned. The whole conversation usually lasted no more than an hour.

Rychie told me that the staff at Red Hawk has begun to share teaching practices in a way that hasn't happened before. One team, for example, watched a 2nd grade teacher lead students through activities designed to familiarize them with the components of nonfiction texts. The team spoke positively about the teacher's pacing, use of wait time, consistency of routines, use of visuals, and movement around the room. Although the students seemed engaged, the teacher had concerns about how much she talked. She decided to shorten the teacher talk by permitting some students to move into independent work a little earlier, freeing up time for her to provide extra support to those who needed it. Feedback from the team helped the teacher deepen her understanding of the lesson, but everyone learned by watching the teacher lead her students.

During team conversations at Red Hawk Elementary, the use of video prompts teachers to think about their own practice, learn new ways to teach from their colleagues, and implement the new practices themselves. Rychie noted that "there have been a lot of really rich 'aha' moments."

Using Video So Teachers Can Coach Themselves

Kimberly Nguyen, a special education teacher in Delton Kellogg Schools, Michigan, was part of a group of teachers studying my book *High-Impact Instruction: A Framework for Great Teaching* (Knight, 2013). She decided to use video to analyze her practice. She watched a video of two classes she taught: the group of students that was most engaged and the one that was least engaged.

Kim was surprised to see that she was a different teacher in each room. "With the engaged group," Kim said, "I'm much more animated, and I interact more. With the second group, I struggle with my mood, and my response time is lower. In that class, I'm really boring."

After watching the video twice, Kim reported that, for both classes together, 41 percent of her comments were positive, with only 17 percent of them involving effective, specific praise. She also found that 59 percent of her comments were negative, with 17 percent of those interrupting the lesson so significantly that it stopped the lesson.

The video gave Kim a crystal-clear picture of her reality, and she was able to set a specific, student focused goal derived from real data for both individual students and each class as a whole. Kim told us, "Children this age [grades 1–4] need a lot more activity. . . . My kids do really well with direct and explicit instruction, but they need the components of freedom and movement. So it will be a challenge to figure out how to put those things together and start using more cooperative learning strategies [along with the] explicit learning strategies. I think that's going to be the best combination."

A Clear Picture of Reality—and a Goal

Three decades ago, Robert Fritz (1984) provided a simple but powerful explanation for the dynamics of professional growth. To grow, Fritz explained, we need two things: a clear picture of current reality and a goal we want to achieve. The difference between our reality and our goal creates a tension that we can only resolve by either achieving the goal or giving up. A compelling goal makes us discontented with our reality; it pulls us forward to a better version of ourselves.

When it comes to professional practice, getting a clear picture of reality is easier said than done. The instructional coaches and teachers we interviewed are often delighted by what they see in their videos, and in other cases, they're disappointed. But in almost all cases, they're surprised (and in many cases, shocked). Watching yourself on video is similar to hearing your voice on an audio recording but amped up to the power of 10.

There are at least three reasons why we don't have a clear picture of what it looks like when we teach. First, teaching is such an all-encompassing intellectual task that it's hard to step back and reflect on exactly what's happening in a given moment. Second, teachers, like all human beings, are prone to get used to what they see everyday—psychologists refer to this as habituation. Over time, our understanding of our class can become less accurate. Finally, all of us are prone to seek out data that support our preconceived understanding of reality—what psychologists refer to as confirmation bias. Consequently, most teachers really don't know what it looks like when they teach. Video reveals an accurate picture of what's going on in the classroom.

Six Guidelines for Success

Because video is so easy to use and because it can lead to measurable, positive changes in student attitude, behavior, and achievement, education leaders and policymakers might be tempted to push its use in a heavy-handed, compulsory

THE IMPACT CYCLE

way. That's a recipe for disaster. Before moving forward to create their own video program, leaders should consider the following guidelines.

1. **Ensure psychologically safe environments.** People who choose to teach invest a lot of themselves in their work. For most educators, teaching is a major part of their identity. When something like a video recording of our lesson causes us to rethink "the story we tell ourselves about ourselves" (Stone, Patton, & Heen, 1999, p. 112), it can be disturbing. "Relinquish[ing] a cherished aspect of how you see yourself," Stone and colleagues wrote, "can be a loss that requires mourning just as surely as the death of a loved one" (p. 114).

Watching ourselves on video can truly be unsettling. First, people are never satisfied with their appearance. (I've yet to hear someone say, "I'm much younger and thinner than I realized!") More important, though, watching a video of themselves forces people to rethink who they are and what they do as professionals. As education consultant Jean Clark, from Cecil County, Maryland, explained when we talked about how her school district used video, "It's painful to realize that what we thought is reality isn't reality, that who we thought we were is not who we are. That's a powerful realization that changes the direction of where we are going. This is very hard to do because you have to be vulnerable. But it's authentic . . . and that's the way we become adults."

Because watching video is so emotionally challenging, people will not embrace its use unless they're in psychologically safe environments. As management expert Amy Edmondson (2012) explained, "In psychologically safe environments, people believe that if they make a mistake, others will not penalize them or think less of them for it. They also believe that others will not resent or humiliate them when they ask for help or information. This belief comes about when people both trust and respect each other, and it produces a sense of confidence that the group won't embarrass, reject, or punish someone for speaking up (pp. 118–119)."

2. **Make participation a choice.** No doubt some leaders will be tempted to make video compulsory across a school or system. This is problematic. First, telling people they must do something almost ensures that they won't want to do it. As Timothy Gallwey (1974) has written, "When you insist, they will resist."

Second, making video compulsory could damage school culture and decrease trust. Almost all teachers feel stress and anxiety when they're first asked to record themselves and share the video with others. Making video compulsory could lead to resentment, hostility, and resistance; and that doesn't sound like a psychologically safe environment. Finally, when leaders take away choice, they decrease the professionalism of teachers. Ensuring that teachers have choice about their learning doesn't mean that educators should have the option of choosing not to learn. Continual improvement is a defining characteristic of professionalism, so teachers who want to be considered professionals must continue to learn. By the same token, if we want our children to be taught by professionals, we must treat teachers as professionals, and that means giving them a lot of choice about what and how they learn.

THE IMPACT CYCLE

3. **Focus on intrinsic motivation.** The way a school uses video will depend on how leaders understand motivation. Leaders who believe that teachers will only change when they're pressured, extrinsically motivated, or, in worst-case scenarios, embarrassed, may wish to use video as a tool to pressure teachers to change. Such a primitive understanding of motivation will likely make things worse.

Teresa Amabile (Amabile & Kramer, 2011) and a host of other researchers (see Pink, 2009) have found that for complex work like teaching, extrinsic motivation actually decreases effectiveness. After reviewing thousands of data points from surveys, interviews, and observations of corporate teams, Amabile summed up her findings as follows: "Managers who say—or secretly believe—that employees work better under pressure, uncertainty, unhappiness, or fear are just plain wrong. Negative inner work has a negative effect on the four dimensions of performance: People are less creative, less productive, less deeply committed to their work, and less collegial to each other when their inner work lives darken (Amabile & Kramer, 2011, p. 58)."

When video recording is shared in a way that supports each educator's intrinsic desire to improve, it can be a powerful tool for rapid, significant improvement. Because it accelerates professional learning, video can awaken or deepen a teacher's desire to achieve his or her personal best.

4. **Establish boundaries.** When I discuss video with teachers, the most common question they ask me is, "Who's going to see it?" Teachers usually recognize that they can learn a lot by watching a video of one of their lessons, but they want to be assured that they won't have to conduct that learning in public, especially because they can't be sure what the video will reveal. For this reason, districts should adopt the policy that a video recording belongs to the person being recorded, who alone should determine whether it can be shared.

Leaders need to establish clear boundaries because boundaries create the rules of the game. Some possible boundaries for those who watch a video might be to focus on data, be nonjudgmental, respect the complex nature of teaching, be positive, be respectful, be supportive, and offer suggestions for improvement only after being asked.

5. **Walk the talk.** One of the most powerful ways leaders can promote the authentic use of video is by using video themselves. Instructional coaches can video record themselves coaching and then use the video to identify goals for improving their practice. The instructional coaches involved in our Kansas Coaching Project unanimously said that the most important type of professional learning for coaches to experience was watching themselves on video.

Principals can record themselves leading a school meeting or professional development session to identify ways to improve. Coaching expert Steve Barkley suggests that principals video record themselves teaching a lesson in a classroom, use the video as part of a staff meeting, and then set up for themselves a coaching conversation with an instructional coach. Simply put, when principals record a lesson and agree to be coached, they send a powerful message that they're not asking anyone to do anything they wouldn't do.

THE IMPACT CYCLE

6. **Go slow to go fast.** When it comes to change, the temptation is always to try to go faster and do more, rather than take the time to do things right. This can result in a reckless implementation that doesn't lead to sustained change. A poorly implemented innovation decreases people's readiness for change and can ultimately make things worse.

Leaders should start with a few volunteer teachers, ideally informal leaders in the school. Those volunteers should receive sufficient coaching and time to really learn from their videos. At the same time, leaders need to repeatedly communicate a few simple messages: People only need to use video if they choose, those who are recorded on a video own that video, and no one has to share anything unless that person is comfortable doing so.

Most important, leaders have to communicate that in a professional culture, everyone must be learning. By providing a clear picture of classroom teaching and a way to measure progress toward a goal, video can make professional learning have a real impact on student learning.

Reflection Questions for "What You Learn When You See Yourself Teach"

1. How can video be used?

2. Why is it we don't have a clear picture of reality?

3. What, in your opinion, are the most important conditions for success?

4. How can schools become *learning schools* through the use of video?

NOTES

_____
_____
_____
_____
_____
_____
_____
_____
_____
_____
_____

CHALK TALK ACTIVITY

 Purpose: To collaborate on ideas gathered from a text.

Process:

1. Select a text, or texts, to go with this activity.

2. Develop questions about the text or use the subtitles provided in the text. Write each question, or subtitle, on a sheet of chart paper (one chart paper for each question/subtitle).

    a. Hang chart paper around the room.

3. Participants will read the text individually. If using more than one text, allow participants to choose which text they use for the activity. They could also read both!

4. After the participants have had time to read the text individually, they will each collect one chart marker, carry their text with them, and move around the room to answer the questions on the chart papers. If subtitles were used on the chart papers instead of questions, explain to the participants that they will leave their ideas or thoughts about that subtitle on the chart paper. If participants are answering questions, explain expectations: how long answers need to be, how to write on the chart paper (in bullets, anywhere, etc.).

    a. Explain that Chalk Talk is a silent activity; as they move around the posters, they are writing notes silently!

    b. Invite people to build off each other's ideas by adding on, underlining, circling words, or putting check marks to indicate that they agree with statements already on the poster.

    c. Everyone will rotate to each poster.

    d. Designate a time for this part of the activity.

5. After everyone has visited each poster, invite the participants to partner up and move back through the posters, reading the final versions and discussing what they see with their partners.

6. Once enough time has passed for partners to rotate and discuss the posters, invite the partnerships to go to the poster they found most interesting. Invite the groups that have formed at each poster to turn in and share what is most interesting to them about that poster. Allow groups to stay in this part of the activity for as long as they need. Once time has passed, ask for a volunteer from each poster to share their group's thinking with the room.

7. Once the activity has come to a close, invite everyone to go back to their seats and talk at their tables or with a partner about what their next action might be after today's learning.

Modifications:

– This can be modified for virtual participation by creating a slideshow to share with the group. Each slide of the slideshow would be one "poster" from the above directions. Using text boxes, participants can share their thoughts on each slide.

THE IMPACT CYCLE

<u>Guiding Question:</u> What do goals look like in instructional coaching?

<u>Resources:</u> "PEERS Goals" article, Principles of Coaching video: What's a Good Goal, PEERS scenarios, Circle, Square, Triangle Reflection activity

<u>Activity:</u>

1. Begin by reading about goals in instructional coaching with the "PEERS Goals" article.

2. Reflect on the reading by using the reflection questions that appear after the article.

3. Afterward, layer on the Principles of Coaching video: What's a Good Goal, and then continue reflecting by using the questions that follow the video.

4. Use the PEERS scenarios sheet to continue thinking about PEERS Goals.

5. Wrap up this learning path by completing the Circle, Square, Triangle Reflection activity that appears after the PEERS Scenarios.

PEERS Goals

Originally published in *Instructional Coaching Group Blog,* November 2015.

 Goal setting is an essential part of coaching. Coaches often partner with teachers to set SMART goals, which are variously understood to be Specific, Measurable, Attainable (or Actionable/Assignable), Realistic (Relevant), and Timely (or Time Bound).

I believe teachers and coaches can set better goals if they consider a different acronym, **PEERS**, which highlights a few additional factors that are very important when setting goals. Teachers that create goals that address the PEERS factors will likely find that their goals will have more impact. I introduced PEERS goals in my book *Focus on Teaching*, and here I include a slightly modified version of what I first wrote about in that book.

Powerful

People who want to make an important difference in students' lives should sort through every possible goal by asking a simple question: Will this goal make a real difference in students' lives? Thus, a teacher might list several possible goals, such as increasing student time on task to 95%, increasing students' vocabulary quiz scores to a 90% or higher average, decreasing student disruptions to fewer than four per 10 minutes, improving the quality of students' writing and so forth.

Easy

Powerful goals that are difficult or impossible to implement are not as helpful as powerful goals that are *easy to implement.* Difficult-to-implement goals, no matter how powerful, often end up on the scrap heap of unrealized good intentions.

The best goals are goals that are powerful and easy, because they have the greatest likelihood of being implemented, and because they provide more time for teachers, who are very busy, to work on other important tasks.

In *Influencer: The Power to Change Anything,* Patterson and his colleagues explain why easy and powerful goals are so important: "When it comes to altering behavior, you need to help others answer only two questions. First: Is it worth it? . . . And second, Can they do this thing? . . . Consequently, when trying to change behaviors, think of the only two questions that matter. Is it worth it? . . . Can I do it?"

Emotionally compelling

In their book *Switch: How to Change Things When Change Is Hard*, Heath and Heath (2010) suggest that *effective goals* need to be more than SMART—they need to compel people to action by moving them emotionally.

According to the authors, effective goals "provide a destination postcard—a vivid picture from the near-term future that shows what could be possible."

Reachable

Teachers and coaches need to consider whether or not their goal, however admirable, is one that can actually be reached. A reachable goal is one that builds *hope.*

Shane Lopez, a researcher at the University of Kansas and The Gallup Organization, has been described as the world's leading expert on hope. In *Making Hope Happen: Create the Future You Want for Yourself and Others*, Lopez (2013) writes that hope requires three elements.

First, hope requires a goal that sets out an idea of "where we want to go, what we want to accomplish, who we want to be." Second, to feel hope, we need agency, our "perceived ability to shape our lives day to day . . . [our knowledge that] . . . we can make things happen." Finally, hope requires pathways, "plans that carry us forward."

A goal that fosters hope is a goal that has a reasonable chance of being achieved because (a) teachers believe they can achieve it (agency) and (b) it includes a strategy or strategies that can help them achieve it (pathways).

Increasing student achievement by 20% on the state reading assessment is an admirable goal, but it is not helpful unless teacher and coach can identify a strategy that will help them reach the goal. Decreasing non-instructional time from 22% to 5% by teaching students expectations for transitions, for example, is a more effective goal because it shows the destination as well as the pathways that teachers can realistically expect will get them there.

THE IMPACT CYCLE

A reachable goal also has to be one that people will know they have reached. That is, as SMART goals have shown for years, the goal has to be measurable; it has to have a finish line.

Student-focused

Finally, effective goals are student-focused rather than teacher-focused. When teachers choose teacher goals ("Let's use graphic organizers at least twice a week"), they may implement the goal, but have no idea whether or not it made a difference for students. Additionally, no measure of excellence is built into the goal so people may implement the goal poorly and still meet the goal.

A student-focused goal, on the other hand, provides clear feedback on whether or not changes make a difference for students. Additionally, student-focused goals carry with them a built-in measure of quality. If a teacher ineffectively implements a teaching practice, it is unlikely that he will achieve the goal. The teacher will have to keep refining his use of the practice until he is able to implement it effectively, so that its use can lead to achievement of the goal.

Reflection Questions for "PEERS Goals"

1. What is the biggest takeaway about goals that are used in instructional coaching?
2. Who chooses the goal, and why?
3. What do student-focused goals tell us about change?
4. What new ideas do you have about working with teachers after reading this?

NOTES

_____

_____

_____

_____

Principles of Coaching Video

What's a Good Goal?

https://youtu.be/2i7bYFMvKyU

Watch this video to continue learning about PEERS goals and how they can enhance instructional coaching.

THE IMPACT CYCLE

Reflection Questions for the Video "What's a Good Goal?"

1. What additional information did you gain from watching the video?

2. What ideas from the video affirmed what you have read about?

NOTES

_____

_____

_____

_____

_____

_____

THE IMPACT CYCLE

PEERS SCENARIOS

 Directions: Use the scenarios to reflect on PEERS goals and practice writing strong PEERS goals.

Examples of a Strong PEERS Goal Are as Follows:

(1) At least 85% of students will improve by 2 rubric points from their pretest scores on the concluding paragraph portion of the argumentative essay post-test.

(2) All students will report themselves to be either "strategically compliant" or "authentically engaged" during 5 self-reported data collections on classroom activities during the fractions unit.

Scenario #1

Coach Allen is partnering with Sage, a third-grade teacher who is concerned about engagement in her classroom. After capturing the current reality on video, Allen moves through the identify questions to support Sage in developing a PEERS goal. During the conversation, Sage shares, "I just want to be able to engage students during the start of my lesson. I feel like I can't get them engaged to begin, so their engagement just stays low throughout the whole lesson."

Task: What might a PEERS goal sound like for Sage?

Scenario #2

Lee, a high school instructional coach, was walking down the hallway when Jamie comes running up to her. Jamie says, "Lee, I need your help. I just don't know how to do feedback in my writing block. I'm behind on my grading, and the essays are piling up. I have to do something to get back on track and get these students some feedback on their writing." Lee invites Jamie to begin an Impact Cycle together, honoring his desire to focus on feedback in his writing block.

Task: What might a PEERS goal sound like for Jamie?

Scenario #3

Harper and Ceci have begun a new partnership and are using the Impact Cycle to guide them in their work together. After collecting current reality on Harper's class, Ceci uses the identify questions and they come up with a goal together, but Ceci needs to review the goal to ensure it is a strong PEERS goal.

The goal: The teacher will teach students strategies for solving problems quickly so that students complete all problems in the time allotted.

Task: What elements of PEERS are present in the goal? What is missing? What would this goal sound like if it is was a *strong* PEERS goal?

Scenario #4

Shaun and Camille are new coaches who are learning more about PEERS goals. They have written a few but are now going back through the PEERS elements to see if they have missed anything.

The following are the goals they have written:

1. Students will explain the procedure they followed in completing their labs more often.

2. Students will demonstrate growth in their analysis of the story on the reading rubric by the end of the marking period.

3. 6 out of 8 partnerships will be actively engaged and holding each other accountable during math stations by self-reporting a 4 or higher on the engagement scale survey 4 out of 5 times after 5 data collections.

4. 100 percent of students will be engaged during small group math instruction.

5. The teacher will implement guided reading more effectively.

Task: Which of the goals Shaun and Camille have written is a strong PEERS goal? Which ones need more work, and what elements of PEERS might be missing? Choose one or two goals to transform into PEERS goals.

Scenario #5

Nate and Brian are in a coaching cycle together and are using the identify questions to establish a PEERS goal for their work together. The following is a transcript of their conversation from the identify questions.

Nate: *On a scale of 1–10, how close is this lesson to your ideal?*

Brian: *It was a 3—nothing seemed to go well. Normally the students are more engaged.*

Nate: *What went well?*

Brian: *Kids were positive and answering questions during the discussion portion of the lesson.*

Nate: *What would have to change to make this closer to a 10?*

Brian: *The transition from the lesson to independent work would need to be more concise and smoother. It seems like they get it during the lesson, but as soon as they get to work, they have so many questions so I'm spending a ton of time repeating myself.*

Nate: *What would you see your students doing differently if it was a 10?*

Brian: *After the lesson, students would get straight to work without asking questions I have already answered or distracting each other.*

Nate: *Describe what that would look like.*

Brian: *I'd finish my lesson, and then students would turn back to their seats and get straight to work, using materials they already have out and ready, with no side conversations.*

Nate: *How could we measure that?*

Brian: *I do not know. Is there a tool I could use?*

Nate: *We can look at tools for you to use to measure that. Should this be your goal?*

Brian: *Yes, I would love to see smoother transitions so kids can get their work done.*

Nate: *If you could reach your goal, would it really matter to you?*

Brian: *YES. I feel like this would move us closer to a tighter block, which would help kids turn their work in more often.*

Nate: *What strategy would you like to try to achieve your goal?*

Brian: *Maybe I need to work on giving clearer directions?*

Task: What would the PEERS goal sound like?

Scenario #6

Manuel is working with Amira, Chase, and Austin on coaching cycles in their classrooms. They are proficient teachers, and their students typically do well. The teachers have talked about what they want their goals to be in their coaching cycles with Manuel, and they all want 100 percent of students to achieve their goals. Manuel meets with each of them individually to hear more about their goals but grows concerned about how big the goal is and that there might be an opportunity to dig deeper to clarify the goal. Manuel decides he will ask each of them, individually, to reflect on their goals using some questions he has prepared:

1.   What might be a smaller goal?

2.   How can we make the goal more specific?

THE IMPACT CYCLE

3. How can we make the goal more powerful?

4. What is it we *really* want students to know or do?

5. How long will the goal take?

The goals the teachers have set are:

Amira: 100% of students will demonstrate use of writing expectations while in Writer's Workshop 100% of the time.

Chase: 100% of students will be able to explain their mathematical reasoning.

Austin: 100% of students will be engaged in the peer editing and revising processes of writing.

Task: Use the five questions Manuel has created to analyze each teacher's goal. Then, rewrite their goals below into strong PEERS Goals.

Amira's new goal:

Chase's new goal:

Austin's new goal:

CIRCLE, SQUARE, TRIANGLE REFLECTION ACTIVITY

●	■	▲
What is something that is still circling around in your head about PEERS Goals?	What is something that squares with your beliefs or practices related to instructional coaching?	What are three important points about PEERS Goals?

<u>Guiding Question:</u> What is important about the learn and improve stages of the Impact Cycle?

<u>Resources:</u> "4 Steps for Focusing Coaching Sessions" article, Case Study: Learn and Improve

<u>Activity:</u>

1. Read the article "4 Steps for Focusing Coaching Sessions."

2. Use the reflection questions that appear after the article to reflect and discuss.

3. Next, read through the case study.

4. Wrap up this learning path by answering the reflection questions that appear after the case study.

4 Steps for Focusing Coaching Sessions

When showing teachers new methods, zero in on what really matters.

Originally published in *Educational Leadership*, 80(7). April 1, 2023.

> *"Teaching is not one-size-fits-all; it's one-size-fits-one."*
>
> —Eric Liu, Guiding Lights (2004)

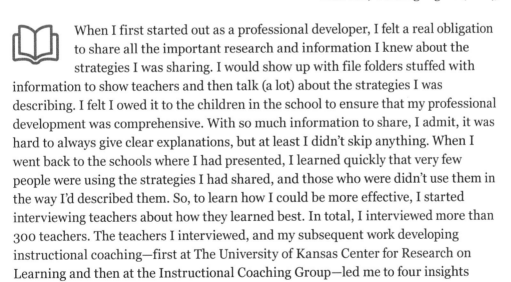 When I first started out as a professional developer, I felt a real obligation to share all the important research and information I knew about the strategies I was sharing. I would show up with file folders stuffed with information to show teachers and then talk (a lot) about the strategies I was describing. I felt I owed it to the children in the school to ensure that my professional development was comprehensive. With so much information to share, I admit, it was hard to always give clear explanations, but at least I didn't skip anything. When I went back to the schools where I had presented, I learned quickly that very few people were using the strategies I had shared, and those who were didn't use them in the way I'd described them. So, to learn how I could be more effective, I started interviewing teachers about how they learned best. In total, I interviewed more than 300 teachers. The teachers I interviewed, and my subsequent work developing instructional coaching—first at The University of Kansas Center for Research on Learning and then at the Instructional Coaching Group—led me to four insights about how to most effectively share with teachers information to help their practice.

1. Use checklists for focus.

When I talked with teachers about how they learned, they told me they didn't benefit from slide after slide of information. They wanted me to zone in on the most important information and present it in a clear way that they could use. What teachers really needed, I discovered, were checklists. The most effective checklists offered simple, easy to implement information that gave teachers clear steps to follow. Checklists gave teachers actionable knowledge that they could translate into practice in their work with students. Not every teaching strategy required a checklist, but for more complex practices, checklists were incredibly helpful. Using checklists aided me as a presenter, too, helping me remember key components of strategies and keeping me from skipping over strategies and keeping me from skipping over important information as I excitedly ran through explanations. Another bonus: creating checklists deepened, synthesized, and simplified my understanding of the teaching strategies I shared. Checklists also helped me overcome the common cognitive bias known as the curse of knowledge, the struggle most of us experience when we try to explain something we know extremely well. As Heath and Heath write: Once we know something, we find it hard not to imagine what it was like not to know it. Our knowledge has "cursed" us. And it becomes difficult for us to share our knowledge with others, because we can't readily re-create our listeners' state of mind.

2 . Leave room for adaptation.

As my colleagues and I started to study instructional coaching, we quickly learned that, powerful as checklists are, they aren't a one-size-fits-all solution. Teachers need to adapt strategies so that those strategies are best suited to their teaching style and most helpful for their students (as the words at the beginning of this column, from Citizen University founder Eric Liu, reflect). Explanations must be precise, but also provisional, leaving room for teachers to adapt practices so they're helpful for each individual in their unique setting. We also learned that it's not effective to position people as passive receivers of knowledge. Over time, we learned that as we described strategies, we had to also communicate that teachers should feel free to adapt, reject, or accept any aspects of the strategies they planned to try. Simply put, teachers should always decide how they will implement a strategy with their students in their classroom. To allow for adaptation and teachers' choices, we learned to be flexible as we shared strategies. When coaches use the approach I suggest, they run through the steps and stop after each item to ask the collaborating teacher if they would like to do that step as it is, skip it, or change it. Then the coach records the teacher's modifications right on the checklist.

3. Share ideas carefully.

Coaches don't help teachers by keeping their ideas to themselves, especially if they think a teacher's modifications will create problems. Good coaches still share ideas, but in ways that don't shut down collaborating teachers. My colleagues and I learned that if we told teachers exactly what to do or not do, we cut them out of the thinking about the strategy, decreasing their ownership of the work and, ironically, making them less likely to adopt what we shared. (We also learned that most of us think our advice is more helpful—and more wanted by others— than it actually is!) Good coaches still share ideas, but in ways that don't shut down collaborating teachers. Over time, we learned to introduce ideas provisionally by asking, "Do you mind if I share something I'm wondering?" As we shared our thoughts, we'd be clear that teachers should make all the decisions about how they implement strategies. In reality, of course, teachers will almost always do what they choose, regardless of what the coach says.

4. Offer objective standards for effective implementation.

Yes, checklists have to be adapted, but a poorly implemented strategy almost always gets poor results. So, teachers need to know what effective implementation looks and feels like. For that, they need a standard for excellence. That standard, I've learned, shouldn't be the coach's opinion; it should be a measure of student success. When teachers set powerful, student focused goals related to achievement or engagement and implement new strategies to hit their goals, they have to keep refining their implementation until the goal is met. Only effectively implemented and adapted strategies will get the results teachers want for learners. Toward True Change! When coaches take this nuanced approach to explaining strategies—when they are precise but provisional as they explain strategies and offer ideas as only suggestions—and when teachers set student-focused goals to guide their actions, students will see real results. True change doesn't take a deck filled with hundreds of slides. It requires simplicity, precision, adaptation, and—crucially—a focus on student success.

Reflection Questions for "4 Steps for Focusing Coaching Sessions"

1. What is helpful about checklists?

2. What are we communicating when teachers can make their own adaptations?

3. How might coaches share instructional strategies with teachers?

4. How can coaches move toward true change?

CASE STUDY: LEARN AND IMPROVE

 Allison and Emily are working through The Impact Cycle together. Allison, the coach, is feeling confident and excited about the work ahead. She and Emily established a clear picture of current reality, set a PEERS goal, and were getting ready to head into the learn and improve stage of their coaching cycle. Since Emily had chosen using effective questions as her teaching strategy, Allison was preparing a checklist to use during the learn stage so that Emily could get a better idea of how to ask great questions during her instruction. As Allison was making the checklist, she thought back to her experience with using questions in her own classroom before she became a coach. She jotted down a list of all the things she would do to make sure her questions were effective and then created a checklist based on that list. In their next meeting, Allison shared the checklist with Emily.

Emily was so excited to have a checklist but quickly became overwhelmed when looking at what Allison had brought. The ideas on the checklist were intimidating, and Emily wasn't quite clear on the strategy. Together, they went through the checklist, but Emily still felt unsure. The next day, Emily was supposed to implement questioning in her instruction, and Allison was going to observe from the back of the room. They had agreed on a data collection tool to monitor the types of questions Emily asked, so Allison was going to gather observational data toward the goal.

After school, they met for their improve conversation where Allison shared that Emily skipped many of the steps on the checklist. She asked what questions she had, because she was looking for Emily to use all the steps from the checklist as they were listed. Emily said she would try again the next day, so they set up their next classroom observation.

In their next improve conversation, Allison shared that Emily still forgot to do some of the steps from the checklist. Emily shared that she actually felt much more confident in how she used questions in her conversation with students. She remarked that her students' engagement increased, and that she was proud of the progress she saw in her class that day. Since they were tracking the types of questions asked, Emily presented Allison with a list of questions she had written for that lesson, and check marks next to the ones that she asked during the lesson. Emily shared that she felt like she asked a variety of questions: open questions when discussion was necessary and closed questions to bring focus to the students' thinking. She felt very pleased with her progress, but Allison pointed out that she was still missing parts of the checklist.

Reflection Questions for the Learn and Improve Case Study

1. What went well in this scenario?

2. What was challenging about this coaching partnership?

3. What would you have done if you were the coach?

4. What does the learning from the article and case study leave you thinking about the learn and improve stages of the Impact Cycle?

NOTES

<u>Guiding Question:</u> What are the potential challenges with learning, and how can we overcome them?

<u>Resources:</u> "Escape From the Zero-Learning Zone" article, Empathy Anchor activity

<u>Activity:</u>

1. Read through the Empathy Anchor activity to become familiar with the process.

2. Engage in the Empathy Anchor activity using the article in this learning path.

3. Wrap up this learning path by using the reflection questions that appear after the article.

Escape From the Zero-Learning Zone

Why educators frequently turn away from opportunities to learn, and what we can do about it.

Originally published in *Educational Leadership*, 76(3). November 1, 2018.

"Who dares to teach must never cease to learn."

—John Cotton Dana

The world is rich with learning opportunities, especially for educators. Teachers can learn from video recordings of their lessons, instructional coaching, conversations with their principals and peers, formative assessment and other data, and student feedback. Similarly, principals can learn from 360-degree feedback; video recordings of meetings they lead or presentations they give; conversations with teachers and students; and data on achievement, school climate, or teacher satisfaction, such as from Gallup's Q12 Engagement Survey (Gallup, 2016).

We know that learning is essential for professional success, self-efficacy, healthy relationships, and well-being. However, when opportunities to learn present themselves, we frequently turn away. Offered the chance to learn, we choose instead to move into what I call the *Zero-Learning Zone*.

What Is the Zero-Learning Zone?

We step into the Zero-Learning Zone whenever we act, consciously or unconsciously, in ways that block our own learning. For example, we might be shy about how we appear on camera and therefore turn down the chance to learn from video recordings of a lesson. We might say no to an opportunity to work with a coach; dismiss feedback from a colleague, principal, or student; adopt beliefs that isolate us from new ideas; blame others; or make excuses that shift responsibility away from ourselves and onto someone else. There are many reasons why we take a pass on an opportunity to learn, but before we explore how to get out of the Zero-Learning Zone, we have to take a look at how we get there in the first place.

Blindspots. We often miss the chance to learn because we do not see that we need to learn. James Prochaska, an expert on the personal experience of change, and colleagues identified the first stage of change as pre-contemplation—not realizing we need to learn so that we can change our situations (Prochaska, Norcross, & DiClimente, 1994). Because of perceptual errors such as confirmation bias, habituation, stereotypes, primacy effect, and recency effect, we don't see reality clearly. As researcher and social psychologist Heidi Grant Halvorson (2015) has written in *No One Understands You and What to Do About It,* "The uncomfortable truth is that most of us . . . can't see ourselves truly objectively" (p. 4). A principal, for example, might not see how much time he wastes on unimportant issues during staff meetings until he watches a video recording of a meeting.

We don't think the learning is worth it. Two factors need to be in place for us to grow and change (Patterson et al., 2008). First, we need to believe we can do what we are considering. Second, we need to believe that what we are considering is worth the effort. If either factor is missing, we are much less likely to embrace the opportunity to learn or change. Teachers who are introduced to new teaching practices may forgo implementation because they can't see the practice as working or because they can't see themselves mastering the new strategy.

Identity. Our deepest learning experiences usually challenge us to re-think "the stories we tell ourselves about who we are" (Stone & Heen, 2015, p. 23) and reconsider what kind of people we are, our efficacy, ethics, and overall place in the world. But we are resistant to any experience that causes us to re-evaluate what we think to be true about ourselves. It's much easier to just say no. "Learning about ourselves can be painful—sometimes brutally so," write Stone and Heen, "and the feedback is often delivered with a forehead-slapping lack of awareness for what makes people tick. It can feel less like a 'gift of learning' and more like a colonoscopy" (p. 7).

Hope (or, more precisely, its absence). Gallup Senior Researcher Shane Lopez (2013) summarizes a three-part process for hope, first identified by University of Kansas researcher Rick Snyder. To have hope we need goals, "pictures of the future [that] identify an idea of where we want to go, what we want to accomplish, who we want to be" (p. 24). Second, hope involves agency, our belief that we have control over our lives and that we can meet our goals. Finally, we need to have multiple ways of getting to the goal. Lopez suggests that when we lose hope, it is often because we lack one or more of these three factors. And when people do not have hope, the easiest place to go is the Zero-Learning Zone.

Fear. When I discussed the Zero-Learning Zone with colleagues, a word I heard frequently was fear. We might be afraid that we are going to embarrass ourselves or fail. This emotion also overlaps with the other Zero-Learning Zone factors. For example, we may fear the unknown impact that learning might have on our identity. A loss of self-efficacy. Confronting our own hopelessness and blind spots. You get the idea.

A well-known education researcher told me that he believes fear blocks learning when people embrace a partial answer to a challenge or problem, creating the illusion of a comprehensive solution. That "solution" can become so entwined with our identity that we seek out proof that our ideas work, rather than information that would help us learn. A partial, if flawed, solution can feel better than risk or uncertainty. But real learning only occurs when we confront our fears and move forward.

Getting Past Zero

Given the complexity of learning and our own flawed perceptions of ourselves, we shouldn't be surprised if we find ourselves in the Zero-Learning Zone. Ron Heifetz (2002) captured our predicament well in his book (with Marty Linsky) *Leadership on the Line* when he wrote about adaptive change, a particular form of deep learning:

> Adaptive change stimulates resistance because it challenges people's habits, beliefs, and values. It asks them to take a loss, experience uncertainty, and even express disloyalty to people and cultures. Because adaptive change forces people to question and perhaps redefine aspects of their identity, it also challenges their sense of competence. Loss, disloyalty, and feeling incompetent: That's a lot to ask. No wonder people resist. (p. 30)

But while learning is challenging, perhaps even threatening, it is also essential. To live truly fulfilling lives, we need to be curious. Choosing not to learn is choosing intellectual impoverishment, something teachers cannot afford. Teaching is a learning profession, in part because each individual child is a unique learning opportunity, and also because to ensure students receive the learning they need and deserve, we need to keep striving to be better. What's more, if we expect our students to learn, we need to show that we are learning.

Fortunately, there are many things we can do to move out of the Zero-Learning Zone. Here are a few:

Flip your perspective. One way to move forward as a learner is to gain a different perspective on how you lead and teach, or how your students learn. The easiest way to do this is to video record yourself doing something important, such as teaching a lesson. If you're not ready for video, try the audio record function on your phone. Interview students to hear their perspectives on your teaching. This will force you to see or hear things outside of your own perspective and, yes, learn.

When we act to get a different perspective on our actions, by looking at video or interviewing students, for example, we are intentionally stepping outside the Zero-Learning Zone. It takes courage to choose to learn, and real learning requires a real picture of reality that comes from flipping our perspective.

Create specific goals. Well-crafted goals can provide guideposts that nudge you out of your comfort zone. As Heidi Grant Halvorson (2012) says, "Taking the time to get specific and spell out *exactly* what you want to achieve removes the possibility of settling for less—of telling yourself that what you've done is good enough. It also makes the course of action you need to take much clearer" (p. 6). Our research on coaching at the Kansas Coaching Project at the University of

Kansas identified five variables that make for effective goals. We summarize these variables as PEERS goals: Powerful, Easy to Achieve, Emotionally Compelling, Reachable and Student-Focused. Most frequently, the PEERS goals that teachers set are achievement-related (students can write a well-organized paragraph), engagement goals (students demonstrate that they have hope on weekly quick, informal assessments of their attitude), or behavior goals (transition time takes up less than 5 percent of class time).

Utilize design thinking. Design thinking is a methodology for creating and problem solving that applies the strategies of design to real-world challenges and opportunities. A teacher who applies design thinking to achieve a goal in her classroom might, for example, decide that she wants a higher level of engaged conversation during classroom dialogue. Taking the stance of a designer, she might identify the goal to be that 75 percent of students contribute high-level comments during classroom dialogue; try out and adapt various approaches to facilitating discussion, such as encouraging more active listening, using different questions or more provocative and relevant thinking prompts, providing more affirmation of students, or establishing clearly defined academic-discussion norms; gather data each time she tries out a different approach; make modifications based on the data; and continue to test and adapt until the goal is met.

One of the advantages of design thinking is that it reduces the stress and anxiety of attempting change without a framework, and therefore helps to push teachers out of the Zero-Learning Zone. Rather than trying to get things perfect the first time, teachers taking the design approach experiment, gather data (possibly through video), try again, and repeat, learning all the time.

Conduct a hope audit. As mentioned earlier, the three factors that are essential for hope are agency, goals, and pathways to the goals (Lopez, 2013). If we feel that we may be losing hope, we may find it useful to conduct an audit to see if we are coming up empty in one of those three areas. Ask yourself: Do I have a clear, specific goal? Do I have strategies I can use to hit the goal? Do I believe I can hit the goal? If your answer to any of these questions is "no," then you need to identify resources that can help you find hope and reach that goal.

A teacher who is starting to lose hope that all of his students will learn to write a well-organized paragraph can conduct a hope audit by first considering the goal: Has he clearly stated what a well-organized paragraph looks like? If not, perhaps he could create a checklist for what an effective paragraph should look like. Next, he could look at pathways: What strategies could he use to increase student success? Maybe he could have students self-assess their writing, work with partners, or look at more examples. Or the teacher could do more modeling or provide better feedback. Finally, he must consider agency: After implementing these changes, does he believe his students can improve? If not, what different strategies or goal adjustments need to change?

Keep it simple and targeted. Learning may seem overwhelming if we try to accomplish too much all at once. Choose one learning target and stick with it until it is accomplished. An excellent example of targeted learning was described on the now-defunct Teach TV web site in the United Kingdom. The video showed an elementary teacher explaining how each Friday she made a list of all the students in her class. For the students whose names she forgot or had to struggle to remember, she made notes about their unique strengths. The next week she took special care to think about the students she'd forgotten and reminded them and herself of their strengths so that she didn't forget those students the next Friday.

Treat yourself with compassion. Teachers are often harder on themselves than anyone else would ever be, and certainly harder on themselves than they would ever consider being with a friend. I believe educators need to be more compassionate toward themselves. Daniel Pink (2018) offers a simple way for doing that. He suggests that when we are disappointed by something we've done, we should write ourselves an email expressing compassion or understanding, imagining "what someone one who cares about you might say" (p. 143). When we step out of the Zero-Learning Zone we will have times when we screw up or experience fear. To keep learning, we need to adopt what Pink refers to as "the converse corollary of the Golden Rule: . . . to treat [ourselves] as [we] would others" (p. 143).

Leading Our Own Learning

Teacher-led learning has great potential because we can influence and inspire students when we model our own learning. When we improve, we have greater impact on students' achievement and well-being. Additionally, when we lead our own learning, when we see more and learn how to act more effectively, our lives improve. Learning is our lifeblood, and we live better when we learn more.

To experience that learning, however, we need to step outside of the Zero-Learning Zone. We need to demonstrate the courage it takes to watch ourselves on video, interview students, experiment with prototypes and iterations, stay hopeful, draw on the resources that already exist, and forgive ourselves when things don't work out. What matters is that we intentionally keep learning. When we do, our children's lives will be better, and so will our own.

THE IMPACT CYCLE

Reflection Questions for "Escape From the Zero-Learning Zone"

1. Have you ever found yourself in the Zero-Learning Zone? What do you think was the cause of your stalled learning?

2. What is one topic or subject that you'd like to learn more about? What steps can you take today to find out more about it?

3. What opportunities can you and your colleagues take advantage of to see yourself and your teaching from a different perspective?

NOTES _____

_____

_____

_____

_____

EMPATHY ANCHOR ACTIVITY

 Purpose: To consider other perspectives about a topic.

Process:

1. Select a text of focus for a group to read and discuss together.

2. Establish a timekeeper for the group.

3. Share that in this activity, people will be choosing an empathy anchor: a person they will keep in their thoughts as they read this article. The participants can choose a specific person (while keeping their name private to protect confidentiality), a group of people, an entire staff, or so on. For example, someone might choose to hold the perspective of a new teacher. Another person might think about a partner they are working with in a coaching cycle or on a project. People can also think of their teammates. The idea is to think of yourself and *one other person or group* as a way to empathize deeply with yourself and others based on the topic.

4. Invite the group to read the text, thinking about themselves and their empathy anchor (the other perspective they have selected). For example, if I am reading about climate change, I might think about how it impacts my life and the life of the new generation (the new generation would be my empathy anchor).

    a. After time to read, the facilitator might provide time for people to write ideas about themselves and their empathy anchors regarding the topic about which they have read.

5. Ask participants to form partnerships, triads, or small groups and share in two rounds.

    a. Round 1: What did this bring up for you as you read? What are the implications for your practice?

    b. Round 2: What did this bring up for your empathy anchor as you read? What might be the implications for your work with that person/group?

6. After groups have had time to share, bring the participants back together and ask them to individually reflect on what they will do next based on today's conversation.

Modifications:

– The facilitator might predetermine empathy anchors for a group. For example, perhaps the facilitator is interested in thinking about groups within a school or individuals on a team.

– The final reflection can be changed into a whole group sharing activity.

<u>Guiding Question:</u> What is the Impact Cycle, and how do I share about this process with others?

<u>Resources:</u> The Impact Cycle checklist, the Impact Cycle Video Reflection activity

<u>Activity:</u>

1. Read through the Impact Cycle Video Reflection activity to become familiar with the process.

2. Read the Impact Cycle Checklist. Reflect on or discuss each line on the checklist to ensure clarity of the stages and steps in the Impact Cycle.

3. Engage in the Impact Cycle Video Reflection activity.

4. Wrap up this learning path by using the reflection questions that appear after the video reflection activity.

THE IMPACT CYCLE VIDEO REFLECTION ACTIVITY

 Purpose: To reflect on how coaches communicate the stages and steps of the Impact Cycle.

Materials: In this activity, participants will be recording themselves in a conversation. Cell phones make great tools for this, and no other tool is needed. Simply find a way to prop up the phone and record the conversations that will happen in pairs. The video will be reviewed by the partnership only, not shared with anyone else or in the group setting.

Process:

1. Invite participants to choose a partner for this activity.

2. Once all participants have a partner, explain that they will be audio- or video-recording conversations with each other to reflect on their communication skills. Recording yourself can be uncomfortable, so share that they have a choice: They can choose to only audio record themselves, or they can video record themselves. They can choose their preference when it comes time to record. Consider, too, choosing a space for this learning opportunity that has room for pairs to spread out and not be close to each other during the recording process. An invitation to leave the room and meet back after they record themselves in their conversations might also be an option, to ensure the learners feel safe using video.

3. In the partnerships, have participants decide who will be the coach first and who will be the coachee first (the teacher being coached). There will be two rounds and an opportunity for each partner to serve in both roles.

4. In Round 1, the coach will go through the checklist with the coachee, dialogically explaining the Impact Cycle using the checklist. The goal is to

practice how coaches will communicate the stages and steps of the Impact Cycle with a teacher.

    a. The coach will use their phone to record (audio or video) themselves explaining the checklist.

5. Once the first round is complete, the pair will switch roles and repeat the process, ensuring that the second-round conversation is also recorded so that both partners in the pair have a video or audio recording of themselves.

6. After both rounds, ask individuals to watch *their own* video back and make notes about what they notice from their explanation of the Impact Cycle checklist. Questions that can guide this reflection include the following:

    a. What did I do well?

    b. What was challenging for me?

    c. What might I do the next time I share the checklist with a teacher?

7. After the individuals have had time to reflect, ask them to return to their partner and share their noticings with each other.

8. Once the activity has come to a close, invite them to continue using video as a way to reflect on their practice.

Modifications:

– Groups of three can be used if it makes it easier to record the coach/coachee conversations.

– Not everyone will be comfortable with using video. Invest in the psychological safety of the learning environment, allow people to choose their groups/partners, and respect the confidentiality of the videos by allowing people to record on their own devices.

– The facilitator might choose to model this activity using the Impact Cycle checklist first, so that the participants have an idea of what this explanation could look like.

Reflection Questions for Learning Path #7

1. On a scale of 1 to 10 (1 being very uncomfortable and 10 being very comfortable), how comfortable are you with sharing the Impact Cycle process (and checklist) with teachers? What led you to choose that rating?

2. What stood out to you the most during the video reflection? How will you use this to inform your coaching?

3. How could you use video to continue learning about your practice?

4. What will you do next?

THE IMPACT CYCLE

NOTES

CHAPTER 4. THE IMPACT CYCLE   197

THE IMPACT CYCLE CHECKLIST

Checklist: Impact Cycle

IDENTIFY:	✓
Teacher gets a clear picture of current reality by watching a video of their lesson or by reviewing observation data, student interviews, or student work.	
Coach asks the identify questions with the teacher to identify a goal.	
Teacher identifies a student-focused goal.	
Teacher identifies a teaching strategy to use to hit the goal.	
LEARN:	✓
Coach shares a checklist for the chosen teaching strategy.	
Coach prompts the teacher to modify the practice if the teacher wishes.	
Teacher chooses an approach to modeling that they would like to observe and identifies a time to watch modeling.	
Coach provides modeling in one or more formats.	
Teacher sets a time to implement the practice.	
IMPROVE:	✓
Teacher implements the practice.	
Data is gathered (by teacher or coach in class or while viewing video) on student progress toward the goal.	
Data is gathered (by teacher or coach in class or while viewing video) on teacher's implementation of the practice (usually on the previously viewed checklist).	
Coach and teacher meet to confirm direction and monitor progress.	
Coach and teacher make adaptations and plan next actions until the goal is met.	

THE IMPACT CYCLE

<u>Guiding Question:</u> How can I enroll teachers into coaching cycles?

<u>Resources:</u> "Strategies for Enrolling Teachers in a Coaching Cycle" article, Enrolling Teachers activity

<u>Activity:</u>

1. Read through the article, and answer the reflection questions.

2. Partner up, and complete the activity.

3. Wrap up the learning path by using the reflection questions that appear after the activity.

Strategies for Enrolling Teachers in a Coaching Cycle

Originally published in *Instructional Coaching Group Blog*, November 2015.

One important consideration for coaches is how to enroll teachers in coaching cycles. It's not always an easy task because teachers can often feel belittled or minimized if a directive or top-down approach is used in the coaching relationship or by their school's administration. Instead, we promote a partnership approach. From the beginning of the teacher-coach relationship, it's important to make sure that the coach respects the teacher's autonomy and fosters a dynamic where the teacher does most of the thinking and the coach provides support to reach their goals. If the teacher is treated as an equal and remains in control of what they do, then they will be more open to the process and improvement will follow.

Here are some effective strategies to enroll teachers using a partnership approach:

One-to-One Conversations

A one-to-one conversation provides a chance for a coach to have an informal interaction with a teacher about what coaching is and how it works. For clarity, a one-page document describing instructional coaching can help facilitate these conversations by providing a reference point for details about the process and answers to common questions teachers may have. These types of conversations can be as long or short as necessary, and they are also a great opportunity to explain that the teacher, not the coach, will make all of the decisions about the coaching cycle. This chance to address anxieties or preconceptions regarding coaching can do a lot to assuage the concerns of skeptical or intimidated teachers. Coaches can also gather unique information about the teacher, their school, and their students' needs to tailor their approach specifically to them.

Workshops

Teachers learn all sorts of useful strategies and ideas through workshops. But after a workshop has concluded, it can be overwhelming to try to remember everything that was learned and then implement it. Coaching can be used as a way to help teachers put those new ideas into practice. In fact, workshops that don't include coaching are rarely beneficial because teachers are left with a wealth of new knowledge and no specific plan for applying it in their classroom.

Informal Conversations

Coaches can also enroll teachers throughout the school year through informal conversations. With this strategy, it is very important that every encounter is not all about coaching. No one likes getting a sales pitch, so the more authentic a coach can be in their interactions with a teacher throughout the year, the better. If they are able to offer genuine support for a teacher facing a challenge, then that teacher will be likely to seek out coaching.

Small- or Large-Group Presentations

In some cases, a small- or large-group presentation can be very effective to get teachers on board with coaching. The next post in the "Preparing for the New School Year" series will take a closer look at using presentations to enroll teachers and provide some examples of powerful presentations. Be sure to check out next week's post to learn more on this strategy! Most coaches will find that a combination of these strategies will be necessary, but ultimately, the most powerful way to enroll teachers is through word of mouth. The more teachers who are able to achieve their goals and reach students, the more teachers will seek out coaching.

THE IMPACT CYCLE

Reflection Questions for "Strategies for Enrolling Teachers in a Coaching Cycle"

1. What other ideas do you have for enrolling teachers into coaching cycles?

2. Which of these have you tried, would you like to try, or do you believe will be challenging to try?

3. Jim shares that 1:1 conversations are the most effective. Why might this be the most effective way to enroll teachers into a coaching partnership?

4. What might need to change to increase the number of teachers who are involved in coaching cycles?

THE IMPACT CYCLE

NOTES

_____
_____
_____
_____
_____
_____
_____
_____
_____
_____
_____
_____
_____
_____
_____
_____
_____

ENROLLING TEACHERS ACTIVITY

 Materials needed: chart paper, markers, sticky notes

1. Divide participants into pairs or small groups.

2. In pairs or small groups, use sticky notes to write down all the ways that coaches can enroll teachers into coaching cycles. Complete this step individually, and then come back together as a pair or small group to share ideas.

3. Using all the sticky notes from the pair or small group, sort them into like groups. In other words, are some sticky notes saying the same ideas? Are there similar trends in the sticky note ideas that could belong to the same big idea?

4. On the chart paper, create categories that have emerged from sorting the sticky notes. For example, you might have a category labeled "1:1 conversations," or "administrator referral."

    a. Inside each category, list notes about that enrollment strategy. Questions that can generate these notes include the following:

        i. What conditions might need to be in place for this enrollment strategy to be successful?

        ii. How will teachers respond to this enrollment strategy?

        iii. How can coaches prepare for this enrollment strategy?

        iv. What documents, forms, or presentations might the coach need to have ready for this enrollment strategy?

5. Once all pairs or small groups have completed their posters, have everyone come back together and share what they have created as a big group.

Reflection Questions for Learning Path #8

1. What are we left thinking about enrolling teachers?

2. Which strategy will work best for the teachers in our school/system?

3. How can coaches prepare?

THE IMPACT CYCLE

NOTES

END OF CHAPTER REFLECTION

Now that you have explored learning opportunities about the Impact Cycle, take time to reflect on this Success Factor overall. Use the following reflection questions, or reflect in your own way, and fill the lines with your ideas.

REFLECTION QUESTIONS

1. On a scale of 1 to 10, 1 being not at all and 10 being significant, what impact did these learning paths have on your practice? What led you to choose the rating you did?

2. How will learning more about the Impact Cycle influence your current and future partnerships with teachers?

3. What will you do next with your ideas?

NOTES

_____

_____

_____

_____

_____

_____

_____

_____

_____

_____

_____

_____

_____

_____

_____

Data

"Data fosters student learning and well-being, guides teachers' professional learning, and builds hope. Data is not a dirty word—just the opposite. When coaches partner with teachers and gather data effectively, data is powerful, positive, and empowering."

—Jim Knight

Success Factor #5: Data

It is often said that "data makes the invisible visible." When coaches focus on using data as an interpretive lens, it can result in powerful discoveries around engagement and achievement. Used effectively, data can reveal aspects of the learning experience that we would not otherwise see (Knight, 2022). Success Factor #5: Data helps coaches and teachers bring focus and intentionality to their coaching interactions and precision to goal setting by providing a clear finish line (Knight, 2022).

So Why Should We Be Talking About Data Within Schools and Systems?

Data should build hope because it helps instructional coaches get a clear picture of reality, set goals, and measure progress. If used well, data can help teachers see their students' needs more clearly, accelerate their professional learning, and even foster hope. Data are central to instructional coaches' work. They help both teachers and coaches see more of what is happening in the classroom, help teachers establish goals and measure progress toward goals, and build teacher efficacy by demonstrating the progress that is being made (Knight, 2022).

Resources Included in This Chapter

ARTICLES	ACTIVITIES	VIDEOS
"Students on the Margins"	Student Work Exploration	Feedback
"Should Coaches Give Feedback? It's Complicated"	Making Meaning From Student Data	
"Data Shouldn't Be a Dirty Word"	Expanding Perspectives Activity	

DATA

Optional Learning Paths

Learning Path #1

Guiding Question: Why is it important to take a dialogical approach to discussing data?

Resources: "Students on the Margins" article, Student Work Exploration, Feedback video

Activity:

1. Share the article electronically or make enough copies for all participants to have the article and read prior to the meeting to guide their data collection to use in the meeting.

2. Have participants collect student data to bring to the meeting to discuss (engagement or achievement). You could also bring a mock data set for all to use as they engage with the activity.

3. Facilitate the Student Work Exploration activity Steps 1 through 3.

4. Revisit your plans for next steps by asking "What can we do to increase your commitment?" Identify next steps, when they will happen, and who will do them.

Learning Path #2

Guiding Question: How should data inform goal setting in coaching conversations?

Resources: "Should Coaches Give Feedback" article, Making Meaning From Student Data activity

Activity:

1. Read the article "Should Coaches Give Feedback" prior to the meeting for background knowledge.

2. Read through the Making Meaning From Student Data activity to make sure the process is clear, and practice in partners using either a created data set or the data set participants have brought to the meeting.

3. Use the last three questions (in the activity) to discuss thoughts and next steps.

Learning Path #3

Guiding Question: How can better understanding the "how" and "why" of data impact coaching interactions and goal setting to improve student outcomes?

Resources: "Data Shouldn't Be a Dirty Word" article, Expanding Perspectives activity

DATA

<u>Activity:</u>

1. Read the article "Data Shouldn't Be a Dirty Word."

2. Read through the Expanding Perspectives activity to become familiar with the process.

3. Complete the activity to further explore the article and facilitate dialogue.

4. Debrief the process, and discuss implications for future data conversations.

Guiding Question: Why is it important to take a dialogical approach to discussing data?

Resources: "Students on the Margins" article, Student Work Exploration, Feedback video

Activity:

1. Before using this learning path, read through the Student Work Exploration activity, and share what participants can do to prepare. Schedule time to go through this learning path once the participants have a sample data set or data from students. You could also bring a mock data set for participants to use as they engage with the activity.

2. Read the article, and use the reflection questions to discuss the text.

3. Use the Student Work Exploration activity to learn from student work.

4. Revisit your plans for next steps by asking "What can we do to increase your commitment?" Identify next steps, when they will happen, and who will do them.

Students on the Margins

How instructional coaching can increase engagement and achievement.

Originally published in *The Learning Professional: The Learning Forward Journal, 40*(6). December 2019.

 My friend and mentor Don Deshler has directed more than 200 studies in his career and, in the process, significantly shaped how we understand and respond to students who are at risk for failure.

One study in particular changed the way Deshler thought about his research. To see the school experience through students' eyes, he and his fellow researchers at the University of Kansas Center for Research on Learning each observed one student for a full school day.

"The results," Deshler told me, "were gut-wrenching. Students who were at risk lived on the margins, even in the hallways and cafeteria. I saw the loneliness in the kids' eyes. It made me question how much I had missed about the experiences kids have in school. I wondered if we'd had blinders on about what students needed because we didn't really see that school was such a lonely experience for far too many students."

What Deshler learned by observing students is similar to what I have learned as I have been studying instructional coaching for more than 20 years. If we are to help teachers move students away from the margins and into the heart of schools, coaching needs to address student engagement, in addition to and as part of student

DATA

achievement. Both are important, and both should be central to any effective instructional coaching program.

WHY ENGAGEMENT MATTERS

Engagement is an essential part of a meaningful life, no less so for students than for adults. Students who are in healthy relationships are engaged by their friends and family. Students who are productive learners engage in learning activities. Most important, students who stay in school do so because they are engaged, as research clearly shows (Centers for Disease Control and Prevention [CDC], 2009; Finn, 1993; Finn & Rock, 1997; Knesting, 2008). Therefore, all of us who work to improve schools must make sure that students are engaged.

KIND	MEASURES	TEACHING STRATEGIES
Behavioral	• Time on task • Instructional time • Responses to questions • Disruptions	• Behavioral expectations • Positive reinforcements • Corrections

Cognitive	• Experience sampling
	• Interviews
	• Responses to questions
	  ○ Correct
	  ○ Quality
	  ○ Level
		• Thinking prompts
		• Effective questions
		• Authentic learning
		• Student voice
		• Guiding questions
		• Formative assessment

Social-Emotional	• Weekly exit tickets • Interviews	• Understand emotional connection • Student voice • Listening • Compassion • Collaborative power vs. coercive power • One-to-one interactions with students

For more information on measures, see J. Knight (2018).

For more information on teaching strategies, see J. Knight (2013).

Coaches should play a role in building student engagement because they influence what teachers do and therefore what students experience. Indeed, one peer-reviewed study we conducted found that instructional coaching had a significant impact on student engagement, with an effect size of 1.02 (D. Knight Hock et al., 2018).

DATA

INSTRUCTIONAL COACHING

Instructional coaches partner with teachers to improve teaching to have a positive impact on student learning and student well-being (J. Knight, 2018). Effective instructional coaches see coaching as a partnership or professional conversation between equals within which collaborating teachers make the decisions about what happens in their classroom.

Coaching, according to van Nieuwerburgh (2017), is "a managed conversation between two people" (p. 5) during which coaches artfully use specific skills, such as purposeful listening, powerful questions, paraphrasing, and summarizing to empower people to "unlock . . . [their] potential to maximize their own performance" (Whitmore, 2017, pp. 12–13).

Effective instructional coaching involves not only strategic knowledge, but an intentional process. Research by my colleagues and me (e.g., J. Knight, 2018) suggests that effective coaches use a coaching cycle process that involves three stages: identify, learn, and improve.

During the identify stage, instructional coaches partner with teachers to identify a clear picture of the current reality in the classroom (including how engaged students are), a goal, and a strategy that teachers can use to try and hit the goal.

To help teachers get a clear picture of their practice, coaches often video record lessons and share the video with teachers. This is especially helpful for engagement because it allows teachers to examine students' actions and reactions.

Coaches and teachers then create goals that we refer to as PEERS goals: powerful, easy to implement, emotionally compelling for teachers, reachable (involving a measurable outcome and an identified strategy teachers can use to attempt to hit their goal), and student-focused.

During the learn stage, coaches get teachers ready to implement a new strategy by describing the strategy precisely but provisionally. That is, coaches explain the strategy while also encouraging teachers to make adjustments to meet the unique needs of their students.

Coaches also often provide some kind of model so that teachers can see the strategy being implemented, either by the coach, another teacher, or on video.

Finally, during the improve stage, teachers try out the strategies and coaches and teachers make adaptations together until the original goal, or a modified goal, is met.

MEASURING ENGAGEMENT

Instructional coaches who partner with teachers to set student engagement goals and monitor progress toward those goals must be able to describe and measure engagement and be familiar with strategies to improve it.

Researchers have identified three major categories of engagement: behavioral, cognitive, and social-emotional. (See the table on p. 29.) Here are ways to measure each category and provide teaching strategies teachers can use as they strive to empower students to hit engagement goals.

DATA

BEHAVIORAL ENGAGEMENT: On-task behavior

When students are behaviorally engaged, they are doing what they are supposed to be doing—that is, they are on task. The advantage of behavioral engagement is that it is objective and measurable. For example, you can see if students are doing the think, pair, share collaboration you asked them to do.

Unfortunately, it doesn't measure whether students are actually learning. However, that does not mean that behavioral engagement is a useless measure. When many students are off task, getting them on task is often a necessary starting point.

> **Measuring behavioral engagement.** Coaches can use at least four simple measures to assess behavioral engagement and obtain information they can share with teachers: the teacher's questions.

> **Improving behavioral engagement.** Three strategies are most frequently mentioned in the literature for increasing behavioral engagement: expectations, reinforcement, and corrections.

Expectations clarify how students are expected to behave during all activities and transitions. Reinforcements—teachers communicating that they see students acting appropriately—are essential since teacher attention is an important motivator for student behavior.

Finally, fluent corrections are essential because when inappropriate behavior is not corrected, it frequently grows and spreads in a classroom. Coaches may choose to work with teachers on using one or more of these strategy types to address off-task behavior.

COGNITIVE ENGAGEMENT: Authentic engagement

When students are cognitively engaged, they are experiencing the thinking their teacher intended them to experience from an activity. Schlechty (2011) makes a useful distinction between what he refers to as authentic engagement and strategic compliance.

When students are strategically compliant, they are doing something for a strategic reason rather than to learn. In contrast, when students are authentically engaged, they find meaning and value in learning tasks and are attentive, committed, and persistent to complete them.

Measuring cognitive engagement.

Since cognitive engagement mostly occurs "inside" the student rather than outside, we have found that the best data come from asking students to communicate their opinions about their engagement in learning activities.

This may involve the coach interviewing students, asking students to respond to exit tickets, or using what we refer to as experience sampling, which prompts students to report their level of engagement at different times during a lesson on a form such as the one above.

DATA

FIGURE 5.1   Experience Sampling Form

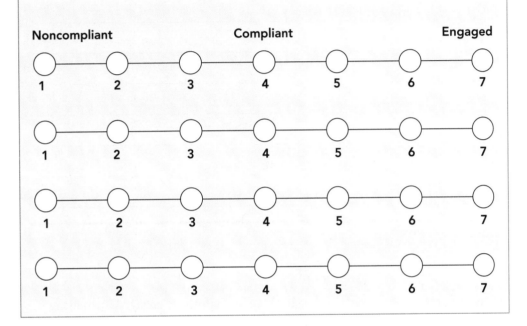

Date: _____

Instructions: Each time you hear the bell, please rate how engaging the learning activity is in which you are involved. You are only to rate whether or not the learning activity is engaging for you

Noncompliant   Compliant   Engaged

1   2   3   4   5   6   7

1   2   3   4   5   6   7

1   2   3   4   5   6   7

1   2   3   4   5   6   7

Assessing Hope: Elementary

Date: _____

How sure are you that you will learn in class this week?

(circle one of the following emojis)

(Continued)

(Continued)

What can I do to help you learn?

_____

_____

_____

_____

_____

_____

_____

_____

_____

_____

Source: J. Knight (2013).

DATA

Improving cognitive engagement.

When students are learning, they are likely to be cognitively engaged. Increasing cognitive engagement, like increasing achievement, usually involves at least three teaching strategies that coaches can support teachers to use: a clear description of learning outcomes, formative assessment, and feedback. Other strategies include thinking prompts, effective questions, authentic learning, and student voice.

EMOTIONAL ENGAGEMENT: Connectedness, belonging, and physical and psychological safety

When students are emotionally engaged, they feel they belong in their school, they are physically and psychologically safe, their experiences in school are positive and meaningful, they have friends, and they have hope.

According to many of the educators my colleagues and I meet, emotional engagement is a prerequisite for all learning. That is, if a student feels alone, afraid, or hopeless, we need to address those challenges before he or she can engage deeply in academic learning.

Measuring emotional engagement. As with cognitive engagement, we need to ask students about their emotions to understand them. One way to do this is to have students complete a weekly informal assessment about their emotional state and ask what could be done to make their experiences more positive.

Coaches and teachers can work together to use these informal assessments of students' positive emotions, relationships, safety, or hopes to establish and monitor progress toward a goal. For example, using surveys, coach-teacher pairs can set goals such as "at least 90% of my students will report each week that they feel able to learn in my classroom."

Improving cognitive engagement.

When students are learning, they are likely to be cognitively engaged. Increasing cognitive engagement, like increasing achievement, usually involves at least three teaching strategies that coaches can support teachers to use: a clear description of learning outcomes, formative assessment, and feedback. Other strategies include thinking prompts, effective questions, authentic learning, and student voice.

EMOTIONAL ENGAGEMENT: Connectedness, belonging, and physical and psychological safety

When students are emotionally engaged, they feel they belong in their school, they are physically and psychologically safe, their experiences in school are positive and meaningful, they have friends, and they have hope.

According to many of the educators my colleagues and I meet, emotional engagement is a prerequisite for all learning. That is, if a student feels alone, afraid, or hopeless, we need to address those challenges before he or she can engage deeply in academic learning.

Measuring emotional engagement. As with cognitive engagement, we need to ask students about their emotions to understand them. One way to do this is to have students complete a weekly informal assessment about their emotional state and ask what could be done to make their experiences more positive.

Coaches and teachers can work together to use these informal assessments of students' positive emotions, relationships, safety, or hopes to establish and monitor progress toward a goal. For example, using surveys, coach-teacher pairs can set goals such as "at least 90% of my students will report each week that they feel able to learn in my classroom."

An example of a simple survey for elementary students is shown in the assessment form at left. (More detailed questions are appropriate for older students and can be found in J. Knight, 2013.)

Also, coaches can interview students about their experiences in school and share the results with teachers. Formal surveys, such as the Gallup student success survey, may provide a more global understanding of student engagement or establish benchmarks. Teachers can assess students' emotional engagement through interactive journals in which students and teachers write back and forth to each other each week.

Improving emotional engagement. All of the strategies to increase behavioral and cognitive engagement should also have a positive impact on emotional engagement. In addition, coaches can help teachers enhance their relationships with students.

For example, teachers can video record their lessons and review them with the coach to reflect on whether they demonstrate empathy and how they manage such variables as power in the classroom. Collaborative power is more likely to build connections than coercive power.

Teachers can demonstrate collaborative power by giving students their full attention, avoiding sarcasm or power tripping, affirming all students, communicating respect, and so forth. Additionally, teachers can increase the number of positive interactions they initiate with students and monitor how they connect emotionally with their students.

Other strategies coaches can work on with teachers include building connections by learning about students' unique interests and activities through surveys and informal conversations; conflict resolution approaches such as restorative justice or collaborative problem-solving; and involving students more directly in decisions about what and how they learn.

Simply listening to students' voices has been shown to significantly increase student success (Quaglia & Corso, 2014) but this is more complicated than it sounds and is an area ripe for coaching support.

BRINGING IT ALL TOGETHER

The Impact Cycle provides the structure for coaching conversations and the engagement definitions, measures, and teaching strategies provide tools for cycles that dramatically increase student engagement.

Identify

After the coach and teacher identify a clear picture of reality, they can set goals based on the measures of engagement described in this article. Following this, they can discuss which strategies to use to lead students to hit their goal.

For most coaches, creating an instructional playbook prepares them to support teachers and communicate their explanations more clearly. An instructional playbook contains checklists and other tools coaches create to help them understand and describe the high-impact teaching strategies they most frequently share with teachers (Knight, Hoffman, Harris, & Thomas, in press).

Learn

During the learn stage, the coach and teacher collaborate to identify how the teacher will implement the new strategy. Coaches usually provide an opportunity for teachers to see the practices in use by modeling them in the teacher's classroom, sharing a video, or covering a class so the teacher can visit another teacher who uses the strategy to be learned.

Improve

When teachers implement a strategy, they usually don't get the results they were hoping for immediately. The coach and teacher usually have to explore various adaptations, including changing the goal, the way a goal is measured, the way a strategy is taught, or the strategy itself.

For example, teachers may start measuring authentic engagement by assessing how many students are correctly answering questions and then switch to experience

DATA

sampling to gain a better understanding of whether students are engaged during a lesson. Throughout the three stages, it is important to understand that each cycle is different. The best coaches, like artists, use the right tools at the right times.

Engagement and achievement

A focus on engagement should not turn us away from the importance of coaching to increase achievement. Everyone wants students to flourish academically, and coaching has to have an unmistakably positive impact on student learning.

However, to meet all the needs of all students and bring all students in from the margins, coaches need to partner with teachers to address engagement because engagement and achievement go hand in hand.

Reflection Questions for "Students on the Margins"

1. What types of goal setting are you supporting in your role currently?

2. Do the teachers you support understand the different types of engagement?

3. What ways of data collection are most energizing to you? Would you try any of the ideas presented in this article?

4. How can you address student achievement through setting engagement goals with teachers focused on student outcomes?

NOTES

DATA

STUDENT WORK EXPLORATION ACTIVITY

 Purpose: to explore data from students, to "see" each student and create new ideas to improve instruction.

Process:

Before beginning this activity, ensure that participants have student work samples or that the facilitator of the activity has a mock set of student data/work samples.

1. Decide if this activity will be done in small groups or whether a large group is more appropriate.

2. See the effort: Begin by inviting all participants to look at the student work and share what they notice about the effort the students are putting forth in the given subject. You can use the following questions:

   a. What are we seeing from students that demonstrates effort?

   b. What are we seeing from students that shows they want to do their best?

3. See the evidence of learning: Next, invite participants to share what evidence, from student work or data, demonstrates their achievement or evidence of their learning. You can use the following questions:

   a. What do we see from students that shows they have grown?

   b. What are we seeing from student work/data that is evidence of well-planned instruction?

4. Listen to the reflection: Now, ask participants to share what this leaves them thinking about instruction or planning. You can use the following questions:

   a. What are we learning from students that can inform our planning?

   b. What did we see from student work/data that might influence how we teach?

5. What does this mean to me? Finally, allow all individuals to spend a minute reflecting on what this exploration of student data or work has taught them. After a minute of individual reflection, invite the group to share out.

 Feedback Video

https://youtu.be/oSfCuv9BCRg

In this video, Jim discusses feedback

DATA

Guiding Question: How should data inform goal setting in coaching conversations?

Resources: "Should Coaches Give Feedback" article, Making Meaning From Student Data activity

Activity:

1. Read the article, "Should Coaches Give Feedback," prior to the meeting for background knowledge.

2. Read the Making Meaning From Student Data activity to make sure the process is clear, and practice in partners using either a created data set or the data set participants have brought to the meeting.

3. Use the last three questions (in the activity) to discuss thoughts and next steps.

Should Coaches Give Feedback? It's Complicated.

When coaching teachers, dialogue works better than directive.

Originally published in *Educational Leadership*, 80(8). May 1, 2023.

 When I was a child growing up in Canada, I wanted to be a hockey player more than anything else. My parents bought me my first skates when I was two years old. My father then took me to the frozen pond on our farm and showed me what to do.

Dad was a real athlete. He skated with strong, confident strides, and he handled the puck with power and finesse. I loved watching him play. He was also a great coach. He showed me how to use the edges of my skates to turn and how to hold my hockey stick to cushion the puck when I received a pass. Then he would watch me and give me very precise feedback. "You're holding the stick too tight," he'd say. His feedback taught me how to play the game. I call the kind of feedback my father gave *top-down feedback*, meaning the coach, seen as possessing the key knowledge, is directing the interaction from the top and passing that knowledge down to the other person.

Why Top-Down Feedback Often Fails

Years later, when I started studying instructional coaching, I assumed coaches would give top-down feedback. An expert coach would tell less-experienced teachers how to improve (just as my dad helped me improve in hockey). And research seemed to backed me up: John Hattie's (2009) analysis identified feedback as one of the most powerful teaching strategies for increasing learning, with an impressive .73 effect size.

DATA

So when my colleagues and I at The University of Kansas Center for Research on Learning started studying instructional coaching, we assumed this "top-down" approach is how we should talk with teachers about data (such as the student writing samples we analyzed or our observations of a teacher's lesson). We were respectful but clear, explaining what teachers did right and wrong and suggesting what they needed to change to get better. We realized quickly, however, that top-down feedback often made learning conversations *more* difficult, not easier. We learned that, as Marcus Buckingham and Ashley Goodall (researchers on work performance) write (2019), "Telling people what we think of their performance doesn't help them thrive and excel, and telling people how we think they should improve actually *hinders* learning."

Top-down feedback, I began to realize, was very helpful when there was a clear right and wrong way to do a task, such as when my dad taught me exactly how to skate backwards or take a wrist shot. But it wasn't helpful (or appreciated) when I tried it to discuss the complex environment of teachers' classrooms.

Buckingham and Goodall (2019) identify three false assumptions behind top-down feedback that explain why such feedback often fails:

- *Assumption 1:* Other people are more aware than you are of your weaknesses. So the best way they can help you is to show you what you cannot see for yourself.

- *Assumption 2:* The process of learning is like filling up an empty vessel: You lack certain abilities you need to acquire, so your colleagues should teach them to you.

- *Assumption 3:* Great performance is universal, analyzable, and describable. Once defined, greatness can be transferred from any one person to another.

These assumptions imply that to improve, teachers should be given a standard set of recommendations. But that oversimplifies the complexities of the classroom and positions teachers as passive receivers of knowledge.

Two Equals Talking Together

Fortunately, there is another way to talk with teachers about data—what I refer to as the Collaborative Exploration of Data. During this kind of conversation, coach and teacher interact as equals, engaging in a dialogue about the data, which functions as a third point for their conversation.

To better understand the Collaborative Exploration of Data, imagine two friends in a museum looking at Mark Rothko's painting *Orange and Yellow*. They might engage in a back-and-forth discussion, listening to each other and asking questions ("What do you think it means?" "Do you like it?" "Have you seen other paintings by Rothko?"). They openly share what they think and, if things go well, both will be energized by the conversation. No one tries to tell the other person what to see. There's no empty vessel to be filled, just two equals thinking together.

Coaching conversations are goal-directed, so they have a different focus than friends talking about art. But they should still feel and sound a lot like two friends talking about a painting. The coach shouldn't tell the teacher what data means but instead ask questions and listen, trying to think *with* the teacher.

DATA

In my 2007 book *Instructional Coaching*, Tricia Skyles, an instructional coach on our research project, describes what it's like when she collaboratively explores data with someone. Although Tricia's words aren't the only way one might talk with a teacher in doing this collaborative approach, they show the general idea:

I turn it into a question first. I lay out my data, usually on an observation form, and say, "Well, here's everything that I saw. How do you think the lesson went? What did you think went really well in the lesson?" and they'll tell me. Then I'll say, "OK, now based on either your experience or this form we've got, what do you think were the components that made that go really well? That made the difference?" And then we'll see, does that match up with what I observed, because I may have missed something. Then I ask, "OK, what do you think some things were either according to your experience or what I have on this observation form . . . that we . . . still need to work on as a team?" And I let them come up with those answers (Knight, 2007, p. 124).

Honoring Complexities

Top-down feedback isn't *always* ineffective. When there really is *one* way to do a practice and a teacher wants to know exactly how to do that practice in the correct way, top-down feedback can be helpful. However, when professional discourse is about the complexities of the classroom, collaboratively exploring data is often more helpful. Sadly, as Robert Kegan and Lisa Laskow Lahey (2001) note, "many a relationship has been damaged and a work setting poisoned by *perfectly delivered* constructive feedback!" (p. 128).

Reflection Questions for "Should Coaches Give Feedback? It's Complicated"

1. How does consideration of dialogue support better data conversations?

2. What kind of goals are you setting around data in your system now?

3. What types of feedback are you asked to provide in your current role? Could ideas offered in this article be applied to those interactions?

NOTES

DATA

MAKING MEANING FROM STUDENT DATA ACTIVITY

 Purpose: to use facts from data to discuss student progress and learning.

Process:

Before beginning this activity, ensure that participants have student work samples or that the facilitator of the activity has a mock set of student data/work samples.

1. Decide if this activity will be done in small groups or whether a large group is more appropriate.

2. Expect: Before looking at the data, take turns sharing what you *expect* to see from this student data.

   a. Allow individual think time before sharing out as a group.

   b. Sentence stems for this part might include: I expect to see . . . ; Some possibilities the student data/work might show are . . .

3. Explore: Now, dig into the data to look at what the students are doing, how they are progressing, what their responses/work tells you, what trends or patterns are emerging, and what stands out to you the most.

   a. Allow individual think time before sharing out as a group.

   b. Sentence stems for this part might include "The data shows . . . ; I observed that . . . "

4. Explain: Once the data have been discussed, explain what this leaves you thinking about how to proceed with instruction and support for students.

   a. Allow individual think time before sharing out as a group.

   b. Sentence stems for this part might include "I am left thinking . . . "; "As we move forward with these students, we might . . . "

5. Reflect: At the end of the activity, allow individuals to share what this activity meant to them and how it will inform their next steps. Questions you might use include the following:

   a. What impact did this have on your instruction?

   b. How can data continue to inform our work?

DATA

Learning Path #3 Resources

How Can Better Understanding the "How" and "Why" of Data Impact
Coaching Interactions and Goal Setting to Improve Student Outcomes?

Guiding Question: How can better understanding the "how" and "why" of data impact coaching interactions and goal setting to improve student outcomes?

Resources: "Data Shouldn't Be a Dirty Word" article, Expanding Perspectives activity

Activity:

1. Read the article "Data Shouldn't Be a Dirty Word."

2. Read through the Expanding Perspectives activity to become familiar with the process.

3. Complete the activity to further explore the article and facilitate dialogue.

4. Debrief the process, and discuss implications for future data conversations.

Data Shouldn't Be a Dirty Word

Coaches can use data to increase learning, engagement, and hope.

Jim Knight and Michael Faggella-Luby

Originally published in *The Learning Professional: The Learning Forward Journal*, *43*(2). April 2022

Data is an inescapable part of our lives. We ask Siri the temperature before we decide what to wear in the morning, we keep an eye on the speedometer as we drive to and from work, and we might even use a sleep app to gauge how effectively we sleep at night. Data is so deeply woven into the fabric of our lives that it is next to impossible to imagine what a data-free life would be like. But despite the centrality of data in everyone's personal lives, when people talk about data in schools, their comments are often negative. For example, aware of the negative feelings the word "data" evokes for many, coaches often try to find other ways to refer to it.

A certain degree of distaste for the word is understandable. In educational systems with an intense focus on achievement scores, teachers can get the sense that numbers are all that matters and that learning is not nearly as important as test scores.

In some instances, educators feel that data isn't useful because standardized test results arrive too late in the school year to change practice for the group of students the data represents. And in worst-case scenarios, leaders sometimes share data in a way that erodes teacher morale, especially when scores are lower than hoped and teachers don't know what they can do to improve results.

But we believe "data" should not be a dirty word. In fact, we believe that gathering, interpreting, and sharing data are all essential parts of effective instructional

DATA

221

coaching. Data should be embraced, not shunned, because it can improve student learning and well-being, accelerate professional growth, and build teacher morale.

Data can help teachers see their students' learning and well-being needs more clearly. For example, data on something as simple as the percentage of noninstructional time occurring in a classroom can lead to important insights into how learning is and isn't occurring during lessons. When teachers reduce noninstructional time by 20%, for example, that is comparable to adding a full-day of learning for students each week.

Data also accelerates professional learning by revealing what is and isn't working for students. A simple exit ticket collected at the end of a lesson that asks students to respond to a content-related question can help teachers see whether they need to adjust their instruction—for example, by providing more feedback, modeling new skills, or giving students more opportunities to practice with a partner—so that more students succeed. When students and teachers both see progress, real learning can occur.

Finally, the way data is shared during coaching can build morale by fostering hope. As psychologist Shane Lopez (2013) has explained, hope has three dimensions: goals; pathways to the goals, which involve monitoring progress and making adjustments; and agency, our "perceived ability to shape our lives" (p. 25).

Data is central to all three dimensions. That is, data helps teachers identify preferred futures or goals by making the invisible visible. Data helps people see if their pathway to a goal is working or needs to be modified. And finally, data helps build agency (in both students and teachers) by helping people see their progress as they move closer and closer to identified goals.

As Teresa Amabile and Steven Kramer (2011) write, "Of all the things that can boost emotions, motivation, and perceptions during a workday, the single most important is making progress in meaningful work." In a very real sense, when they share data effectively, coaches build hope in others.

DATA RULES

Data takes many forms in schools, but if teachers and coaches intend to reap the benefits described above during coaching, schools must gather and share data effectively; sadly, too often, they do not. For the past two years, we have been studying how data can be used by teachers and coaches to increase learning and hope. We've summarized our findings in the following data rules.

Teachers should choose the types of data to collect and analyze. Teachers are more likely to embrace data and, therefore, benefit from it, when they choose it themselves. Coaches can ask teachers the simple question, "How will you know you've hit the goal?" as a helpful starting pointing for identifying what data to gather. If data is going to increase hope, it needs to be the kind of data that teachers see as important.

Measures must be valid. Data isn't helpful if it measures the wrong thing. Asking people to complete a multiple-choice quiz to assess their ability to ride a bike isn't nearly as effective as actually watching them attempt to ride a bike. Coaches and teachers should use the appropriate kind of assessment for the learning that is being assessed. For example, quizzes and checks for understanding might work well for assessing student knowledge, but rubrics are likely more effective for assessing skills.

DATA

Data gathering should be reliable.

Reliability means that different people get the same results when they gather the data. Within coaching, this means that the coach and teacher get the same results regardless of who collected the data. This is important because when people engage in dialogue about data, they need to be certain they are talking about the same things. Miscommunication is almost inevitable when data is not gathered reliably or when those involved have different definitions for the data.

Coaches and teachers should prioritize objective over subjective data. Data is most powerful when it is objective. Although subjective data can be helpful, most of us find it easier to process factual data rather than someone's opinion. Furthermore, research suggests that observers often overestimate the validity and reliability of their observations (Buckingham & Goodall, 2019), so our subjective observations may not be as helpful as we assume.

Data is more useful when it is gathered frequently. One of the most important uses of data is to help teachers see whether what they are doing is working, and frequent data collection helps them make real-time connections between their practice and students' learning. Teachers who frequently give students exit tickets with questions about content, for example, are able to see if their teaching is working or if they need to make adjustments to how they teach so students master the content before moving on to new content. Also, data only builds hope when it shows teachers and students that they are making progress. For these reasons, we suggest data is gathered at least once a week.

Data should be easy to gather.

Since assessments need to be conducted frequently, they need to be as easy to implement as possible. There are many excellent assessments that yield excellent data for teachers but aren't helpful because they are too difficult to implement regularly and reliably.

Data is most powerful when teachers are involved in gathering it. When teachers, rather than coaches or others, gather data, it cuts out the middle person, and data becomes more immediate and powerful. For example, if teachers watch video recordings of their lessons and code what types of questions they ask in class, it's more powerful than when coaches observe lessons and code the data and share it with teachers. When teachers see for themselves the impact of their teaching, they are much more likely to believe they and their students can achieve their goals.

KINDS OF DATA COACHES CAN GATHER

The data rules can be applied to the gathering of many different types of data, but during instructional coaching, three types are especially important: student achievement, student engagement, and instructional practices.

STUDENT ACHIEVEMENT

We usually describe achievement data as either summative or formative. Teachers give summative assessments at the end of a learning period to get an overall measure of achievement and give formative assessments to measure student understanding at regular intervals during instruction.

DATA

Formative assessment is most useful for guiding professional learning since it provides timely data for instructional decision-making. Formative data can help coaches and teachers consider the following types of achievement.

Knowledge. Formative assessments of knowledge can include daily or semiweekly short quizzes or checks for understanding, such as exit tickets, response cards, Likert-scale responses, or other types of assessments that teachers can use quickly and informally during teaching.

Other options include prompts being embedded within a set of Google slides or requiring a written response via an index card or sheet of paper placed on students' desks that the teacher can collect at the end of the lesson.

Skills. Checks for understanding are valid measures of learning, but they're less effective for measuring skills. Teachers and coaches are better off using rubrics to assess the extent to which students have mastered skills. The three essential components of a rubric include a set of evaluative criteria, quality explanations of criteria at specific levels, and a means of scoring.

Rubrics can be holistic, analytical, or single point in nature. Holistic rubrics employ a single scale with multiple criteria (e.g., capitalization, organization, punctuation) to assign a single score. Analytical rubrics provide criteria for each component of the assignment separately, leading to a total score but also clear individual component feedback. Finally, single-point rubrics are used to guide student self-assessment.

Big ideas. Teachers and coaches can use all the types of data described above to measure whether students have learned big concepts or principles. Analytic rubrics, in particular, can be used to assess more complex forms of student writing.

STUDENT ENGAGEMENT

Instructional coaches may not immediately think of engagement data as important, but it is, in fact, essential, because lack of engagement is the main reason students drop out of school (see J. Knight, 2019, for more information on coaching and engagement). Unfortunately, engagement is often mistakenly seen as a single element. However, it is helpful to view the whole student and gather data on the behavioral, cognitive, and emotional elements.

Behavioral engagement is the most directly observable type of engagement due to external behaviors during learning. For example, physical responses associated with engagement are easily observed when students are on task, using appropriate materials, challenged but not overwhelmed, and able to ask or answer relevant questions. Teachers can collect observable data on student disruptions or time on task during a particular learning activity (e.g. during circle time). Teachers might also use a clipboard with a seating chart to keep track of which students respond to questions and engage in group discussions.

Cognitive and emotional engagement is more challenging to observe. For example, it is difficult to observe how much mental investment (cognitive engagement) a student puts into a given activity before giving up. Similarly, it is tough to gauge the range of positive or negative emotions students experience during different parts of a lesson, including interest, anxiety, or happiness.

DATA

However, there are ways to get inside student thinking and feeling before, during, and after learning experiences. One excellent source of data on cognitive engagement is exit tickets, which ask students to share their thinking and, therefore, provide formative feedback. Typically, students respond to a prompt on a slip of paper, index card, or prepared worksheet (digital solutions are also helpful).

Similarly, admit slips, used to assess students' attitudes when they enter class, prompt students to share their thoughts about their interest in the lesson, their emotional response, or other helpful points of clarification before the start of class for immediate teacher attention.

Another alternative is the use of interactive journals, in which teachers and students write back and forth to each other. Finally, to learn more about their students' social-emotional experiences and reactions, teachers may use engagement interviews, probing students' belonging and connection, sense of safety, and hope.

INSTRUCTIONAL PRACTICES

Gathering data that assesses student learning and engagement keeps the focus where it needs to be—on students—but teachers frequently want to adapt how they teach to help students succeed, and that requires teachers to look at their own practices. Two ways to do this include coding the questions teachers ask and recording the amount of teacher talk throughout a lesson. Teachers can gather this type of data by reviewing video of their lessons, and coaches can do it while observing teachers' lessons or reviewing data.

Teacher questions are vital components of classroom talk. When they are asked effectively, questions can support students' thinking and provide teachers with ongoing assessments of students' understandings. Data collected should include the type, kind, and level of questions asked. The two major types of questions are open questions—those that involve infinite correct answers (Who is your favorite author?)—or closed questions with specific, discernible answers (Who wrote "The Pearl"?).

Questions can be further categorized by kind: opinion questions that don't have personal or individual answers or right/wrong questions that must be answered correctly. Finally, teachers can assess levels of thinking required to answer a question by noting if the question focuses on student knowledge, skills, or big ideas.

Teacher talk refers to the verbal interactions that take place between a teacher and a student, or group of students, and is usually intended to facilitate learning. Coaches and teachers can assess three types of teacher talk: teacher monologue, involving no interaction with students; teacher-initiated interactive talk, involving segments of verbal interaction with students as initiated by the teacher; and student-initiated interactive talk, involving segments of verbal interaction with students as initiated by the students.

Alternatively, student-initiated interactions may arise from individual student questions about the material and take the form of either prompted or unprompted opportunities from the teacher. Student responses may be individual or shared. To ensure that teacher talk does not dominate the learning environment, data can be collected to note timeframes for teacher talk only, guided practice with teacher-led student talk, and student talk only.

THE POWER OF DATA

All data is imperfect, and none of the forms of data discussed here is without limitations. However, moving forward with a little bit of light is better than moving forward in darkness. Data fosters student learning and well-being, guides teachers' professional learning, and builds hope. Data is not a dirty word—just the opposite. When coaches partner with teachers and gather data effectively, data is powerful, positive, and empowering.

Reflection Questions for "Data Shouldn't Be a Dirty Word"

1. How can we use data to shift the way we lead, coach, or facilitate?

2. Which "data rule" challenges you the most? Why?

3. Which "data rule" gives you the most energy?

4. What might need to change in your school/system around data collection or data conversations?

DATA

NOTES

EXPANDING PERSPECTIVES ACTIVITY

 Purpose: To hear different perspectives and approaches to the content of a text.

Process:

1. Start by selecting a text for a group discussion.

2. Explain the process:

   a. Participants will be placed in groups of four (modify as needed for small groups or based on the needs of your learners).

   b. Each of the four members will select one "perspective" to hold as they read the article. That means that as participants read, they are reading with that perspective in mind, allowing it to shape how they interact with the text.

   c. Once everyone has read the article, the group will take turns sharing out. As each person shares their perspective, the rest of the group is invited to respond to, add to, or build upon the ideas.

3. Then, have participants choose their perspective:

   a. Appreciate: the appreciate perspective reads the article to search for ideas that they appreciate the most out of everything that has been shared.

   b. New thinking: the new thinking perspective searches the article for new ideas, content, or skills that can be shared with others.

   c. Still processing: the still processing perspective finds and shares ideas that are challenging, concepts that push their thinking, or concepts that they might not completely agree with at this time.

   d. Take action: the take action perspective reads to find concepts that inspire them to start, stop, or explore new actions.

4. The groups read the article, holding on to their perspectives.

5. Once the group has read, they begin sharing out, one perspective at a time. Invite all participants to respond to each perspective to add to or build upon the shared ideas.

6. At the conclusion of the activity, the following reflection question can be used for individual or group reflection: How have you expanded your perspective today?

DATA

END OF CHAPTER REFLECTION

Now that you have explored learning opportunities about Data, take time to reflect on this Success Factor overall. Use the following reflection questions below, or reflect in your own way, and fill the lines with your ideas.

REFLECTION QUESTIONS

1. On a scale of 1 to 10, 1 being not at all and 10 being significant, what impact did these learning paths have on your practice? What led you to choose the rating you did?

2. What is a major aha you had as you learned about Data as a Success Factor?

3. What will you do next with your ideas?

NOTES

_____

_____

_____

_____

_____

_____

_____

_____

_____

_____

_____

_____

_____

_____

_____

_____

_____

_____

The Instructional Playbook

Success Factor #6: The Instructional Playbook

The Instructional Playbook is a tool for identifying and explaining high-impact teaching strategies. When the coach gets to the learn phase of the Impact Cycle, there may be some confusion about where to look for strategies, how to vet them, and how to learn them. The Instructional Playbook is meant to ameliorate some of those challenges by providing a Table of Contents, One-Pagers to summarize and explain the strategy, and checklists to translate the strategy to action (Knight, 2022).

So Why Should We Be Talking About Instructional Playbooks Within Schools and Systems?

Because the coach takes on the role of "Chief Explainer" during the learn phase of the Impact Cycle, coaches must know deeply and be able to explain thoroughly a few, high-impact strategies to be used to hit the PEERS goal set by the teacher and coach. The Playbook helps the process of understanding and learning by scaffolding the steps and processes for coaches and teachers to make sure they implement the strategy deeply and thoroughly enough to gather data to determine whether the strategy is useful for hitting their goal.

Resources Included in This Chapter

ARTICLES	ACTIVITIES	CHECKLISTS	VIDEOS
"High-Quality Teaching > High-Fidelity Teaching"	Inventing Improvements	Dialogical Explanations	Buy-in vs. Alignment
"Should Coaches Be Experts?"	Chief Explainer		Checklists

Optional Learning Paths

Learning Path #1

Guiding Question: How might I make sure the teachers I coach use high-quality teaching strategies that yield learning?

Resources: "High Quality Teaching > High-Fidelity Teaching" article, Buy-in vs. Alignment video

Activity:

1. Read the "High Quality Teaching > High-Fidelity" Teaching article.

2. Watch the Buy-in vs. Alignment video.

3. Use the discussion questions to share thoughts and ideas about the article and video.

Learning Path #2

Guiding Question: How can I be the Chief Explainer and still engage in dialogue?

Resources: "Should Coaches Be Experts?" article, "Dialogical Explanations Checklist," any Instructional Strategy checklist for practice (many found in *Impact Cycle* and *The Instructional Playbook* as well as www.instructionalcoaching.com), Checklists video

Activity:

1. Read the "Should Coaches Be Experts?" article. Use the discussion questions at the end of the article.

2. Watch the video on Checklists.

3. Use a checklist to dialogically role-play, explain the strategy, and make it "provisional." Let each participant have a chance to coach and be coached.

4. Video record your dialogical role play. Prepare to watch these videos in Step 7.

5. Check the language of the checklist, the feasibility/ease of implementation, and vet to be sure it matches what research experts say about the strategy.

6. Discuss the process and how checklists play an important role in the creation of an Instructional Playbook.

7. Watch your individual videos and note, using the checklist, where you were dialogical and where there might be improvement. Share snippets of your videos with each other, and discuss what you notice and where there is room for growth.

Learning Path #3

<u>Guiding Question:</u> What are the high-impact strategies and categories we might include in our Instructional Playbook?

<u>Resources:</u> Inventing Improvements activity

<u>Activity:</u>

1. Use the Inventing Improvements activity to brainstorm strategies and categories for the Table of Contents for your Instructional Playbook.

<u>Guiding Question:</u> How might I make sure the teachers I coach use high-quality teaching strategies that yield learning?

<u>Resources:</u> "High Quality Teaching > High-Fidelity Teaching article," Buy-in vs. Alignment video

<u>Activity:</u>

1. Read the "High Quality Teaching > High-Fidelity Teaching" article.

2. Watch the Buy-in vs. Alignment video.

3. Use the discussion questions to share thoughts and ideas about the article and video.

High-Quality Teaching > High-Fidelity Teaching

To lift student learning, teachers often need to tweak the strategies we show them.

Originally published in *Educational Leadership, 80*(2). October 18, 2022.

When I started as a professional developer, I felt a great responsibility to tell teachers they had to implement what I was sharing exactly as I described it. I'd personally seen students get results from the strategies I was explaining and research that had been done. I thought if teachers wanted to get the results described in the research, they had to teach the strategies with fidelity. I gave teachers an instructor's manual with a script and went through it with them, explaining in great detail exactly what teachers were to do. "You really shouldn't try this," I'd say, "unless you commit to doing it correctly."

But when I observed teachers implementing the strategies, I discovered that, in fact, no two teachers used the strategies the same. Those who implemented the practices I'd outlined had to adapt the strategies to fit them into their classrooms. Some teachers even turned away from the strategies just because I told them that these practices *had* to be followed with fidelity. Most troubling, even *I* wasn't teaching the strategies with fidelity. I didn't have time to do everything in my teachers' manual, so I had to do the best I could, given the time I had.

The Problem With Fidelity

After my first years presenting, I made up my mind to learn as much as I could about professional learning. I interviewed a lot of teachers and wrote about some of their perceptions of PD for a research study. Looking back on those interviews, I see three reasons why a narrow focus on fidelity likely wasn't effective then—and won't be today.

Stressing fidelity diminishes teachers. Telling teachers exactly how they are supposed to teach leaves little room for them to share their own ideas, knowledge, and expertise. At worst, too much focus on fidelity can lead teachers to feel like they're working on an assembly line putting widgets together rather than engaging in the complex, important art of inspiring and educating tomorrow's leaders. Also, a fidelity-focused approach is grounded in the assumption that you can get people to learn just by telling them how to do something. However, everything we know about learning and motivation shows us that we can't force people to learn. Most adults—I am one of them—are skilled at nodding in agreement while passively choosing not to do something.

One size doesn't fit all. When researchers describe complex work, they often use parenting as an example. If raising one child is complex work, how much more complex is it to teach 20 or 30 students in a classroom? In an environment as complex as a classroom, a one-size-fits-all approach won't work. Each child brings their own complex needs, beliefs, habits, and skills. What works for one group or individual student will likely need to be taught differently for another group or individual.

The checklist becomes the focus. Intensive focus on fidelity can turn educators' attention away from what really matters in the classroom: student learning and well-being. The only reason for teaching with fidelity should be to have an unmistakable, positive impact on students. But it's possible that a teacher could do every move described on an implementation checklist and still fail to engage students.

FINDING A BALANCE ON FIDELITY

Accepting poor quality implementation of practices isn't the solution. We all want students to have higher achievement and more well-being, so we want every student to experience excellent instruction—and better teaching does lead to better learning. So how can we encourage professional growth (and for one to be professional, growth needs to be present) if we ignore fidelity? I have three suggestions.

Listen to teachers. Rather than force-feeding teachers about practices, start by asking *them* to set the direction for their professional growth by setting goals that will make a powerful difference in students' lives. Coaches can help teachers set those goals by asking questions that invite teachers to reflect deeply on how they teach and how students learn. Simply asking, "What are your students not doing now that you want them to do?" can open the door to powerful goals relevant to teachers and students.

Encourage teachers to adapt strategies. This suggestion appears to be the exact opposite of teaching with fidelity, but complex tasks like teaching require adaptive responses. Adapting practices is often fairer to students—and teachers—because we all have diverse needs. But how do we know that the changes a teacher makes will still lead to effective teaching?, you might ask. Read on to the next suggestion.

Focus on students. To get the most effective teaching, we must make student learning and well-being the standards for defining high-quality teaching, *not* teachers hitting the boxes on a checklist. When teachers set compelling student-focused goals for engagement or achievement, they establish an objective standard for judging how effectively they are implementing new practices. The standard for excellence in teaching should always be student growth.

Coaches can encourage a focus on student growth by asking a teacher a simple question: "When you implement this strategy, what should be different for students?" Their answer should guide that teacher to set a student-focused, rather than strategy-focused, goal that can drive their professional learning. Once the goal is set, a coach and teacher can gather ongoing data on student progress and modify the teaching strategy until the student-focused goal is achieved. Rarely will a poorly implemented practice be the catalyst for great student growth.

Encouraging teachers to use their professional judgment to adapt recommended strategies to hit a student-focused goal might not represent perfect fidelity, but it should lead to our children learning more. Sounds like high-quality instruction to me.

Reflection Questions for "High-Quality Teaching > High-Fidelity Teaching"

1. When might fidelity be necessary?

2. How can a coach balance fidelity with autonomy?

3. Which of the seven Partnership Principles stand out for you when you read this article?

4. What else is on your mind after you read this article?

NOTES

_____

_____

_____

_____

_____

_____

Buy-in vs. Alignment Video

https://youtu.be/PmrHE087oe4

Coaching is about alignment, not buy-in. Jim distinguishes between these two approaches and explains the difference between push and pull coaching.

INSTRUCTIONAL PLAYBOOK

<u>Guiding Question:</u> How can I be the Chief Explainer and still engage in dialogue?

<u>Resources:</u> "Should Coaches Be Experts?" article, Dialogical Explanations Checklist, any instructional strategy checklist for practice (many found in *Impact Cycle* and *The Instructional Playbook* as well as www.instructionalcoaching.com), Checklists video

<u>Activity:</u>

1. Read the *Should Coaches Be Experts?* article. Use the discussion questions at the end of the article.

2. Watch the video on Checklists.

3. Use a checklist to dialogically role-play, explain the strategy, and make it "provisional." Let each participant have a chance to coach and be coached.

4. Video record your dialogical role play. Prepare to watch these videos in Step 7.

5. Check the language of the checklist, the feasibility/ease of implementation, and vet to be sure it matches what research experts say about the strategy.

6. Discuss the process and how checklists play an important role in the creation of an Instructional Playbook.

7. Watch your individual videos and note, using the checklist, where you were dialogical and where there might be improvement. Share snippets of your videos with each other, and discuss what you notice and where there is room for growth.

Should Coaches Be Experts?

Good coaches have expertise but don't act like experts.

Originally published in *Educational Leadership, 79*(4). December 6, 2021.

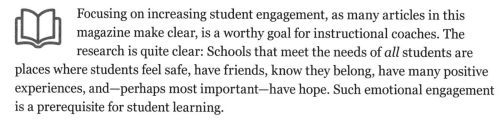 Focusing on increasing student engagement, as many articles in this magazine make clear, is a worthy goal for instructional coaches. The research is quite clear: Schools that meet the needs of *all* students are places where students feel safe, have friends, know they belong, have many positive experiences, and—perhaps most important—have hope. Such emotional engagement is a prerequisite for student learning.

What, then, is the best way for coaches to partner with teachers to increase student engagement? Do coaches need to be experts to have the biggest impact?

Many educators and coaching experts say no. When coaches position themselves as experts giving advice, they often overestimate the value of their advice, and turn off the people they coach by trying to solve their problems for them. Many coaches and teachers will likely nod their head in agreement with author Michael Bungay

Stanier's haiku: "Tell less, ask more. Your advice is not as good as you think it is" (Stanier, 2016, p. 59). The true job of a coach is not to solve people's problems, but, as Sir John Whitmore (a leader in education coaching) has famously said, to unlock "people's potential to maximize their own performance" (Whitmore, 2017, pp. 12–13).

Effective Coaches Know a Lot About Engagement

And yet, coaches have access to an ever-growing body of research describing how to increase student engagement. For example, instructional coaches can help teachers define engagement by distinguishing between (a) behavioral engagement (students look like they are on task), (b) cognitive engagement (students are getting out of their activity what the teacher intended for them to), and (c) emotional engagement (students feel they are connected and that they belong in school; they have friends, positive experiences, and hope) (Knight, 2019).

Also, instructional coaches can help teachers gather data on engagement in their classes. They can do so by assessing behavioral engagement (through measures such as students' time on task, how many kids are being disruptive, and academic responses), cognitive engagement (through exit tickets and experience sampling, which involves students giving feedback on their engagement during a lesson), and emotional engagement (through interviews, checks for understanding, and monitoring students' interactive journals).

Finally, instructional coaches can partner with teachers to increase student engagement by sharing high-impact teaching strategies. For example, teachers who want to increase behavioral engagement can learn how to write, teach, and reinforce expectations for all activities and transitions. Teachers who want to increase cognitive engagement can be guided to use strategies that encourage student voice and make learning more relevant, or to try strategies that increase the impact of frequent formative assessment and feedback. Teachers who want to increase emotional engagement can look at—and work to improve—how they create a learner-friendly classroom culture, or how they use power in the classroom, or how they build emotional connections with students. And these are just a few ideas coaches might share on how to increase student engagement.

Use Your Expertise—But Honor

So, should effective coaches ignore this body of helpful research and knowledge? I think most of us could agree that *not* drawing on this knowledge would be counterproductive. Yet I understand why some may dislike the "expert" label; the word *expert* conjures up images of an experienced, powerful professional tutoring an amateur novice, hardly a good analogy for professional-to-professional interactions.

What's more, telling teachers what to do—and expecting them to do it—is not an evidence-based model for change. In fact, a strictly directive model can do more harm than good, by increasing teacher dependence, decreasing teacher morale, and de-professionalizing teaching.

I believe instructional coaches can and should have expertise—they just shouldn't act like experts. This may sound paradoxical, and maybe it is. But it's a very real approach to coaching. Indeed, anyone who is coaching or mentoring a fellow educator needs a more sophisticated understanding of how to share knowledge between professionals if they want to provide ideas and strategies in a way that's embraced and implemented.

Effective instructional coaches honor the professionalism of teachers by ensuring that *teachers* make the decisions about what happens in their classrooms. This, as I stress in my work with schools, starts with *teachers* setting goals designed to have an unmistakably positive impact on students' learning or well-being.

Counterintuitive Communication

This kind of partnership coaching also involves an almost counterintuitive way of communicating. Most of us get a great deal of pleasure out of telling others how to solve their problems. But effective coaches know they need to refrain from fixing people and focus on creating conditions where people unlock their own potential. This means that coaches should only share their expertise when it is clearly needed. If a teacher knows what strategy she or he wants to use to move toward an established goal, that strategy should be the starting point for change.

However, if a teacher isn't sure what to do, then a coach can say something like, "Do you mind if I share some ideas I've got about strategies you might use?" Then, after sharing the strategy, the coach needs to communicate in a tentative way that ensures that the teacher only chooses a strategy they genuinely want to implement ("This is just one idea you might try here"). I've found in my coaching experience that teachers won't adopt a strategy as their own unless they choose it.

When explaining a teaching strategy, the coach should describe it clearly while also encouraging the teacher to think openly about how they might want to modify the strategy for use with their students. In this way, coach and teacher move away from an overly optimistic, one-size-fits-all notion and toward an interaction that is just as dialogical as goal setting.

Expertise matters. Those of us who guide teachers do need to ensure that teachers have access to the expertise coaches or others have (such as about student engagement). But we also need a new kind of discourse about expertise, a professional discourse in which all educators (teachers, coaches, administrators, and others) honor each other's professional discretion. When teachers are seen as professionals, they act in professional ways, which means they make many decisions about their practice. Our students deserve to be taught by professionals. Encouraging teachers to view themselves that way begins with the way we talk.

Reflection Questions for "Should Coaches Be Experts?"

1. Can you think of a time in your school or district when a directive approach to coaching or PD had a counterproductive effect on teachers?

2. If so, how could the training have been done differently?

3. Can you describe examples of responsible accountability in your school? What conditions helped create them?

4. What could you change in your coaching or supervision to better honor teachers' autonomy? How comfortable are you about making that change?

NOTES

_____

_____

_____

_____

_____

_____

_____

_____

_____

_____

_____

_____

_____

_____

_____

Checklist Video

https://youtu.be/3zGQZ2qs2yI

In this video, Jim talks about the benefits of checklists and how to be precise and provisional with the use of checklists to honor the capacity of the professionals with whom we partner.

INSTRUCTIONAL PLAYBOOK

CHIEF EXPLAINER ACTIVITY

 Purpose: To practice making a strategy checklist provisional with a partner.

Process:

1. Review the Dialogical Explanations checklist to see how a coach can engage in dialogue about a teaching strategy with a teacher.

2. Talk about what you notice, wonder, and understand from the Dialogical Explanations checklist.

   a. Note: using this checklist should make the teacher's thinking visible.

3. Select a checklist for a teaching strategy that you would like to use in the partner activity. This is the checklist that you will practice making provisional using the Dialogical Explanations checklist/guidance.

4. Find a partner and complete the following steps:

   a. Decide who will be the coach first and who will be the teacher first.

   b. Remember to use the Dialogical Explanations checklist to guide your conversation as you make your chosen checklist provisional with your partner.

   c. Take turns explaining (and making provisional) the teaching strategy checklist you have chosen (from Step 3).

   d. Debrief after each turn with these questions:

      i. What did you notice?

      ii. What areas for growth did you see?

      iii. What celebrations do you have?

      iv. What else?

Extension: To increase the impact of this protocol, use a device to record the partner conversations, and use the video to reflect using the debrief questions!

CHECKLIST: DIALOGICAL EXPLANATIONS

COACHING BEHAVIOR	✔
Explain that the purpose of the conversation is to describe the parts of the strategy and record any modification that the teacher would like to make.	
Provide a quick overview of the strategy, and ask the teacher to read the checklist to see what the strategy involves.	
Ask if the teacher has any questions or thoughts about the checklist.	
Go through each item on the checklist, and ask the teacher if the explanation is clear and if she would like to modify it at all. Write down on the checklist any modifications the teacher would like to make.	
If the teacher suggests modifications that the coach thinks might diminish the effectiveness of the strategy, share your thoughts with the teacher, while still positioning the teacher as the decision maker in the conversation.	
Sum up how the strategy will be taught asking if there is anything that is still unclear.	
Ask, "Now that we've gone through this, on a scale of 1–10, how confident are you that you can implement this practice?"	
If the teacher doesn't feel confident, continue the explanation and dialogue until the teacher is ready to implement.	

INSTRUCTIONAL PLAYBOOK

Learning Path #3 Resources

What Are the High-Impact Strategies and Categories
We Might Include in Our Instructional Playbook?

<u>Guiding Question:</u> What are the high-impact strategies and categories we might include in our Instructional Playbook?

<u>Resources:</u> Inventing Improvements

<u>Activity:</u>

1. Use the Inventing Improvements activity to brainstorm strategies and categories for the Table of Contents for your Instructional Playbook.

INVENTING IMPROVEMENTS ACTIVITY

 Purpose: To review, scrutinize, and improve a "work in progress" by requesting support from other colleagues in a trusting, low/no-stakes environment.

Process:

1. A request for this activity can come from an identified need/desire of either a person or group you are working with that is having trouble making progress or moving forward with their work.

2. To complete this activity, a second team will need to be identified separate from the requesting team (ranging in size from three to six people) to look at the work/issue. A moderator/facilitator is designated from the newly formed team. The moderator observes the second team as they problem solve while recording information that is being created, asking questions along the way, and potentially providing summary points during the discussion.

3. After this second team is formed, the requesting party shares its work in progress while the other group listens. (This usually takes 5 or 10 minutes.) The invited team may need to ask clarifying questions before moving on.

4. The requesting team takes responsibility for focusing the discussion and states what it needs or wants as a desired outcome. This focus can be in the form of a specific request or as generic as "How can we make this better?" or "What is our next step?"

5. The invited team then discusses while the requesting team listens and takes notes. There are no hard and fast rules here. Occasionally (but not usually) the requesting team joins in the discussion process. The emphasis is on improving the work, which now belongs to the entire group. The atmosphere is one of "we're in this together," and our single purpose is "to make a good thing even better."

6. When the requesting team knows it has gotten what it needs from the invited group, they stop the process, briefly summarize what was gained, thank the participants and moderator, and return to the "drawing board."

END OF CHAPTER REFLECTION

Now that you have explored learning opportunities about the Instructional Playbook, take time to reflect on this Success Factor overall. Use the following reflection questions or reflect in your own way, and fill the times with your ideas.

REFLECTION QUESTIONS

1. On a scale of 1 to 10, 1 being not at all and 10 being significant, what impact did these learning paths have on your practice? What led you to choose the rating you did?

2. What is a major aha you had as you learned about the Instructional Playbook as a Success Factor?

3. What will you do next with your ideas?

NOTES

NOTES

System Support

*"We need to be working on all different parts of the system in order
to successfully change the whole system."*

–Peter Senge, The Fifth Discipline

Success Factor #7: System Support

Coaching has tremendous potential to have a powerfully positive impact on students' learning and well-being (Knight, 2022). Success Factor #7: System Support is about creating a setting where coaches can flourish by understanding stages of implementation and ensuring leadership support. Systems need to establish a districtwide understanding of coaching that ensures theoretical alignment while clarifying coaches' roles and addressing confidentiality. Building leaders are instrumental in creating a learning culture and learning architecture that clearly helps learning flow through the system efficiently.

So Why Should We Be Talking About System Support Within Schools and Systems?

Coaches are not the only people who need to understand what coaching is and is not. In settings where district leaders, teachers, and other educators don't understand coaching, coaches will struggle to succeed (Knight, 2022). Systems and leaders within them should reflect and agree on a set of principles that guide coaching and ensure that their messaging around coaching supports coaches. Systems and organizations should support educators to become proficient in the practices they learn through having procedures in place to hire outstanding professionals for these roles.

Resources Included in This Chapter

ARTICLES	ACTIVITIES	SCENARIO	VIDEOS
"Hey Instructional Coach, What Do You Do?"	Four Is Text Activity	A Broken Trust	Measuring Impact
"What Can We Do About Teacher Resistance?"	The Exploring Viewpoints Activity		Two Questions to Understand Teacher Resistance
"The Problem of Nominal Change"	Expanding Perspectives Activity		Confidentiality
"Coaching"	KLE Activity		
"5 Key Points to Building a Coaching Program"	In Closing		
"Working With Instructional Coaches"			
"Instructional Coaches Make Progress Through Partnership"			
"What Good Coaches Do"			
"Pull Versus Push Professional Development"			
"Moving From Talk to Action in Professional Learning"			
"The Life-Changing Magic of Going In-Depth"			

Optional Learning Paths

Learning Path #1

Guiding Question: How does an instructional Coaching role impact a school system, and how can leadership support the role?

Resources: "Hey Instructional Coach, What Do You Do?" article, Four *I*s Activity, Measuring Impact video

Activity:

1. Show the video about measuring impact to the group. After the video, talk about how this might align with the article on the coaching role.

2. Engage in the Four *I*s Activity.

3. End the meeting with an open discussion framed around a question such as, What does this mean for the instructional coaching role in our system?

Learning Pathway #2

Guiding Question: Why do people resist change, and how might we engender resistance?

Resources: "What Can We Do About Teacher Resistance?" and "The Problem of Nominal Change" articles, the Exploring Viewpoints activity

Activity:

1. Show the video from Principles of Coaching, titled "Two Questions to Understand Teacher Resistance" to the group. After the video, talk about how this might align with your ideas about why people resist change and helping.

2. Then, use the Exploring Viewpoints activity to guide a conversation around the role of coaches and the articles "What Can We Do About Teacher Resistance?" and "The Problem of Nominal Change"

3. During the activity, ask the questions "Why do people resist change?" or "What is resistance?" or create your own.

4. Debrief, and discuss the perspective presented and how the information in the articles and video can support your ideas and next steps for support in your system (if helpful, you can use the reflection questions at the end of the article).

Learning Path #3

Guiding Question: What is needed for coaches to flourish in a system?

Resources: "5 Key Points to Building a Coaching Program" and "Coaching" and "Working With Instructional Coaches" articles, Expanding Perspectives activity

Activity:

1. Read through the Expanding Perspectives activity to become familiar with the process.

2. Complete the activity to further explore the articles and facilitate dialogue. (You could split the group into three groups and assign each group an article, have each group complete the activity, and then debrief together.)

3. Debrief the process, and discuss implications for future conversations around coaching in your system. You could use the reflection questions at the end of the chapter to guide this conversation.

Learning Path #4

Guiding Question: How does confidentiality impact how coaches are perceived in a system?

Resources: "Instructional Coaches Make Progress Through Partnership" article, A Broken Trust case study, Confidentiality video

Activity:

1. Show the video from Principles of Coaching, titled "Confidentiality" to the group. After the video, talk about how this might align with your ideas about why systems should develop a confidentiality policy.

2. Then, use the *A Broken Trust* scenario to guide a conversation around the implications of confidentiality and breaking trust in a system.

3. Debrief, and discuss the perspective presented and how the information in the scenario and video can support your ideas. You could use the reflection questions at the end of the article to guide the discussion if you wanted to have a more deeply articulated debrief.

Learning Path #5

Guiding Question: What do coaches do?

Resources: "What Good Coaches Do" article, KLE Activity

Activity:

1. Read the activity to become familiar with the practice, and start with the first few steps before reading.

2. Read the article, "What Good Coaches Do," and continue using the KLE activity.

3. Wrap up this learning path by using the reflection questions that follow the article.

Learning Path #6

<u>Guiding Question:</u> How can you redefine professional learning that improves depth of knowledge and is grounded in partnership?

<u>Resources:</u> "Pull Versus Push Professional Development," "Moving From Talk to Action in Professional Learning," "The Life-Changing Magic of Going In-Depth" articles, The In Closing activity

<u>Activity:</u>

1. Read the activity to become familiar with the practice, and start with the first few steps before reading.

2. Distribute the articles "Pull Versus Push Professional Development," "Moving From Talk to Action in Professional Learning," and "The Life-Changing Magic of Going In-Depth" and continue using the In Closing activity.

3. Wrap up this learning path by using the reflection questions that follow the article.

Guiding Question: How does an instructional Coaching role impact a school system and how can leadership support the role?

Resources: "Hey Instructional Coach, What Do You Do?" article, Four *Is* activity, Measuring Impact video

Activity:

1. Show the video about measuring impact to the group. After the video, talk about how this might align with the article on the coaching role.

2. Then, engage in the Four *Is* Activity

3. End the meeting with an open discussion framed around a question such as, What does this mean for the instructional coaching role in our system?

Hey Instructional Coach, What Do You Do?

Gaining a deeper understanding of coaches' roles and impact.

Originally published in *Educational Leadership, 79*(1). September 1, 2021.

 As a new school year begins, many educators are stepping into new careers as instructional coaches. Others are welcoming instructional coaches to their schools. Although people in either position likely have a lot of enthusiasm about this newish role in schools, that enthusiasm might be tempered if an important question goes unanswered: "What does an instructional coach do?"

I've spent more than two decades describing, studying, and validating coaching. I'd like to share a bit about what I've learned as I've tried to answer that question.

Not Quite Like Sports Coaches

Relying on a coach has become a popular form of professional learning in almost all walks of life. There are life coaches, athletic coaches, surgical coaches, even dating coaches. These types of coaching all share one goal—helping someone else get better at something important, whether it's finding purpose in life or hitting a knuckle ball.

Different professions, however, require coaches with different skills and approaches.

Instructional coaching is a specialized approach to supporting others' learning. Like other coaches, instructional coaches (ICs) are intent on helping professionals, teachers in this case, get better at what they do. They know a lot about their chosen field—teaching. In other ways, however, what an instructional coach does is significantly different than what, say, a hockey coach does.

Coaching Tip

By asking reflective questions, listening, and making nondirective suggestions, effective coaches empower teachers to come up with their own solutions, the essential outcome.

Five Maxims

I've found five maxims clarify the special skills, beliefs, and processes used by instructional coaches.

1. A coach is a teacher talking with a teacher. Although effective instructional coaches have expertise, they don't act like experts—they act like partners. The word partner tells us a lot about what coaches do. A partnership conversation is one between two people who have equal power. Partners don't make decisions for each other. In the best situations, partners listen to and respect each other. This means that instructional coaches interact in ways that ensure that collaborating teachers make the decisions about what happens in their classrooms. ICs don't simply observe a teacher's classroom and tell the teacher what they did right and what they need to work on. Rather, coaches create the conditions that empower teachers to take control of their own learning. (The remaining maxims describe setting ideal conditions for teacher learning.)

2. Learning involves seeing reality as it is, not as we wish it to be.[1] The perceptual errors that we all make and the defense mechanisms most of us employ combine to make it very difficult for us to see reality as it really is. Almost always, when professionals watch themselves on video, they're astonished by what they see—sometimes delighted, sometimes disappointed, rarely unsurprised. That's why players on just about every school football team watch themselves on game film after every game. Video is rocket fuel for learning because it gives us a clear picture of reality.

When educators don't have a clear picture of reality, they risk spending a lot of time learning strategies that don't address the real needs of their students. Equally important, since motivation is usually fueled by awareness of a discrepancy between our reality and our goals, a clear picture of reality is essential for a person to feel motivated about any opportunity for growth.

3. If there's no goal, it's just a nice conversation. I heard this saying from coaching expert John Campbell (who attributes it to coaching researcher Tony Grant). Effective instructional coaching is a goal-directed action. Goals give direction to coaching; they provide a finish line, and when they matter to teachers, goals propel the entire coaching process. If teachers don't have a goal, or if they are pursuing a goal they don't care about, the entire coaching process can be a waste of time. But when teachers pursue a powerful, student-focused goal that truly matters to them, unmistakable improvements happen in students' lives and learning.

4. It's not about me.[2] Whenever we work with others, we can feel strongly tempted to solve their problems for them. We lean in, our pupils dilate a little, and we feel a surge of energy to help this person clean up their mess. "Oh, I've had that issue," we might say, "let me tell you what you should do."

The problem is, as our energy goes up, the collaborating teacher's energy often goes down. If a coach does all the thinking for a teacher, it creates dependence, making it less likely that the teacher will be empowered to address issues independently.

By asking reflective questions, listening, and making nondirective suggestions, effective coaches empower teachers to come up with their own solutions, the essential outcome. I'm reminded of what coaching expert Tony Stoltzfus says in his workshops: a less optimal solution the coachee develops often produces better results than the "right answer" coming from the coach.

5. Real learning happens in real life. A person who wants to learn how to swim might get a lot out of watching swimming instructional videos on YouTube. Eventually, though, he will have to get wet. Learning that we remember, that helps us do more and be more, usually only happens when we apply new knowledge, skills, or beliefs to our personal experiences or work. The same is true for teachers.

Coaches walk a tightrope between support and dialogue to ensure that such real-life learning occurs. On the one hand, they have a deep knowledge of effective teaching practice. On the other hand, they share that information tentatively and only when requested, so they empower teachers to carry out their own decisions and plans in their classrooms.

A New Kind of Teacher Learning

The learning catalyzed by instructional coaching doesn't happen in workshops, but in classrooms. It's driven by teachers' energy. While this may seem radical, we can validate why instructional coaching works by thinking of our own experiences. We know that the most important changes we make in life are ones we choose for ourselves, and that we respond best to people who treat us like equals. We know that growth requires a clear picture of reality and a goal—and happens day-to-day. Most important, we know that when teachers learn more, students learn more. That's why we need instructional coaches—and a deep understanding of what coaches do.

End Notes

1. This maxim is a variation on a quotation often attributed to General Electric CEO Jack Welch, "Face reality as it is, not as you want it to be."

2. This maxim comes from coaching researcher Christian van Nieuwerburgh.

4 *Is* PROTOCOL

Purpose: to think deeply about your responses to a text.

Process:

1. Begin by selecting a text and giving everyone time to read the text in its entirety.

2. Afterward, invite the participants to review the reading and find parts of the text that fit these 4 ideas:

    a. What from the text is *interesting* to you?

    b. What part of the text would you say is the most *important* idea?

    c. If you were to disagree with part of the text, what would you say *instead* of what was presented?

    d. What *inspired* you from this reading?

3. Once the participants have had time to gather their ideas for the 4 *Is*, conduct a group discussion. This can happen in several small groups or in one large group, depending on the number of participants.

4. To wrap up this activity, invite the participants to individually complete this sentence: "*I* am left thinking. . . . "

Measuring Impact

https://youtu.be/2i7bYFMvKyU

In this video, Jim talks about what coaches do.

Reflection Questions for "Hey Instructional Coach, What Do You Do?"

1. How can instructional coaches support teachers through partnership?

2. Is there a clear description for coaches in your system?

3. What might need to change in your school/system to better understand the coaching role?

NOTES

<u>Guiding Question:</u> Why do people resist change and how might we engender resistance?

<u>Resources:</u> "What Can We Do About Teacher Resistance?" and "The Problem of Nominal Change" articles, the Exploring Viewpoints activity

<u>Activity:</u>

1. Show the video from Principles of Coaching, titled "Two Questions to Understand Teacher Resistance," to the group. After the video, talk about how this might align with your ideas about why people resist change and helping.

2. Then, use the Exploring Viewpoints activity to guide a conversation around the role of coaches and the articles "What Can We Do About Teacher Resistance? and "The Problem of Nominal Change."

3. Within the activity, use the questions "Why do people resist change?" or "What is resistance?" or create your own.

4. Debrief, and discuss the perspective presented and how the information in the article and video can support your ideas and next steps for support in your system (if helpful, you can use the reflection questions at the end of the article).

What Can We Do About Teacher Resistance?

If school leaders understand the nature of resistance, they can improve their relationships with teachers and increase teacher implementation of proven practices.

Originally published in *Phi Delta Kappan, 90*(7), 508–513. 2009.

 When efforts to improve student learning fail, teachers often end up being blamed. Teachers were resistant to new ideas, say the leaders who were working with them. Rather than blame teachers and ask, "Why do teachers resist?" perhaps those of us who lead change should ask, "What can we do to makes it easier for teachers to implement new practices?"

Two pioneers in unpacking the meaning of resistance, Miller and Rollnick, have this to say about resistance in counseling and therapy relationships:

To use the term "resistance" as explanatory seems to suggest that things are not going smoothly because of something that one person (the client) is doing. . . . In a way, it is oxymoronic to say that one person is not cooperating. It requires at least two people to not cooperate, to yield dissonance. (Miller & Rollnick, 2002, p. 45)

We can learn a lot about professional learning if we apply the same kind of thinking to our understanding of "resistant teachers." Consider six questions that can bring to the surface reasons for this dissonance between teachers and change agents.

QUESTION #1:

Are the Teaching Practices Powerful?

In The Evolving Self, Mihalyi Csikszentmihalyi describes what's required for one idea to supersede another. "Ideas, values, technologies that do the job with the least demand on psychic energy will survive. An appliance that does more work with less effort will be preferred" (Csikszentmihalyi, 1993, p. 123, emphasis added).

Csikszentmihalyi's suggestion that people adopt new ideas or tools that are easier or more powerful also applies to teachers leaving behind old ways of teaching for more effective approaches. Teachers aren't likely to implement new practices unless they are powerful and easy to implement. Indeed, that seems like wise practice.

The issue of ease of use will be addressed in question two. Let's begin by considering the need for powerful teaching tools. Of course, few teachers will be motivated to implement a teaching practice if it does not increase student achievement, make content more accessible, improve the quality of classroom conversation, make students happier, increase love of learning, or have some other significant positive impact. Nevertheless, teachers report that they're frequently asked to change in ways that don't make a difference.

This situation can arise for at least three reasons. First, not all teaching practices are created equally. Before recommending practices for their schools, consumers of educational interventions must consider the quality of research that supports those practices, the effect sizes or other measures of statistical significance from supportive research studies, and the experiences of other educators. Indeed, change leaders should propose new ways of teaching only if they're confident they will have a positive impact on student achievement.

Second, educators should consider student achievement and behavior data from their schools before proposing new ways of teaching. Decision makers should strive to find teaching tools that are the best match for the needs of their students. A highly effective program in one school might be totally ineffective if adopted in a school facing different challenges. School improvement is not a one-size-fits-all solution.

Third, even proven, effective programs that are a good match for a school's needs still may not be powerful if teachers don't get sufficient support for high-quality implementation. Our research at the Kansas Coaching Project (Knight & Cornett, 2009) indicates that teachers are unlikely to implement a practice successfully, if they implement at all, if they have had only workshops without coaching or other forms of follow-up support. Many teaching practices are sophisticated, and teachers can't be expected to learn them without an opportunity to watch model demonstration lessons, experience job-embedded support, and receive high-quality feedback. Without support, a powerful practice, poorly implemented, is no better than one that is ineffective.

Even when teachers want to implement new programs, they may not have the energy needed to put that program into practice.

QUESTION #2:

Are the Practices Easy to Implement?

Most teachers face what Michael Fullan and Andy Hargreaves (1996) have referred to as a "press of immediacy." In a typical day, teachers grade stacks of papers, create lesson plans, complete reports, attend meetings, contact parents, stay at school for sporting events, do bus duty, supervise the cafeteria, attend IEP meetings, and on and on. On top of that, they complete all of those tasks while doing work that requires a great deal of emotional fortitude. The result is that even when teachers want to implement a new program, they may not have the energy needed to put that program into practice.

Research on the personal experience of change (Hall & Hord, 2001; Prochaska, Norcross, and DiClemente 1994) suggests why change leaders need to make it easier for teachers to implement new practices. The personal experience of change is complex. Few of us adopt new habits of practice without some struggles, and if those new practices also involve a large number of tasks and learning challenges, professional learning probably won't happen. Consequently, when change leaders remove barriers, they increase implementation.

Our experience suggests that several types of support are especially helpful. Teachers say they benefit greatly when they get to see demonstrations of new ways of teaching before they try to implement them.

Learning also is much easier when someone breaks down new approaches into easy-to-implement steps. Change agents must have a thorough, deep understanding of the practices they share so they can effectively explain those practices to teachers. Finally, teachers are more inclined to adopt new programs when all teaching materials (overheads, readings, handouts, or learning sheets) are created for them.

The importance of easy and powerful interventions has been nicely summarized by Patterson and his colleagues: "When it comes to altering behavior, you need to help others answer only two questions. First, is it worth it? . . . And second, can they do this thing? . . . Consequently, when trying to change behaviors, think of the only two questions that matter. Is it worth it? . . . Can I do it?" (Patterson et al., 2008, p. 50).

Even if a proposed program is "worth it" and easy to do, we still aren't out of the woods. Teachers will adopt powerful and easy practices only if they believe that they are powerful and easy. Consequently, change leaders need to be able to convince teachers that they are so. Unfortunately, the most common forms of persuasion often fail.

QUESTION #3:

Are They Experienced?

I have shown hundreds of change leaders a scene from the documentary *The Waters of Ayole*. The short film describes the efforts of United Nations aid workers to support villages as they take care of village water pumps, literally a matter of life or death for many villagers. In the scene, four village leaders are asked what they thought when they learned they were getting a pump for their village. "At first, we weren't particularly pleased," they say. "We thought it might be a trick." "And people refused to come to meetings." "When the machines arrived . . . we were afraid they might scare us away from our village." "Without seeing the water, we weren't convinced." Even when the water gushed out, "without having drunk any of it, we still weren't convinced." What finally convinced the villagers? "The day water came from the pump and we drank it. Then we said these people really did something for us." Even when offered something that is lifesaving, people may resist until they actually experience the phenomenon.

Patterson and his colleagues explain that when it comes to change, experience trumps talk every time. "The most common tool we use to change other's expectations is the use of verbal persuasion . . . [however] When it comes to resistant problems, verbal persuasion rarely works. Verbal persuasion often comes across as an attack. It can feel like nagging or manipulation. If people routinely enact behaviors that are difficult to change, you can bet that they've heard more than one soliloquy on what's wrong with them—and to no effect" (Patterson et al., 2008, p. 50).

If talk is cheap, or at least ineffective, then it's experience that persuades. Tom Guskey has made exactly the same observation:

> The crucial point is that it is not the professional development per se, but the experience of successful implementation that changes teachers' attitudes and beliefs. They believe it works because they have seen it work, and that experience shapes their attitudes and beliefs . . . the key element in significant change in teachers' attitudes and beliefs is clear evidence of improvement in the learning outcomes of their students. (Guskey, 1999, p. 384)

When it comes to change, teachers have to drink the water, so to speak, before they will believe. This has real implications for change leaders. First, they should provide teachers with experiences that demonstrate the value of a program. For example, if a school employs coaches, the coaches can present model lessons in teachers' classrooms. Other forms of professional learning, such as Japanese lesson study or peer observation with feedback, also enable teachers to see and experience new practices. Video recordings and experiential learning activities can also be used effectively during workshops, study groups, and other professional learning activities.

Perhaps most important, if we know that teachers usually need to experience success to believe in a teaching practice, that should change how we communicate with teachers. Trying to talk teachers into new ways of teaching without providing experiences can actually decrease implementation, creating what Miller and Rollnick (2002) refer to as an "ironic process," an approach that "causes the very outcome that it was meant to avert" (p. 37). A better tactic is to offer teachers opportunities to experiment with practices so that they can make up their own minds about their effectiveness.

Ignoring teacher autonomy often ensures that teachers don't implement new practices.

If the practices are powerful and easy, most teachers will implement them. If the practices aren't powerful or easy, there is very little anyone can say to persuade teachers to change. Indeed, the respectful way in which we talk to teachers can make a big difference in whether they implement a practice.

QUESTION #4:

Are Teachers Treated With Respect?

Commenting on how another professional works is almost always difficult because so much of a person is woven into how she or he works. This challenge may be even more difficult for educators because few professions are more personal than teaching. Change agents need to be aware that they walk on sacred ground when they suggest new ways of teaching, especially when they criticize a teacher's current teaching practices.

In more than 200 interviews that I've done with teachers about professional learning, teachers have been close to unanimous in criticizing professional developers who fail to recognize teacher expertise. The old model of an expert talking to a room full of strangers is, in fact, in some cases literally worse than nothing because teachers may leave traditional sessions feeling frustrated, disappointed, or patronized and worse off than they were before the session. One teacher's comments summarize the views of many of these teachers: "It's not like we are undergraduates. There are many people on our staff who are bright and who do read what's going on in the field, who do take classes on their own time, not because they have to but because they love to teach. And I do think it's kind of demeaning [when a presenter appears not to] know about that."

Few change leaders actually intend to be demeaning, but intentions don't matter. What matters is how teachers perceive change leaders. Perception is reality, and if teachers feel that their identity (their own sense of how good, competent, or talented they are) is under attack, their most frequent reaction is to resist (Stone, Patton, and Heen 2000).

Change agents, then, are likely to be more effective if they are masters of effective communication. They need to listen respectfully (Goldsmith & Reiter, 2007) and communicate positive comments so frequently and so authentically that they foster what Kegan and Lahey (2001) refer to as "a language of ongoing regard" (p. 101). Perhaps most important, they need to communicate recognition for the professionalism of teachers. For that reason, change leaders must understand the role of reflection and thought in professional practice.

QUESTION #5:

Are Teachers Doing the Thinking?

Thomas Davenport has deepened our understanding of professional practice by describing the attributes of knowledge workers who, he says, "think for a living. [Knowledge workers] live by their wits. Any heavy lifting on the job is intellectual, not physical. They solve problems, they understand and meet the needs of customers, they make decisions, and they collaborate and communicate with other people in the course of doing their own work" (2005, p. 15). Few people do more thinking on the job than a teacher standing in front of 27 students, so it seems safe to say that teachers are knowledge workers.

Davenport extends his analysis by stating that a defining characteristic of knowledge workers is that: "Knowledge workers like autonomy. . . . Thinking for a living engenders thinking for oneself. Knowledge workers are paid for their education, experience, and expertise, so it is not surprising that they take offense when someone else rides roughshod over their intellectual territory" (2005, p. 15). This is precisely the case with teachers. Ignoring teacher autonomy often ensures that teachers don't implement new practices.

On the surface, having a small group of educators and administrators do the thinking for teachers is understandable. Schools need programs implemented consistently across a district, and it's not especially efficient for many teachers to be deeply involved in curriculum revision. However, if change leaders ignore teachers' need for autonomy, they run the risk of alienating their audience.

Respecting teachers' professional autonomy does not mean all teachers have complete freedom to teach in whatever way moves them. There have to be some non-negotiables in schools. Schools could expect all teachers to develop classroom management plans, use common assessments, or adopt particular textbooks or curricula, for example. However, handing a pacing guide to teachers and giving them no say in its development and no choice about implementing it is a recipe for disaster. When someone else does all the thinking for teachers, there's little chance that teachers will implement the practice.

One particularly self-destructive pattern that prevents real change from taking hold in schools is the attempt, attack, abandon cycle.

QUESTION #6:

What Has Happened in the Past?

How teachers view professional learning in their schools on any given day will inevitably be shaped by how they have experienced professional learning in the past. If professional learning has been truly professional, respected teachers' need for autonomy, offered powerful and easy practices, and been supported through coaching and other forms of job-embedded learning, then teachers will approach professional learning with positive, high expectations. When these elements are missing, however, history can become a major roadblock to implementation.

One particularly self-destructive pattern that prevents real change from taking hold in schools is what I call an "attempt, attack, abandon cycle." During the attempt, attack, abandon cycle, change leaders introduce a new practice into a school. However, very little support is available to help teachers try the new practice, so many teachers never implement it and others attempt it but poorly. Before the program has been implemented effectively, and before it's had sufficient time to be fully implemented, various individuals in the school or district begin to criticize or attack the program. As a result, many teachers implementing the program begin to lose their will to stick with it. Inevitably, even though the practice was never implemented well, district leaders label it unsuccessful and abandon it, only to propose another program that's sure to be pulled into the same vicious cycle, to eventually be attacked and abandoned for another program, and on and on. Thus, schools stay on an un-merry-go-round of attempt, attack, abandon, without ever seeing any meaningful, sustained change in instruction taking place (Knight, 2007).

Hargreaves and Fink (2005) have identified lack of continuity as another self-destructive pattern in schools. When districts swing from one instructional approach to another, when school leadership is consistently changing, the lack of consistency and focus can undermine a teacher's enthusiasm for new ideas. Of course, if the history of professional learning is one that ignores all of the above questions, there is an even greater likelihood that teachers will adopt the age-old refrain, "This too shall pass."

Suggestions for Leading Change

I hope the above questions show how the approach taken by change leaders can have a significant positive or negative impact on whether teachers adopt better ways of teaching. Indeed, if we carefully consider change issues, we might wonder why teachers don't resist change more than they do. If we ask teachers to implement practices that may not have a powerful impact on students, if we don't make it easier for teachers to adopt new ways of teaching, if we tell teachers why innovations are important without providing them opportunities to experience success, if we do the thinking for teachers, if we ignore the personal and professional aspects of change, and we do this year after year while continually changing the focus for professional learning, can we really expect teachers to be enthusiastic about changing their practices?

Fortunately, our six questions carry within them suggestions for how we can increase the likelihood that teachers will adopt and implement proven practices.

1. Seek high-leverage teaching practices that are proven and powerful. Those who propose new ways of teaching need to be certain that what they bring to teachers will have an unmistakable positive impact on students' and teachers' lives.

2. Use data to select and monitor the impact of practices. Data can be a valuable tool for the selection of effective teaching practices. Ignoring data can waste a great deal of effort on tools that don't address students', teachers', and schools' most pressing needs.

3. Provide quality coaching. The preliminary research on coaching (Knight & Cornett, 2009) suggests that teachers rarely implement without sufficient support involving precise explanations, modeling, and encouraging feedback.

4. Balance precise explanations with provisional comments. Professional developers can make it easier for teachers to learn new practices if they precisely describe how teachers should use new practices in the classroom. However, they should also explain those practices provisionally to allow teachers the freedom to adopt practices to fit their unique pedagogical approach or the particular needs of their students.

5. Obtain commitment by offering teachers choices and valuing their voices. The more teachers can have a say in how and what new practices they implement, the more likely they will be to embrace new ways of teaching.

6. Focus professional learning on a few critical teaching practices. Professional learning that involves too many approaches can lack focus or overwhelm teachers (Davenport, 2005). A better idea is to collaboratively identify a few critically important practices and then work together to ensure that they are implemented successfully.

7. Align all activities related to professional learning. Professional learning communities, coaching, teacher walkthroughs, program book studies, and all other forms of professional learning should focus on the same critically important practices that everyone agrees are important within the school.

8. Increase relational trust. Professional learning is most successful in settings that foster support and trust. As Michael Fullan has stated, "the single factor common to every successful change initiative is that relationships improve. If relationships improve, things get better. If they remain the same or get worse, ground is lost" (2001, p. 5).

Conclusion

This article began with a simple question: "What can we do about teacher resistance?" One answer is that those of us who are change leaders should be careful about how we share practices with teachers. Professional developers who adopt the suggestions included here should see much less resistance and much more meaningful and valuable professional learning. More important, when teaching practices improve, there is every reason to believe student achievement will improve as well.

Reflection Questions for "What Can We Do About Teacher Resistance?"

1. How can consideration of why people resist shift the way we lead, coach, or facilitate?

2. Which of the reasons presented in the article do you see most commonly in your work? How do you respond?

3. What might need to change in your school/system to engage around the topic of resistance?

NOTES

The Problem of Nominal Change

Originally published in *Educational Leadership, 81*(7). April 1, 2024.

 According to the Oxford English Dictionary, something that is nominal "exists in name only . . . merely named, stated, or expressed, without reference to reality or fact." Having now spent more than twenty-five years working with organizations, I've come to see that the word nominal describes how change occurs in schools. Leaders say they are implementing PLCs, or Visible Learning, or gradual release, or instructional coaching, but what is implemented in schools bears little resemblance to the skills, beliefs, knowledge, and processes that authors describe as quality implementation. Too often schools implement high-leverage practices in name only.

I think I have at least a partial understanding of why nominal change is common. Few people are busier than educational leaders, and they are anxious for change in their schools. Taking months to plan an intervention effectively seems hard to justify when students are dropping out and you're already overwhelmed with work. Also, people tend to lose interest in innovations over time. Trying out something new is more interesting than going the distance with an intervention we've been working on for years. I have felt these forces myself as I've led my organization.

There are, however, negative consequences from nominal change. If new practices aren't implemented effectively, they won't make a difference. When new practices don't have a positive impact, organizations move to other new interventions, which in turn get poorly implemented and eventually forgotten. This nominal change cycle of (a) introducing new practices, (b) implementing them nominally, and (c) moving on to other new practices (that will eventually be implemented nominally and rejected) erodes teachers' commitment to any new initiatives. Over time teachers come to adopt a simple mantra: "this too shall pass."

Fortunately, there are several steps leaders can take to get out of the nominal change cycle. I've summarized them below.

1. **Begin With the End in Mind.** Leaders need to be crystal clear on why they are implementing a new strategy and what will be different when that strategy is effectively implemented. Clarity around the desired outcome should be a north point on a compass guiding everyone's actions when a new practice is implemented.

2. **Identify a Champion.** If an organization is going to implement a new practice like coaching or PLCs, someone needs to lead the implementation, and that person needs to have time to do that leadership work. Champions need to know what a new practice looks like when it is implemented so that they can provide the in-depth support needed for quality implementation. To help them develop their deep knowledge, champions may need their own coaches.

3. **Add by Subtracting.** Most champions, principals, coaches, and teachers do not have a lot of extra time in their day. If they are going to add something new to their day, they will need to remove something else. Powerful change can't be an add-on. Time has to be created so that the new practice can be implemented effectively, and that means other practices need to be removed.

4. **Ensure Deep Knowledge.** Most practices involve many different components. We have found that coaching, for example, involves knowledge (of teaching strategies and data gathering), skills (at least ten essential coaching skills), beliefs (based on the extensive research on how people change), and a process (in this case, a coaching cycle). If coaching is going to be implemented effectively, champions, coaches, principals, and teachers all need to know exactly what it is, how long it takes, and what it looks like.

5. **Plan.** Leaders who want to be successful need to take the time to plan how people learn to do what is needed for a practice to be implemented. Coaches, for example, who are going to develop the skill of questioning to set powerful goals, probably need to practice that skill at least ten times. Those practice attempts won't happen unless leaders plan when and how they will happen.

6. **Try, Test, Improve.** The best laid plans, of course, still need to be tested, adapted and improved. Educators need to measure what works and what doesn't work and make improvements until the practice is helping teachers and students hit their goals.

7. **Listen to Teachers and Students.** It is a strange reality that the people who are closest to the change often have the least say in what is implemented. Doing change "with" teachers instead of "to" teachers can make an enormous difference in teacher's commitment and quality of implementation. Also, teachers first-hand experiences into what is and isn't working with an intervention can be extremely valuable for making improvements. Similarly, students' feedback can prove incredibly helpful for anyone improving new practices. When it comes to understanding what works and what doesn't work in schools, students are often a great untapped resource.

To Sum Up

There is no lack of good ideas on how to improve schools. But there is a lack of quality implementation. Nominal change wastes the time of everyone in a school including students. However, change doesn't have to be in name only. Like so many things in life, taking the time to plan, learn, and improve can be a difference maker—and when it comes to schools, the difference is better learning and well-being for students.

Reflection Questions for "The Problem of Nominal Change"

1. How can understanding of how people change shift the way we lead, coach, or facilitate?

2. How can we involve students when goal setting or use their feedback to help us coach/lead?

3. What might need to change in your system/school to put the focus on planning and learning to support improvement/student outcomes?

NOTES

_____

_____

_____

_____

_____

_____

_____

_____

_____

_____

_____

_____

_____

_____

_____

_____

_____

_____

_____

_____

THE EXPLORING VIEWPOINTS ACTIVITY

 Purpose: To enrich conversations and make learning more powerful through examining diverse perspectives.

Process:

1. Participants are encouraged (and helped) to select identifying perspectives according to the group's purpose. Clearly this involves judgment, but no one's self-selected perspective should be argued with; however, all should be willing to negotiate. It must be noted that we all have multiple ways we could describe ourselves and, for this activity we will settle on one or two. For example, "I am an administrator who is committed to the 10 Common Principles" or "I am a new teacher in my first year." This process may take about 7 minutes. (You could also have people consider and decide on perspectives in advance of this conversation.)

2. Next, a question is presented that has emerged from the work of the group or that has emerged as an important one to the group. For example, "What is engagement, actually?"

3. Participants write their first thoughts in response to the question. This part of the process could take 5 minutes.

4. After this time, each participant gives their preliminary thinking on the question, prefaced with their point of view: For example, "From the point of view of an administrator, I think. . . ." This part of the process could take about 10 minutes.

5. During the second round, each person gives their thinking building on what they heard from the other participants: "Having heard each of your perspectives, I now think. . . ." (10 minutes)

6. The final round allows you to reflect on the quality of the responses: "I noticed that my/our responses. . . ." This part of the activity could take 15 minutes.

 Resistance

https://youtu.be/D3rncu7xF4s
In this video, Jim talks about teacher resistance.

Guiding Question: What is needed for coaches to flourish in a system?

Resources: "5 Key Points to Building a Coaching Program" and "Coaching and Working With Instructional Coaches" articles, Expanding Perspectives activity

Activity:

1. Read through the Expanding Perspectives activity to become familiar with the process.

2. Complete the activity to further explore the articles and facilitate dialogue. (You could split the group into three groups and assign each group an article, have each group complete the activity, and then debrief together.)

3. After, debrief the process, and discuss implications for future conversations around coaching in your system. You could use the reflection questions at the end of the chapter to guide this conversation.

Coaching

The key to translating research into practice lies in continuous, job-embedded learning with ongoing support.

Originally published in the *Journal of Staff Development, 30*(3). Summer 2009.

 In the past decade, interest in the form of professional learning loosely described as coaching has exploded. This growing interest in coaching is likely fueled by educators' recognition that traditional one-shot approaches to professional development—where teachers hear about practices but do not receive follow-up support—are ineffective at improving teaching practices. Much more support is needed to help teachers translate research into practice, and for many districts, that support is coaching.

DEFINITION

What is coaching? Researchers and practitioners have described several distinct approaches with unique goals and methods. Peer coaching (Showers, 1984), classroom management coaching (Sprick, Knight, Reinke, & McKale, 2006), content-focused coaching (West & Staub, 2003), and blended coaching (Bloom, Castagna, Moir, & Warren, 2005) are just a few approaches. Three approaches are especially common in today's schools: literacy coaching (Moran, 2007; Toll, 2005), cognitive coaching (Costa & Garmston, 2002), and instructional coaching (Knight, 2007).

Cognitive coaches engage in dialogical conversations with teachers and others, observe them while working, and then use powerful questions, rapport building, and communication skills to empower those they coach to reflect deeply on their practices. The term literacy coach is used widely to refer to educators who use a variety of tools and approaches to improve teachers' practices and student learning related to literacy. Instructional coaches partner with teachers to help them incorporate research-based instructional practices into their teaching so that students will learn more effectively.

Despite the unique goals and methods of each of these approaches, there are several commonalities:

Focus on professional practice. The purpose of most forms of coaching is to improve the ability of a school to educate students by improving the way teachers teach in the classroom.

Job-embedded. The professional learning experiences facilitated by coaches are usually directly applicable to teachers' classrooms. Teachers who collaborate with coaches make plans, explore content, reflect, and implement new practices that they will use immediately in their lessons.

Intensive and ongoing. Coaching is not a one-shot workshop, but rather differentiated professional support, meeting each teacher's unique needs over time. Coaching often occurs one-to-one and may involve several interactions lasting months.

Grounded in partnership. Coaches see themselves as equal partners or collaborators with teachers. Thus, teachers have choice and control over how coaching proceeds.

Dialogical. Coaches strive to enable dialogue when they coach teachers. Coaching is not about telling teachers what to do but rather about engaging in reflective conversations where coach and teacher think together.

Nonevaluative. Although coaches frequently observe teachers teaching, and, indeed, teachers may observe coaches teaching, coaches do not set themselves up as evaluators of teachers. Rather, they discuss teaching with teachers in a nonjudgmental way.

Confidential. Most approaches to coaching describe the relationship as confidential. Coaching will likely be more successful when teachers are comfortable speaking openly about their strengths and concerns.

Facilitated through respectful communication. Coaches need to be excellent communicators who articulate their messages clearly, listen respectfully, ask thought-provoking, open-ended questions, and whose observations are energizing, encouraging, practical, and honest.

CONDITIONS FOR SUCCESS

Between 2005 and 2008, researchers and consultants associated with the Kansas Coaching Project at the University of Kansas Center for Research on Learning have worked with coaches and other educators in schools, districts, and state agencies in more than 35 states. During these workshops and consultations, certain factors repeatedly surface that appear to be critical for coaching success.

Focus and continuity. Districts that attempt to implement too many practices simultaneously overwhelm teachers with the changes they are expected to implement and decrease their enthusiasm for any change. Similarly, when districts frequently adopt and abandon programs and initiatives, teachers often take a wait-and-see approach to professional learning. Coaches will find a better setting for professional learning if districts have a sustained focus on a few high-leverage strategies.

A learning-friendly culture. Teachers are more likely to experiment and learn when they feel respected and free to take risks. Conversely, when teachers feel they are punished more than praised and constantly under scrutiny without sufficient encouragement, their desire to learn may decrease dramatically. Teachers who work in learning-friendly schools will be much more likely to collaborate with coaches.

Principal support. Principals need to support their coaches by attending coaching workshops, observing coaches while they conduct model lessons, speaking frequently about the importance of professional learning and coaching, learning what the coach shares with teachers, and meeting frequently with coaches to ensure that their coaches share their vision for professional learning.

Clear roles. If teachers perceive their coach as an administrator rather than a peer, they may hesitate to open up about their needs or take risks. Therefore, principals and coaches should ensure that coaches work as peers providing support and service to their colleagues, and principals and other administrators should perform important administrative tasks such as teacher evaluations and walk-throughs. Principals respectfully hold teachers accountable, and coaches provide sufficient support for teacher professional learning.

Protect the coaching relationship. Coaching works best when teachers are collaborating with a coach because they want to, not because they are forced to. If a principal tells a teacher they have to work with their coach, the coach may be perceived as a punishment. If a principal strongly encourages a teacher to change, but offers the coach as one of several growth options (others might include books, articles, web sites, and video programs), the coach can be perceived as a lifeline rather than a punishment.

Time. The single most powerful way to increase the effectiveness of coaches is to ensure that they have sufficient time for coaching. In conducting research on coaching at many sites around the nation, my colleagues and I ask coaches to map out how they use time in their roles. Overwhelmingly, their maps indicate that less than 25% of their time is spent in coaching tasks. Principals and other district leaders need to ensure that they do not ask coaches to do so many noncoaching tasks that they rarely have the opportunity for sustained coaching.

Continuous learning. Coaches and administrators should "walk the talk" when it comes to professional learning by continuously improving their own professional practice. Coaches need to have a deep understanding of the practices or content knowledge they share with teachers as well as the coaching practices and communication skills that are necessary for effective coaching. Principals need to understand what coaches do, and how they can contribute to conditions that support coaching. Additionally, both coaches and principals need to be coached so that they are constantly learning how to improve the way they lead instructional improvements in schools.

WHAT THE RESEARCH SAYS

For a recent book chapter, Jake Cornett and I reviewed more than 200 articles, presentations, reports, articles, and books that contain some form of research on coaching (Cornett & Knight, 2008). The bulk of this research was conducted on peer coaching, cognitive coaching, and instructional coaching. In one landmark study, Bush (1984) conducted a five-year study of staff development in California. Bush's research team studied the impact that various approaches to professional development had on whether or not teachers used new teaching practices. They found that when teachers were given only a description of new instructional skills, 10% used the skill in the classroom. When modeling, practice, and feedback were added to the training, teachers' implementation of the teaching practices increased by 2% to 3% each time. When coaching was added to the staff development, however, approximately 95% of the teachers implemented the new skills in their classrooms. (See chart below.)

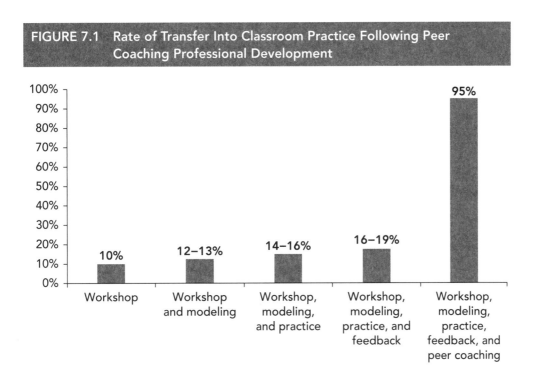

FIGURE 7.1   Rate of Transfer Into Classroom Practice Following Peer Coaching Professional Development

In her book *Cognitive Coaching: A Synthesis of the Research* (2001, p. 1), Jenny Edwards identified nine anticipated outcomes:

1. Increase in student test scores and "other benefits to students;"

2. Growth in teacher efficacy;

3. Increase in reflective and complex thinking among teachers;

4. Increase in teacher satisfaction with career and position;

5. Increase in professional climate at schools;

6. Increase in teacher collaboration;

7. Increase in professional assistance to teachers;

8. Increase in personal benefits to teachers; and

9. Benefit to people in fields other than teaching.

In a recent study of instructional coaching (Cornett & Knight, 2008), 51 teachers attended an after-school workshop on unit planning and teaching routine, based on *The Unit Organizer* (Lenz, Bulgren, Schumaker, Deshler, & Boudah, 1994). Teachers were randomly assigned into two groups, one that received coaching and one that did not. Research assistants observed the classes taught by teachers in both groups, watching for evidence of use of the newly learned teaching practice. In classes taught by teachers who were coached, observers saw evidence of use of the unit organizer during 90% of their visits. However, in classes taught by teachers who were not coached, observers saw evidence of use of the unit organizer in only 30% of the classes.

It is important to note that research on cognitive coaching doesn't necessarily apply to instructional coaching, and vice versa. Nonetheless, a few generalizations seem to be fairly unavoidable. First, in most of the studies we reviewed, the best implementation rate one could hope for following a one-shot workshop was 15%. Second, coaching that focuses on helping teachers implement new practices leads to implementation. Finally, the research on cognitive coaching suggests that this approach has a positive impact on teachers' beliefs about their efficacy as teachers.

Coaches need to have a deep understanding of the practices or content knowledge they share with teachers as well as the coaching practices and communication skills that are necessary for effective coaching.

Reflection Questions for "Coaching"

1. How can understanding of a partnership approach change the way we communicate with others?

2. How can learning different approaches to coaching support coaching flourishing in your system?

3. What might need to change in your system/school to move the culture toward a more partnership approach to coaching?

NOTES

_____

_____

_____

_____

_____

_____

_____

5 Key Points to Building a Coaching Program

Originally published in the *Journal of Staff Development, 30*(1). Winter 2009.

 Across America today, hundreds of instructional coaches are being hired to improve professional practice in schools.

Preliminary results (Knight, 2007) suggest there are reasons to be optimistic about this form of professional development. Since coaches provide on-site professional learning, they can adapt their approach to meet the unique needs of the teachers and students in the schools where they work. And, since coaches can provide professional development that addresses teachers' concerns at different stages of the change process (Hall & Hord, 2006; Prochaska, Norcross, & Diclemente, 1994), coaching can lead to sustained implementation of new teaching practices in schools.

The danger is that schools will implement school-based coaching too simplistically, underestimating the complexity of change initiatives. However, if educational leaders recognize and respond to the complexity of change, in particular by paying attention to five key points in building a coaching program, school-based coaches can make a difference. When coaching programs are designed well, the chances of making a significant difference are greater and the potential of coaching can be realized.

1. TOP-DOWN AND BOTTOM-UP

In a 1997 study, teachers reported that they were four times more likely to implement teaching practices they learned during partnership sessions than those they learned in traditional sessions (Knight, 1998). Partnership takes an approach that:

- Professional developers and teachers are equal partners;

- Teachers should have choices regarding what and how they learn;

- Teachers should reflect and apply learning to their real-life practice as they are learning;

- Professional development should enable authentic dialogue; and

- Professional development should respect and enable the voices of teachers to be heard. In our ongoing study of coaching, however, we have found that a purely partnership approach that exclusively relies on bottom-up initiatives has limitations (Knight, 2007). A bottom-up approach that does not have the principal's guiding hand as the instructional leader will lead to teachers adopting new teaching practices, but unsystematically—with some and not others implementing the change so school improvement may progress incoherently. A purely bottom-up approach also risks placing teachers significantly out of step with district and state mandates. When a bottom-up approach offered teachers complete freedom to choose whether to participate, those teachers who most needed to change frequently were the ones who chose not to participate.

Of course, a purely top-down approach is not a practical alternative. When leaders adopt a purely top-down stance, they risk introducing what counselors refer to as an "ironic process," an approach that "causes the very outcome that it was meant to avert" (Miller & Rollnick, 2002, p. 37). Telling teachers they must work with an instructional coach actually makes it more difficult for coaches to assist teachers.

"When you tell teachers to do something, they resent it," said Ric Palma, an instructional coach in Topeka, Kan. (personal communication, August 29, 2004). "If they do it, they're going to do it in a half-baked . . . manner. And others will just refuse because they don't like to be told what to do."

Instructional coaches need a balance of bottom-up and top-down strategies to be effective. They should position themselves as equal partners collaborating with fellow teachers, basing their professional actions on partnership principles. Principals should support their on-site coaches by focusing school change initiatives to make it easier for teacher and coach to work together on interventions that have the highest possibility of impacting student achievement. Most importantly, the principal and coach must work together to ensure that those who need help get it.

2. EASY AND POWERFUL

In *The Evolving Self*, Mihalyi Csikszentmihalyi (1993) says that for an idea or innovation to supercede another idea or technology, the new idea must be easier and more powerful. "Ideas, values, technologies that do the job with the least demand on psychic energy will survive," the author states (p. 123). "An appliance that does more work with less effort will be preferred."

Similarly, for teachers to abandon an old teaching practice to embrace a new one, coaches must offer a practice that is both more powerful and easier to use than the current strategy.

Teachers will not adopt practices that are difficult to implement. Thus, one of a site-based coach's primary tasks is to do everything possible to make it easier for teachers to implement new teaching practices. Coaches highlight, simplify, and clarify practices described in teacher manuals, prepare materials, make copies or handouts if necessary, model in the teachers' classroom, observe teachers, and provide feedback.

"My job is to remove every barrier that might stand in the way of a teacher implementing" a new practice, said Tricia McKale, a coach in Topeka, Kan. (personal communication, April 8, 2005).

To support school-based coaches in helping teachers adopt change, professional development leaders must provide coaches with the resources and time they need to remove barriers teachers face in implementing new methods. Also, coaches and leaders must evaluate the teaching practices they are sharing with teachers to ensure that they are making a real difference in children's and teachers' lives. When teachers have a chance to implement a practice that really works and that is easy to implement, they usually adopt it quickly.

3. SELF-ORGANIZING AND HIGHLY ORGANIZED

When coaches work with an open mind, without a formalized, structured approach, and see their task as spreading a healthy virus in schools, they are more likely to succeed.

At Landon Middle School in Topeka, Kan., for example, coach LaVonne Holmgren shared writing strategies from the Strategic Instructional Model with a few pioneering language arts teachers when she arrived at the school. After those teachers were successful, others wanted to try the strategies, and soon a majority of the language arts staff was using the strategies. At that point, Holmgren guided the staff in creating a schoolwide curriculum ensuring that all language arts teachers taught grade-appropriate writing strategies. Had Holmgren arrived at the school with a plan to institutionalize the writing strategies, she likely would have met resistance or other road blocks. By allowing the plan to grow and develop based on teacher interest and student need, she got deep commitment to a schoolwide plan that every teacher implemented.

To help accelerate the spread of "healthy viruses," coaches should ensure that:

- They share teaching practices that are powerful and easy to use;

- Their first encounters with teachers are highly effective;

- Teacher leaders within the school have opportunities to be early adopters; and

- They use a variety of communication strategies (newsletters, e-mails, bulletin boards, word of mouth) to ensure that teachers know about successes when they occur.

When someone offers a service that is easy to use and that helps students, teachers become interested in using it pretty quickly. Support coaches by allowing them time to build rapport and respond to teachers' needs. Once a critical mass of teachers use what the coach has to offer, the coach and principal together encourage the creation of more permanent structures.

4. AMBITIOUS AND HUMBLE

Alex LeClaire (a pseudonym) began his coaching career excited about helping teachers use strategies he had found extremely successful in teaching writing. He began the school year with a passionate presentation to teachers about the power of strategic instruction, and he quickly lined up conferences with teachers in their classrooms, in the staff room, and at team meetings to convince them to get on board.

The more LeClaire pushed, the less enthusiastic his colleagues became and the more barriers they put up. As teachers turned away, LeClaire became even more zealous in his attempts at persuasion.

Eventually, he became frustrated and began privately, then publicly, criticizing his colleagues for failing to do the right thing for kids. His criticism, of course, alienated staff even more, and by the end of his first year, LeClaire felt his efforts were wasted, and he blamed the teachers, who he said "were too stubborn to change." Another coach, Lauren Morgan (a pseudonym), was the embodiment of humility. Morgan was determined not to force herself on teachers and to work with only those who wanted to work with her. Morgan was careful not to put herself out in front of the staff; she preferred to stay in the background. Teachers liked her, but they always seemed a little too busy to try her ideas. As time went by, Morgan found she had very few teachers collaborating with her. She waited patiently, but the right time never seemed to come along. Morgan found herself doing more and more busy work within the school and less coaching. At the end of the year, Morgan realized that she had worked with only eight teachers, and most of those had made only a superficial attempt at new practices.

Successful coaches embody a paradoxical mixture of ambition and humility, a mix of attributes similar to those described by Jim Collins (2001) for Level 5 leaders. Level 5 leaders "are incredibly ambitious—but their ambition is for the institution, not themselves" (p. 21). Effective coaches, like Collin's Level 5 leaders, should be "a study in duality: modest and wilful, humble and fearless" (p. 22). Devona Dunekack, a coach in Topeka, Kan., embodies both personal humility and wilful ambition.

"I just ask teachers if they're interested in an extra set of hands," Dunekack said (personal communication, March 16, 2004). "I never put on airs that I know more than them. . . . I'm just not trying to be anything other than a colleague."

Dunekack works to nourish relationships with each teacher in the school, and builds up trust before sharing ideas. She is supportive and kind, but keeps charts on each teacher and the extent of their commitment to coaching. If a teacher does not collaborate with her, Dunekack doesn't take it personally, but sees that teacher as a challenge, and through a forceful kindness, almost always wins over each teacher.

Not surprisingly, more than 95% of the teachers at Eisenhower Middle School collaborate with Dunekack, and Eisenhower students have shown the greatest improvement on state reading assessments in the Topeka district for each of the past three years.

Outstanding coaching programs begin with outstanding coaches. Hiring coaches who embody both ambition and humility helps create a successful experience.

5. ENGAGED AND DETACHED

Lynn Barnes, coach at Jardine Middle School in Topeka, Kan., is an outstanding relationship builder. She is positive, funny, warm, and very supportive of others. She loves, she says, "communicating with people . . . making them feel good about themselves and what they teach" (personal communication, July 14, 2005). Not surprisingly, Barnes considers coaching to be "the perfect job to make people feel good about themselves, to feel good about their profession."

Effective coaches have to care deeply about teachers and students, and they also clearly have to communicate to others that they care.

"You have to build a relationship before you do anything," Barnes said, "and to do that, you truly need to care about the individual you are working with and their students."

Yet coaches have to be careful not to weave too much of themselves into their jobs. As Ronald Heifetz and Martin Linsky (2002) observed, "To lead is to live dangerously because when leadership counts, when you lead people through difficult change, you challenge what people hold dear—their daily habits, tools, loyalties, and ways of thinking. . . . And people resist in all kinds of creative and unexpected ways that can get you taken out of the game: pushed aside, undermined, or eliminated" (p. 2).

Jean Clark, a coach at Bohemia Manor Middle School in Cecil County, Md., learned this firsthand. Shortly after beginning her job, Clark says she stepped into the staff lounge in time to overhear a teacher say,

"The reason why there's evil in this building is because of Jean Clark."

Clark had to learn to remain steady and calm. She came to understand that leading as a coach put her in the line of fire. "It's not about me," she said. "This is their stuff. It's not personal. . . . Some people are going to like me, and some people aren't, and in the end, they will come along whether they like me or not, if they see their children growing." Clark succeeded as a coach, and her school has had the greatest gains in the county in the last two years.

The ability to connect with others is a critical characteristic of effective coaches. Principals and staff development leaders should provide training on how to communicate effectively and how to build that emotional connection with others. Coaches also need a structured support network with other coaches to support them in the face of inevitable resistance.

SUMMARY

More than a decade and a half ago, Seymour Sarason (1990) published *The Predictable Failure of Educational Reform*, a book whose title captured the frustrations experienced by many educational leaders valiantly promoting school Improvement initiatives. The preliminary positive results of coaching and other promising professional development and school reform efforts suggest that there now is, indeed, cause for optimism about future reform efforts. When planners and implementers support coaches by recognizing and responding to the complexity of change, in particular by responding to the five paradoxes outlined here, their chances of success improve greatly.

> ## Reflection Questions for "5 Key Points to Building a Coaching Program"
>
> 1. How can creating a culture of partnership coaching shift the way we lead, coach, or facilitate?
>
> 2. How can leaders support coaches to build a successful coaching model?
>
> 3. What might need to change in your school/system to use the research-based tenets of helping coaches flourish?

NOTES

_____

_____

_____

_____

_____

_____

_____

Working With Instructional Coaches: 7 Ways Principals Can Offer Support

Originally published in *Principal Leadership*. January 2024.

 Educational leaders around the world are recognizing that real improvement in schools requires ongoing, focused, intensive, goal-directed, job-embedded professional development. That is, instructional coaching.

My colleagues and I at the Instructional Coaching Group and at the Center for Research on Learning at the University of Kansas have been studying and supporting instructional coaches for more than two decades. During that time, we've found that administrative support is one of the two most important variables that make or break coaching success (the other is hiring the right person for the job). When coaches and principals work together successfully, there is an excellent chance the coach will have an unmistakably positive impact on students and teachers. The opposite is also true.

In this article, I identify seven actions administrators can and should take to support coaches so that positive change can occur in schools.

1. Understand Instructional Coaching

Since coaches play a central role in any change or improvement plans in a school, principals must understand what coaches do so they can provide the right support. Understanding coaching will likely involve the following: (a) agreeing on a set of beliefs to guide coaching actions (we propose the partnership principles), (b) outlining the skills coaches need for effective coaching conversations (in particular listening and questioning), (c) following a coaching cycle that coaches can move through in partnership with teachers to organize, set, and hit goals (we suggest the Impact Cycle), and (d) drawing upon strategic knowledge about data gathering and high-impact instruction to move through the cycle. When administrators understand the beliefs, skills, processes, and knowledge inherent in effective coaching, they are much better prepared to support coaches in the other actions I describe in this article.

2. Theoretical Alignment

Coaches and administrators work well together when they have theoretical alignment. This is a fancy way of saying that the coach and principal agree on the principles that should guide the coach's actions. When they don't, that can undercut a coach's effectiveness. For example, if a coach has learned that coaching should be a partnership between professionals, with teachers having a lot of autonomy, but the principal sees coaches as experts whose primary job is to fix teachers by telling them what to do, that difference can make it difficult for coaches to act effectively and with confidence.

The ultimate goal of coaching should be to have an unmistakably positive and lasting impact on student achievement and well-being. My research suggests that coaches will be more successful if they work from what I call the partnership principles. When coaches see themselves as partners with teachers, they see teachers as equals who should have a significant say in their own professional learning. Coaches who act as partners engage in back-and-forth (or dialogical) rather than directive (one-way) conversations that focus on reflective work for real-life change in the classroom. Most coaches learn quickly that telling teachers what to do is counterproductive, but involving teachers in identifying goals and strategies increases the likelihood that teachers will commit to their coaching goals.

3. **Role Clarity and Time**

To succeed in their job, coaches need to know the expectations for their job, and they must have sufficient time to do that job. Unfortunately, this is often not the case. And, when there is no clarity around what coaches do, coaches can end up doing low-priority tasks that keep them from partnering with teachers to move through a coaching cycle. We suggest coaches and administrators sit down together and review a list of all the tasks coaches might be asked to do. Then, they need to discuss each task and decide if the coach will—or will not—do it. Administrators and coaches need to prioritize the actions that will have the greatest impact on student achievement and well-being. If coaches are going to spend at least 60% of their time coaching, and at least 10% of their time on their own professional learning, that doesn't leave much time for other tasks.

Administrators will often need to help coaches say no to many tasks if coaches are to focus on the most important work. Potentially valuable tasks such as leading PLCs, conducting walk throughs, overseeing state testing, designing and leading workshops, and so forth may all need to be set aside so coaches can focus on partnering with teachers to make dramatic improvements in learning and teaching practice.

4. **Principal Support**

In almost all organizations, people seek the approval of the leaders to whom they report. When it comes to coaching in schools, this means teachers will be more likely to prioritize coaching if their principals prioritize coaching. At the most fundamental level, principals need to believe that effective professional development leads to important improvements in schools, that professional development isn't just a box to be checked. If administrators don't believe in professional development, something needs to change.

Administrators can also support coaching in many other ways. They can speak publicly about the importance of coaching, they can observe coaches when they offer model lessons, and they can encourage teachers to speak publicly about their positive coaching experiences.

One of the most powerful ways principals can support coaches is for principals to agree to be coached themselves. More and more districts are offering leadership coaching for principals, and some administrators are learning to take a coaching approach to leading by learning and using coaching skills, beliefs, and a coaching process.

Coaching expert Steve Barkley suggests that principals demonstrate the power of coaching by being coached themselves by their school's instructional coach in front of staff during a meeting. To do this, a principal can teach a model lesson in a teacher's classroom, record the lesson, watch it to find some interesting sections, then share those sections at a staff meeting. Then, after sharing the video, the principal can be coached by the school's instructional coach in front of everyone. Barkley says that even in meetings where teachers are usually anxious for the meeting to end as quickly as possible, staff will want to stick around to see their principal be coached. Most importantly, when teachers see how easy and powerful coaching can be, they'll be more likely to embrace coaching for themselves.

5. Support Professional Development for Coaches

Coaching is a new job for most coaches, and it involves different beliefs, processes, skills, and knowledge than coaches used themselves when they were teachers. Coaches won't acquire all that new knowledge and skill without professional development and time for learning. Principals can provide support by looking for resources and ensuring that at least 10% of a coach's work time is spent on professional learning. Also, just as teachers need coaches to translate new ideas into better learning and well-being for students, coaches also need someone who helps them learn and improve their craft. Principals can also provide a great service to coaches by advocating for coaches of coaches.

One final and important form of professional learning for coaches is for them to create instructional playbooks: digital or analog documents that contain (a) a list of the highest-impact strategies to be used by coaches and teachers in a school, (b) one-pagers for those strategies, and (c) checklists that coaches can share with teachers to help teachers get ready to implement new strategies.

6. Confidentiality

Every coach and principal needs to confirm their policy for confidentiality. In the best learning environments, of course, confidentiality wouldn't be an issue given widespread psychological safety. If all teachers feel 100% safe discussing the students in their classrooms and their professional practice, there would be no need for a confidentiality policy.

In most cases, however, teachers may be less than candid about their needs, especially when they are talking with someone who meets with the administrators who will evaluate them. In some schools, the policy is that coaches share no information at all with administrators so that teachers feel more comfortable sharing their concerns and needs. The most common policy is that coaches share what they're working on and with whom, but they do not share evaluative information.

What matters most with respect to a confidentiality policy is that it is clearly stated, agreed upon, and widely understood by everyone in a school. A lack of clarity around confidentiality may lead to coaches sharing information that teachers thought was confidential. For teachers, that can feel like a breach of trust. And trust is crucial for coaches to succeed.

7. Effective Evaluation

In too many settings, coaches are evaluated by people who don't understand effective coaching with an evaluation tool that was designed specifically for teachers. This is a bit like asking psychiatrists to evaluate surgeons with a tool designed for dentists.

Evaluation of coaches should be conducted by people who understand coaching and who use a tool designed and field-tested for coaches. We suggest a 360° evaluation be completed by teachers who have been coached by the evaluated coach, and we suggest the coach's administrator or direct report complete the same evaluation. Coaches themselves should complete a self-evaluation. Such triangulated data can really help coaches improve.

Coaching programs should also be evaluated. At a minimum, schools should assess the impact of coaching by looking at what goals teachers set and hit by working with coaches. Additionally, evaluation should assess the ways in which the school system supports or impedes coaching success. There are many tools for such evaluation described in a book I co-wrote, *Evaluating Instructional Coaching: People, Programs, and Partnership.*

Conclusion

Real change, change that has an unmistakably positive impact on students, likely won't happen without follow-up, collaboration, and goal-directed practice. Coaches play a central role in such efforts, but they can't do it alone. Coaches will struggle to succeed without school leader support. Fortunately, administrators can take concrete and specific actions to support coaches so real change, good change, is always occurring.

Reflection Questions for "Working With Instructional Coaches: 7 Ways Principals Can Offer Support"

1. How can leaders ensure coaches flourish in their role?

2. How can coaches help leaders better understand the coaching role?

3. What might need to change in your school/system for coaches to feel supported and have role clarity?

NOTES

EXPANDING PERSPECTIVES ACTIVITY

 Purpose: to hear different perspectives and approaches to the content of a text.

Process:

1. Start by selecting a text for a group discussion.

2. Explain the process:

    a. Participants will be placed in groups of four (modify as needed for small groups or based on the needs of your learners).

    b. Each of the four members will select one "perspective" to hold as they read the article. That means that as participants read, they are reading with that perspective in mind, allowing it to shape how they interact with the text.

    c. Once everyone has read the article, the group will take turns sharing out. As each person shares their perspective, the rest of the group is invited to respond to, add to, or build upon the ideas.

3. Then, have participants choose their perspective:

    a. Appreciate: the appreciate perspective reads the article to search for ideas that they appreciate the most out of everything that has been shared.

    b. New Thinking: the new thinking perspective searches the article for new ideas, content, or skills that can be shared with others.

    c. Still processing: the still processing perspective finds and shares ideas that are challenging, concepts that push their thinking, or concepts that they might not completely agree with at this time.

    d. Take action: the take action perspective reads to find concepts that inspire them to start, stop, or explore new actions.

4. The groups read the article, holding on to their perspectives.

5. Once the group has read, they begin sharing out, one perspective at a time. Invite all participants to respond to each perspective to add to or build upon the shared ideas.

6. At the conclusion of the activity, the following reflection question can be used for individual or group reflection: How have you expanded your perspective today?

<u>Guiding Question:</u> How does confidentiality impact how coaches are perceived in a system?

<u>Resources:</u> "Instructional Coaches Make Progress Through Partnership" article, A Broken Trust case study, Confidentiality video

<u>Activity:</u>

1. Show the video from Principles of Coaching, titled "Confidentiality" to the group. After the video, talk about how this might align with their ideas about why systems should develop a confidentiality policy.

2. Then, use the *A Broken Trust* scenario to guide a conversation around the implications of confidentiality and breaking trust in a system.

3. Debrief, and discuss the perspective presented and how the information in the scenario and video can support your ideas.

4. Read the article, and use the reflection questions to have a more deeply articulated discussion and debrief.

Instructional Coaches Make Progress Through Partnership

Originally published in the *Journal of Staff Development, 25*(2). Spring 2004.

> *"Quick fixes never last, and teachers resent them. They resent going to in-services where someone is going to tell them what to do but not help them follow up. Teachers want someone who's going to be there, who's going to help them for the duration, not a fly-by-night program that's here today, gone tomorrow."*

> — Lynne Barnes, Pathways to Success instructional coach

Over the past four years, researchers and professional developers from the Kansas University Center for Research on Learning (KU-CRL) have used an approach to staff development that provides teachers with intensive support designed to improve instruction. The Pathways to Success project places full-time instructional coaches in the six middle and three high schools in Topeka, Kan., the district made famous by *Brown v. Board of Education.* An instructional coach is an on-site professional developer working in one school offering, as instructional coach Irma Brasseur said, "on-the-spot, everyday professional development."

"You're right with the teachers and their students, you see what's happening, and you provide a real suggestion or solution for what's happening," Brasseur said.

"We give them something they can use, right with their kids, right in their content area," said instructional coach Lynn Barnes.

It is that practicality that has won widespread teacher support. In the four middle schools where the program began, 98 of 125 teachers are using the research-based strategies instructional coaches introduced. Similar results are occurring in the other middle and high schools as the project spreads across the district. And teachers have seen the effect on their students.

WHAT A COACH DOES

Instructional coaches are university employees who are funded by a five-year federal GEAR UP program, along with other grants written through a district-university partnership. They work with school administrators to implement school improvement initiatives and plan and implement professional development.

An instructional coach's main task is to help teachers see how research-validated practices offer useful solutions to the problems teachers face. Instructional coaches teach teachers about strategies and routines validated

But an instructional coach has to be more than an expert in instructional practices. She or he is part coach and part anthropologist, advising teachers on how to contend with the challenges and opportunities they face while recognizing each school's unique culture. Although coaches must be flexible and adapt their approaches, all usually follow similar procedures:

1. Meet with departments or teams. Instructional coaches begin the change process by meeting with each school department or team. The instructional coach explains that teachers have an opportunity to learn about new research-validated teaching practices designed to make classes more accessible or to help students become better learners. The instructional coach then asks teachers to indicate their interest on an evaluation form.

2. Meet one-on-one with interested teachers. The instructional coach schedules a series of one-on-one or small group meetings to identify what research teachers are interested in learning about and to discuss how that research can be translated into practice. School culture is often opposed to change initiatives, but every school has individuals interested in new ideas.

3. Work on real content. Teachers meet with instructional coaches anywhere from once or twice to every week for a semester, depending on the nature of the strategy being introduced. Each meeting focuses on real applications of the research-based.

4. Model lessons in each teacher's classroom. A major part of an instructional coach's work is modeling initiatives so teachers can see how an approach works in their classrooms. Instructional coaches often model the first lesson in a sequence so teachers can better understand how to make the approach work. "Teachers need to see it," said Barnes. "They need to see you modeling, and that gives them insight into other things that might need to be done—keeping kids on task, redirecting inappropriate behavior, giving feedback, recognizing kids

when they're doing great, keeping the room positive and energized. . . . There's an art to teaching, and a lot of that art is hard to learn from reading teachers manuals."

5. Pay for teachers' time. For teachers to enthusiastically commit extra time to any change effort, they should be paid. Paying teachers demonstrates respect, yet teachers in the project frequently turn down the honorarium. They simply appreciate the recognition that their time is being taken.

6. Make it as easy as possible. If an intervention works and is easy to implement, our experience suggests teachers will use it. Instructional coaches provide all the materials teachers need to implement a strategy or routine, to help teachers transfer research into practice. For example, instructional coaches give teachers a cardboard box called "strategy in a box" filled with everything the teacher needs to implement an intervention—overheads, learning sheets, readings, teaching behavior checklists, and instructional manuals. Coaches also might write lesson plans, help with student evaluations, create overheads, or co-teach to give teachers additional time. "Part of our goal is to release teachers from burdensome, mundane things so they can spend time thinking about being a learner, to make changes to bring out critical teaching behaviors," Brasseur said. "(Teachers) need to get to the point of thinking about teaching."

7. Respond quickly to teacher requests. Since teachers are pressed to organize classes, evaluate students, and keep on top of their content, they require material quickly. Instructional coaches must reply immediately when teachers request new materials. Even a few days' delay may kill the opportunity for implementation. "I take care of as much as I can right within the hour," said Barnes. "Too many times, people put you on hold. When we get right back to our teachers, we show them we care about them."

WHAT DOES THE PROJECT LOOK LIKE?

Instructional coaches have been able to gain support because the coaches respond to teachers' individual needs. One 7th-grade team, for example, was part of a summer CHAMPs workshop offered by an instructional coach. The teachers then collaborated with their school's instructional coach to create materials that specifically addressed problem behaviors they had seen the previous year.

The teachers identified a top 10 list of problem behaviors, then worked together with the instructional coach to write up very specific expectations for how they wanted students to act when they walked in the hall, entered the class, listened to teacher instruction, worked in cooperative groups, used their planners, worked with a substitute teacher, and so forth.

The teachers "figured out a plan together, and then everyone went over it with their classes and reinforced it in the same way," instructional coach Shelly Kampschroeder said. The result was that "the teachers had their act together from the get-go. A lot of the headache behaviors decreased, and you could see a visible change in behavior. The kids got it. . . . Teacher teams definitely make my job easier—some ideas spread like wild-fire."

HOW DO IDEAS SPREAD?

Malcolm Gladwell's (2001) observation that "ideas and products and messages and behaviors spread just like viruses do" is borne out by the experiences of instructional coaches working on Pathways to Success.

Shelly Bolejack's experiences as an instructional coach at Highland Park High School are typical. At first, she doubted whether she'd have a meaningful effect on the school. "I had a lot of time," she said, "and I sat and stared at the wall, thinking, 'What have I done? They don't know me and don't want to work with me.' . . . People were unclear about what I was doing. I felt I had to keep clarifying what was going on. Teachers were reticent and apprehensive, so I kept sharing that I was there to help them."

Bolejack said she kept contacting teachers through conversation, e-mails, and the school newsletter. She made herself available to talk with teachers at any time. She gathered materials, explained the project, answered questions, modeled it, and listened to teachers' issues. Eventually, interest grew.

"Once somebody tries it," she said, "the next teacher tries it, and another teacher talks to another. . . . Teachers have to see that it works. And because the strategies are research-based, since they do work, they sell themselves. Even teachers who felt they haven't been successful can be successful since the strategies are so complete. When they see that success, it makes them want to continue. "Now, less than a year after I started, every single person on the freshman team is doing something with our project. There are times when I'm really busy, but I feel incredible seeing this happen for other teachers."

HOW ARE INSTRUCTIONAL COACHES SELECTED?

Hiring the right instructional coach is important to successful implementation. In addition to being disciplined, organized, and professional, instructional coaches also must be flexible, likable, good listeners with great people skills, and committed to learning. Most importantly, instructional coaches have to be outstanding teachers. A good instructional coach must be able to go into any classroom and provide a model lesson that responds to an individual teacher's needs.

"Now, less than a year after I started, every single person on the freshman team is doing something with our project. There are times when I'm really busy, but I feel incredible seeing this happen for other teachers."

During interviews, project staff included unconventional questions to learn more about candidates' flexibility and people skills in addition to the potential instructional coach's teaching philosophy, relationship-building skills, and ability to think on his or her feet. After the first round of interviews, remaining candidates demonstrated their teaching skills. Each was given a manual for a Pathways to Success intervention, such as Jan Bulgren et al.'s (1993) *Concept Mastery Routine*, and then had 24 hours to prepare a 20-minute lesson on the content. Project staff could see which candidates were able to learn content quickly, think on their feet, prioritize, and, of course, teach. Instructional coaches have primarily been hired from within the district, although some are external candidates. They are assigned to schools in close consultation between project staff and the district administrative team, who meet weekly to discuss the project.

Since they are university employees who report to the Pathways to Success Project director, instructional coaches are protected from being drawn into the numerous school-based bureaucratic tasks that can consume so much of any school employee's time. They are free to spend the vast majority of their time providing intensive professional development. Coaches make it clear they are not administrators, and their job is to provide support, validation, and professional growth for teachers, not to evaluate. At the same time, as full-time workers in a school, they are able to collaborate with the school principal and other staff to create plans for schoolwide or teacher-specific professional development.

HOW DO INSTRUCTIONAL COACHES LEARN THEIR JOBS?

For Devona Dunekack, learning to be an instructional coach was like learning a new language. Dunekack honed her skills and continues to learn in a variety of ways, through formal and informal professional development, by watching other experienced instructional coaches, and by collaborating with other instructional coaches during formal and informal meetings.

"You can't learn to be an instructional coach in a week," she said. "I remember at first I was totally confused because it was a lot to internalize. Understanding all the vocabulary was flipping me out, and I told my friend, 'I will never be smart enough to do this.' But as time has passed, I've learned how to put things together. I'm still learning every day, and my understanding keeps coming by little bits, but now I'm confident that I know what I'm doing." Dunekack, along with other instructional coaches, helped write the Pathways to Success mission and values statement. "The partnership training and writing the mission helped us embrace the same vision and purpose," she said. "We're a strong team because we're all on the same page."

Instructional coaches take part in formal professional development activities, including five day-long sessions per year conducted by the project director on the interventions, and the philosophy and approach of coaching. They are trained in the partnership approach to professional development. The coaches also attend two conferences a year.

And all instructional coaches spend at least an hour or two every two weeks watching other instructional coaches in action. "For me, it's huge that we get to go to another school and see someone else do it," Dunekack said. "We learn a lot when we see each other model."

They read and review the research supporting Pathways to Success interventions. Dunekack said reading articles was a task that didn't seem useful at first, but ultimately it paid dividends. "Now I can speak with confidence about the research," she said, "and thanks to my reading, if my understanding was muddy, the articles cleared it up."

WHAT HAVE WE LEARNED?

Project staff are committed to learning from teachers and adapting as the program proceeds. We continually rethink the shape of interventions and how to work with teachers. Over the last four years, we've learned several important lessons.

Go slow to go fast. Those who expect the most from improvement efforts often underestimate the complexity of change. Pushing for rapid change can alienate staff and sabotage the effort. Instructional coaches found the most efficient way to create change is to spend time creating meaningful relationships that generate successes. Once a few teachers have had positive experiences, word travels.

Focus on relationships.

Instructional coaches work to build healthy relationships with everyone in a school. They work hard to see matters from the viewpoint of the teachers in their school. An effective instructional coach recognizes when teachers need support and also when they are too overloaded to take on anything new. Their goal is to pass ownership of ideas to teachers; the art of being an instructional coach is to know when to do so.

Have a partnership mind-set.

Instructional coaches must genuinely see themselves in equal relationships.

The instructional coach's goal is "to work with teachers where they are, to listen to their point of view, to respond to each teacher as a human being, and to give them something that helps them reach more kids right away," said instructional coach Susan Claflin. "A successful instructional coach will do anything that needs to be done to help teachers implement something that will help kids."

Professional developers who see themselves as experts, more gifted than the teachers with whom they're working, are doomed to fail before they begin.

Offer teachers choices. The heart of professionalism is individual discretion (Skrtic, 1991). When we respect teachers' ability to make their own decisions about how a teaching practice might fit into their classrooms, teachers are much more interested in adopting the practice and teaching it with fidelity. Teachers participate in the Pathways project voluntarily, and we believe this has led to deeper and broader implementation.

RESULTS FROM THE PAST TWO YEARS

Pathways to Success staff have engaged in ongoing formative and summative assessment through all stages of the project. Teachers and project staff use curriculum-based pretest and posttest measures (along with other measures) to assess the effectiveness of each intervention used. Here are a few examples of results from the past two years:

- Jardine Middle School's 7th-grade team learned a classroom management strategy through coaching that reduced the number of disciplinary referrals from 203 in first semester 2002 to 78 in the same term 2003.

- A traditional experimental design was used to study the effectiveness of the self-questioning strategy when taught in general education 7th-grade science classes at Chase Middle School. One teacher taught the reading strategy along with his science content in three of his classes, and used his traditional methods of teaching in his remaining three classes. To study the strategy's effectiveness, we gave each student a pretest and posttest on the content covered in the unit. Students who learned the strategy improved their posttest scores by 60%; students who didn't learn the strategy improved their posttest scores by 40%.

- One study of middle school students who learned a sentence writing strategy (n = 1,302) in classes where the intervention was taught with fidelity showed significant improvement in the number of complete sentences in their writing (according to curriculum-based measures of their writing samples), writing 73% complete sentences on pretests and 87% complete sentences on posttests. In classes where the strategy was taught with less fidelity, students (n = 564) showed much less impressive improvement, writing 76% complete sentences on pretests and 80% complete sentences on posttests.

CONCLUSION

Our research suggests (Knight, 2000) that teachers resist change programs that offer too little support. In four years, the coaches in the Pathways to Success project have had a significant impact on the schools in Topeka. By offering teachers choices, providing support, respecting teachers' time, establishing partnerships, and modeling instructional practices, instructional coaches have enabled schoolwide improvements in instruction. More importantly, the coaches have created dozens of meaningful relationships and friendships, giving teachers an opportunity to talk about and reflect on the art and practice of teaching.

Reflection Questions for "Instructional Coaches Make Progress Through Partnership"

1. How can we use the Partnership Principles to shift the way we lead, coach, or facilitate?

2. How are you offering choice and voice to teachers in your coaching interactions?

3. What might need to change in your school/system to support a partnership over top-down approach to coaching?

NOTES

CASE STUDY: A BROKEN TRUST

 Cathy Winslow sat in her car, staring out through the windshield, lost in thought. A coach for only a few months, Cathy was deeply concerned that she had made the wrong career choice. While Cathy wanted to serve her school as a coach, she was quickly realizing that coaching was more challenging than expected. Early in the school year, Cathy sat down with her principal, Dr. Carolyn Austin, to touch base on the school's coaching program. During the conversation, Carolyn asked Cathy how she thought a few teachers were doing, and Cathy was quick to say how impressed she was with all of them, except for one: Tom Drekker. Cathy elaborated on how challenging Tom was being and how he was constantly resisting her support. She asked the principal what she should do. Cathy and Carolyn talked for a few minutes about the situation, and then moved on to other topics. When Cathy left, Carolyn decided to chat with Tom to see if she could help the situation and ensure Tom felt supported by the coach.

A few days later, Tom confronted Cathy in the hall. In front of several staff, Tom turned on the coach, saying, "If I had known you were a spy for the principal, I never would have let you in my classroom." After his outburst, Tom stormed past Cathy and headed back to his classroom. Word of the confrontation traveled fast, and soon Dr. Austin, the principal, heard about it. She went to see Cathy, and together they went over what could have gone wrong. After a week, Cathy started hearing that people were rethinking their partnership with her because their conversations were not confidential.

 Exploring Confidentiality and Resistance

 https://youtu.be/PRs_zQHS7m0
In this video, Jim talks about confidentiality.

 https://youtu.be/D3rncu7xF4s
In this video, Jim talks about teacher resistance.

<u>Guiding Question:</u> What do coaches do?

<u>Resources:</u> "What Good Coaches Do" article, KLE Activity

<u>Activity:</u>

1. Read the activity to become familiar with the practice and start with the first few steps before reading.

2. Read the article "What Good Coaches Do," and continue using the KLE activity.

3. Wrap up this learning path by using the reflection questions that follow the article.

What Good Coaches Do

When coaches and teachers interact equally as partners, good things happen.

Originally published in *Educational Leadership, 69*(2). October, 2011.

 The way we interact with others makes or breaks most coaching relationships. Even if we know a lot about content and pedagogy and have impressive qualifications, experience, or post graduate degrees, people will not embrace learning with us unless they're comfortable working with us.

Emotional intelligence and communication skills help, but another factor is crucial. After conducting close to two decades of research on instructional coaching, my colleagues and I at the Kansas Coaching Project at the University of Kansas Center for Research on Learning have come to believe that how we *think* about coaching significantly enhances or interferes with our success as a coach. We suggest that coaches take a partnership approach to collaboration.

The partnership approach grew out of themes we found repeatedly in the literature from the fields of education, business, psychology, philosophy of science, and cultural anthropology (Knight, 2011). We have synthesized those themes into seven principles that describe a theory of interaction currently used by hundreds of coaches across North America and around the world.

Seven Partnership Principles

Identifying our principles is important because the way we act grows naturally out of what we believe. The partnership principles of equality, choice, voice, reflection, dialogue, praxis, and reciprocity provide a conceptual language that coaches can use to describe how they strive to work with teachers.

Equality

Equality is a necessary condition of any partnership. In true partnerships, one partner does not tell the other what to do; both partners share ideas and make decisions together as equals.

Problems arise, however, when people feel they don't have the status they believe they deserve. Usually, if we feel that someone who is helping us thinks that he or she is better than we are, we resist their help. For this reason, coaches need to be sensitive to how they communicate respect for the teachers with whom they collaborate.

At the Kansas Coaching Project, where we have watched many video recordings of coaches and teachers interacting, we see talented coaches skillfully act in ways that communicate that they do not see themselves as having higher status than their collaborating teacher. Coaches who act on the principle of equality have faith that the teachers they work with bring a lot to any interaction, and they listen with great attentiveness.

Choice

Coaches who act on the principle of choice position teachers as the final decision makers, as partners who choose their coaching goals and decide which practices to adopt and how to interpret data. Partners don't choose for each other.

Violating the principle of choice often increases the likelihood that teachers will resist change initiatives. As the saying goes, "When you insist, they will resist." Ironically, telling a professional that he or she must act a certain way is often a guarantee that the person will *not* want to do that. Indeed, meaningful commitment to an offer of help is only possible when we have the choice to say no. "If I can't say no," as Peter Block (1993) has written, "then saying yes has no meaning" (pp. 30–31).

Ensuring that teachers have meaningful choices does not mean that teachers are free to stop learning. Everyone in school needs to be actively engaged in professional growth, with the principal being the first learner. Most people, however, want to have a say in what and how they learn.

Voice

Conversation with a coach should be as open and candid as conversation with a trusted friend. When coaches follow the principle of voice, teachers feel free to express their enthusiasms and concerns.

When coaches respect teachers' voices, they seek out and act on teachers' opinions. Teachers' professional learning is driven in great part by the goals that teachers hold for themselves and their students. Thus, coaches might start the coaching process by videotaping teachers' classes, prompting them to watch the videos, and then asking them what *they* would like to focus on in light of what they saw. If teachers don't see how professional learning matters to them or their students, they won't be motivated to implement what they're learning.

Reflection

Much of the pleasure of professional growth comes from reflecting on what you're learning. When professionals are told what to do—and when and how to do it, with no room for their own individual thought—there's a good chance they're not learning at all.

We see a partnership coach as a thinking partner for teachers and coaching as a meeting of minds. When we watch videos of partnership coaches and teachers co-creating ideas during reflective conversations, we see two energized people who laugh, talk enthusiastically, and enjoy themselves.

Dialogue

When a coach and teacher engage in dialogue, they let go of the notion that they must push for a particular point of view. The goal is for the best idea to win—not for *my* idea to win—and the best idea wins most frequently when both partners think their way together through a discussion.

Paulo Freire's (1970) writing has laid the groundwork for much of our understanding of dialogue in education. He describes dialogue as a mutually humanizing form of communication. This means that my discussion partner and I become more thoughtful, creative, and alive when we talk in ways that are two-way rather than one-way.

Because dialogue is only possible when we value the participants' opinions, Freire suggests we enter into dialogue with humility. This often means that we temporarily withhold our opinion so we can hear others. Dialogue may also involve a kind of radical honesty. That is, rather than covering up the flaws in our argument or hiding our ignorance, in dialogue we display the gaps in our thinking for everyone to see. If we want to learn, we can't hide behind a dishonest veneer of expertise.

Praxis

Praxis describes the act of *applying* new knowledge and skills. When we study cooperative learning, for example, and then spend time planning how we'll integrate it into our lessons, we're engaged in praxis. Similarly, when we learn about asking effective questions and then write appropriate open-ended, nonjudgmental questions for our lessons, we're engaged in praxis. And when we learn about a new teaching practice, think about it deeply, and decide not to use it in our class, we're also engaged in praxis.

Reciprocity

Reciprocity is the belief that each learning interaction is an opportunity for everyone to learn—an embodiment of the saying, "When one teaches, two learn." When we look at everyone else as a learner *and* a teacher, regardless of their credentials or years of experience, we're often delightfully surprised by new ideas, concepts, strategies, and passions.

Reciprocity is the inevitable outcome of a true partnership. Seeing our partners as equals means we come into a conversation respecting and valuing them. Freeing our partners to make choices means they're free to surprise us with new ideas. Encouraging them to say what they think means we'll have an opportunity to learn what's important for them to share.

Reflection, dialogue, and praxis increase the chances that we'll learn from our colleagues because we're engaged in work focused on real-life situations and we share ideas about that work. Partnership is about shared learning as much as it is about shared power.

The Actions of Good Coaches

Saying you like the partnership principles and acting on them are two different things. Taking the partnership approach demands that we temporarily relinquish power—and that's never easy. However, when we give up top-down power and adopt a partnership approach to interaction, we replace the empty power that we get by virtue of our position with the authentic power gained through choice.

Coaches who act on the partnership principles engage in the following practices.

They Enroll Teachers

When teachers are forced to work with a coach, they often see coaching as a punishment. However, when teachers are offered coaching as one of many ways in which they can conduct professional learning, they often see it as valuable. Agreeing to continually improve and grow is part of joining the ranks of physicians, pilots, architects, and nurses. To do anything less is unprofessional.

Coaching should be a part of all professional learning that happens in a school. Schools should build time into workshops and professional learning communities so that teachers can plan how to collaborate with a coach to implement new practices. Principals should suggest coaching as one option for professional learning when they talk with teachers after classroom observations. Coaches should also give brief presentations on coaching and meet one-on-one with teachers to talk about how they can support professional learning.

Effective coaching makes it easier for teachers to learn and implement new ideas. Indeed, without follow-up such as coaching, most professional learning will have little effect. When professional learning is central to a school's culture and when coaching is woven into all professional learning, most staff members won't need to be told to work with a coach. Most will choose to work with someone who makes it easier for them to learn new strategies, improve their skills, and reach more students.

They Identify Teachers' Goals

Coaches who take a top-down approach to coaching arrive in classrooms with a predetermined collection of strategies and see it as their job to convince the teacher to use them.

However, when coaches take the partnership approach, their efforts are guided by specific goals that teachers hold for their students. Partnership coaches start by gathering data with or for the teacher. They then collaborate with the teacher to identify a specific student goal. Student goals can be either academic (for example, 95 percent of students will demonstrate mastery of this concept on the next test); behavioral (students will be on task more than 90 percent of the time); or attitudinal (90 percent of students will ask to read a book for pleasure over the break).

They Listen

Ensuring that others know we hear them and that we want to know their ideas communicates that we see them as partners. We can't be partners unless we understand how our partners see things.

During partnership coaching conversations, coaches create a setting in which collaborating teachers feel comfortable saying what they think. Coaches are curious to understand, and they make sure the conversation focuses on the teachers' concerns. In this way, they get to hear the real truth.

They Ask Questions

Coaches ask questions of their partners because they're more concerned with getting things right than with being right. Therefore, they ask good questions to which they don't know the answers—and they listen for the answers. For example, when they ask, "What evidence did you see that shows that your students are learning?" they want to know what the teacher thinks, not guide the teacher to see what they see. They stop persuading, and they start learning.

They Explain Teaching Practices

When coaches explain practices, they should be precise *and* provisional. As Atul Gawande (2010) pointed out in *The Checklist Manifesto*, precision is an essential part of coaching. If we can't explain a practice clearly, we can't expect teachers to implement it effectively.

However, precision that doesn't account for an individual's thoughts and knowledge runs the risk of alienating teachers. Partnership coaches not only give precise explanations, but also ask teachers how they can adapt practices to best fit their teaching style and meet their students' needs. Thus, a coach might share a checklist describing how to model metacognitive reading strategies, with a step-by-step explanation of the process. However, while explaining it, the coach would ask the teacher whether that process would work for her students or for her teaching style.

The reality is that teachers will adapt practices to make them their own. By taking the partnership approach, coaches can collaborate with teachers on creating the best fit. To think that each practice must be done in exactly the same way in every classroom underestimates the complexity of the process. In education, as Eric Liu (2004) has explained, "It's never one size fits all; it's one size fits one."

They Provide Feedback

The term *feedback* often brings to mind traditional top-down feedback. We envision a coach who gives an athlete feedback on how to hit the ball or jump a hurdle. This kind of feedback usually involves giving some positive comments, explaining how to improve, and ensuring that the listener knows what he or she needs to do to improve.

When coaches take the top-down approach in school, they use data to explain what they think the teacher has done well and what she or he needs to do to improve. Top-down coaches do most of the talking because they want to make sure that teachers learn how to do something correctly. However, the problem with top-down feedback is that it's based on the assumption that there's only one right way to see things—and that right way is always the coach's way.

An alternative to top-down feedback is the partnership approach—the collaborative exploration of data. Here, coach and teacher sit side by side as partners and discuss their interpretations of the data that the coach has gathered. Coaches don't withhold their opinions, but they offer them provisionally, communicating their openness to the teacher's point of view.

Partner for Success

The partnership approach builds on an old idea—that we should treat others the way we'd like them to treat us. Chances are we'll want someone who will help us by giving us choices about what and how we learn. We'll likely want a say in our learning, and we'll likely get more out of back-and-forth conversations than one-way lectures. Chances are we'll want our conversations to help us address real-life issues, and we'll be more open to new ideas if the person helping us respects us, has faith in us, considers us educated and capable of making good decisions, and sees us as an equal. Chances are we'll want to be treated like a partner.

Reflection Questions for "What Good Coaches Do"

1. How can we use the Partnership Principles to shift the way we lead, coach, or facilitate?

2. How are you offering choice and voice to teachers in your coaching interactions?

3. What might need to change in your school/system to support a partnership over top-down approach to coaching?

NOTES

KLE ACTIVITY

 Purpose: To interact with a text in a meaningful way.

Process:

1. Select a text to explore.

2. Begin by individually writing down or sharing out with a group everything you KNOW ("K") about the topic. You might use a guiding question to prompt this or even the title of the article.

3. Then, read the text in its entirety; annotating or jotting notes as you go. As you read, or after you have finished reading, write down big ideas that you have LEARNED from the text ("L").

4. After reading, reflect on or discuss the ideas you collected in the "L" category of your KLE activity. Continue to add to your ideas as others share.

5. Next, head to the "E" section of the KLE Activity and write down two or three ideas you would like to EXPLORE further from the reading. For example, you might want to know more about communication skills, the Partnership Principles, or how to help teachers generate PEERS Goals. Make a plan for how you will explore more about those ideas.

K WHAT DO YOU ALREADY KNOW?	L WHAT DID YOU LEARN?	E WHAT DO YOU WANT TO EXPLORE?

<u>Guiding Question</u>: How can you design professional learning that improves depth of knowledge and is grounded in partnership?

<u>Resources:</u> "Pull Versus Push Professional Development," "Moving From Talk to Action in Professional Learning," "The Life-Changing Magic of Going In-Depth" articles, The Final Word activity

<u>Activity:</u>

1. Invite participants to choose which article they read from the three provided for this learning path.

2. Once participants have chosen their article, invite them to read through it. After they are done reading, lead the activity.

3. Wrap up this learning path by inviting individuals to reflect using the reflection questions that follow the article they selected to read.

Pull Versus Push Professional Development

When teachers choose the goals, professional development gains critical momentum.

Originally published in *Educational Leadership, 79*(2). October 1, 2021.

 Chances are you have had experiences with professional development that doesn't work. Maybe teachers—possibly including you—have sat quietly in a compulsory workshop listening to someone talk about "standards" or "best practices" or "test results." Although the teachers were polite, their lack of eye contact with the presenter, or the lack of energy in the room, suggested that what was being described was not going to be implemented. Or maybe you've watched a video of a coaching conversation where the coach tries to give advice to a teacher who rejects each suggestion. The more enthusiastic the coach becomes, the less enthusiastic the teacher is. (Maybe you've even been that teacher.)

When professional learning doesn't work, professional developers are tempted to label teachers as resistant. "Why," they might ask, "won't these teachers do what I say?" But I have found that, in most cases, when teachers don't implement the ideas shared in workshops, it isn't their fault. It's the result of poorly designed professional development.

SLOGGING UPHILL OR PULLED BY ENTHUSIASM?

I like to use a simple analogy to illustrate why professional development sometimes goes wrong. Imagine you are driving your car and you run out of gas. You can see a gas station a few hundred yards ahead at the top of a hill. Needing to get fuel, you and your passengers get out of your car and start pushing. But the car is heavy, and the hill is steep. Although you push harder and harder, eventually you give up. No matter how hard you work, you'll never get the car to the station by pushing.

Now imagine a different scenario. This time your car hits empty at the top of a hill. A few hundred yards ahead, at the bottom of the hill, you see a gas station. This time, to get to the station, you simply let gravity pull your car down the hill, adjusting the steering and touching the brakes to stay on track until you roll, almost effortlessly, into the station.

These two distinct strategies, push versus pull, also describe two different ways of designing professional development and coaching. When professional development is pushed onto teachers through compulsory workshops or advice-giving, it can be a lot like trying to push your car up the hill—a lot of work and not much progress. However, when professional development begins with teachers identifying a goal *they* really want to meet, the professional developer's role shifts from directing to supporting and helping teachers achieve what matters deeply to them. Professional development that's pulled by teachers' goals is PD that will likely get to an identified destination.

I first read about the distinction between push and pull in Robert Hargrove's (2008) *Masterful Coaching*. Hargrove writes that using pull is about "inviting people to discover their greatness" (p. 13) by declaring "an ambitious aspiration for themselves and their organization" (p. 346). "Pull" PD moves forward because of an emotionally compelling, powerful goal that matters deeply to the teacher and that will have a positive impact on students.

"Push" PD, by contrast, is a remnant of old command-and-control models of leadership, in which a few smart people make most decisions and then put systems in place to push people to implement them. One vestige of the command-and-control paradigm is directive coaching: A coach watches a teacher teach, shares some observations, and then tells the teacher what she should do. Sadly, when teachers are simply told what to do, they often comply with the directive by looking for a way to do what they've been told to using the least amount of effort. The coaches in the coaching workshops I conduct understand Pull PD conceptually, but their questions give away that they're having trouble staying away from Push strategies: "What can I do," they often ask, "when teachers won't do what I suggest they should do?"

With Push PD, teachers are expected to implement something with fidelity even though they may not see the value of the innovation—and even if their district has a history of trying and dropping new innovations before they ever take hold. In many cases, teachers who are thinking "This too shall pass" aren't being negative; they are being realistic. Part of being realistic is not investing too much energy in a teaching methodology that will be gone within a year or two.

Beyond Passive Compliance

Not surprisingly, Push PD often engenders resistance. A mountain of research shows that most of us aren't motivated by others choosing goals for us. Push training creates dependency and inhibits creativity, often leading teachers to say, "Just tell me what to do, and I'll do it." Perhaps most troubling, since the Push model fails to encourage individual creativity, it often pushes talented teachers out the door.

Pull PD, however, is guided by teachers' decision making about what happens and should happen in the classroom. It respects teachers and treats them like professionals. When coaches take the Pull approach, they give teachers tools (reflection forms, video recordings of lessons, etc.) so that teachers can determine their own understanding of the reality of the classroom. Then coaches skillfully ask questions that empower teachers to identify important goals. Coaches who take the Pull approach do share ideas and strategies with teachers when it is helpful, but they always make suggestions tentatively, so the teacher is always the ultimate decision maker about what happens in her classroom.

Using a Pull approach doesn't mean being soft on people. Pull usually requires teachers to work hard, to courageously confront reality and step outside of their comfort zone. This effort is inspired by teachers' desire to see good things for their kids.

Pull goes against some deeply engrained ideas about how organizations should be structured and how PD should be delivered, so it can be hard to embrace. Inevitably, too, there will be some forms of professional development that must be shared through a Push approach. But the more teachers have a voice in their learning, the more control they have over their own growth, and, indeed, the more teachers are treated like professionals, the more real change will happen—real change that leads to better experiences for students.

Reflection Questions for "Pull Versus Push Professional Development"

1. How are professional development opportunities designed in your system?

2. Is there opportunity to discuss push versus pull and the implications on adult learning when planning professional development?

3. Do you think providing teachers more choice and focusing less on fidelity would help move desired learning forward?

NOTES

Moving From Talk to Action in Professional Learning

Knowing the stages teachers tend to go through as they implement a new approach makes it easier to support them.

Originally published in *Educational Leadership, 78*(5). February 15, 2021.

Learning and internalizing something new, like a coaching skill or a teaching strategy, is—like most of life—more complex than it first appears. In most cases, we do not go to a workshop or watch a webinar and suddenly find ourselves acting in completely new ways. Change takes time, and the movement toward proficiency is often messy and unpredictable.

For that reason, those of us who support educators who are implementing innovations will provide much better support when we understand what the journey to proficient implementation really entails. To that end, I describe here a model for understanding stages of implementation and suggestions for principals and professional developers like coaches to consider as they support teachers moving from one stage to the next.

The Stages of Implementation

Two teams of researchers have especially shaped the way I understand the stages people move through as they learn and change. I've been influenced by Prochaska et al. (1994), who describe change as involving non-linear movement through six stages (pre-contemplation, contemplation, preparation, action, maintenance, and termination), and Hall and Hord's (2015) eight "Levels of Use," part of their Concerns-Based Adoption Model (non-use, orientation, preparation, mechanical use, routine use, refinement, integration, and renewal).

To develop my own understanding of implementation, I've found it helpful to combine my experience studying change with these models. In the process, I've come up with my own five stages of implementation: (1) Non-Use, (2) Awareness, (3) Mechanical, (4) Routine, and (5) Proficient. A clearer understanding of these stages of implementation, especially what hinders and helps people as they move from one stage to the next, should lead to better professional development—leading to better teaching practice and, consequently, better learning and lives for students.

Non-Use

People are in this stage when they are not carrying out an innovation because they're either unable or unwilling to implement it. They may be unable to implement an innovation simply because they don't know about it, having missed the workshop or skipped the webinar. Educators can also be in the non-use stage because they either actively or passively resist the new learning. Individuals who actively resist learning are very clear that they choose to not implement something that's been suggested for them, perhaps because it conflicts with their professional goals or values. Those who passively resist quietly choose not to implement a strategy for reasons they choose not to articulate.

Awareness

People are at the awareness stage when they know something about an innovation, are not resistant, but also aren't implementing it. Often, educators in this stage have a little knowledge about an innovation but are unclear how to put that new knowledge into practice. And the longer people go without implementing a strategy, the less likely they are to ever implement it. For example, teachers might attend a workshop on restorative justice and be excited about implementing it in their classroom. But as time passes, they will remember less and less about the approach and consequently be less likely to implement it.

Workshops help people develop an awareness of an innovation, but they sometimes provide too much abstract information and too little detailed, practical guidance on how to implement the new practice. In my experience, it only takes about three days to forget most of what was learned in a workshop. However it happens, during the awareness stage, people *talk* about change, but don't do anything differently.

Mechanical

During the mechanical stage, people start to implement an innovation, but they often feel awkward carrying it out because they have to remember a lot of new information in order to change what they're doing. The mechanical stage can feel like walking through a field of deep, wet snow: messy, slow, uncomfortable, and tiring. A teacher who is implementing Fisher and Frey's gradual release model (2008), for example, may struggle with the focus lesson when they model their thinking. They may tell students what they are doing rather than transparently demonstrate their thinking, or they may involve students in discussion too quickly before they have finished modeling.

Additionally, the first time we implement an innovation is usually not our best performance, and it might not immediately yield the desired results. Since the new strategy may not improve student learning or well-being at first, and since implementing something new can feel clumsy, it's not surprising educators often decide to return to their old, comfortable ways of teaching.

Routine

During the routine stage of implementation, people start to become comfortable with aspects of the new strategy or skill they are learning. This can feel reassuring after the struggles of the mechanical stage. Feeling comfortable, people may be tempted to implement the innovation in a structured, quick, and easy to remember way. Once they are confident of some aspect of what they are learning, such as using the identify questions from the Impact Cycle (Knight, 2018), teachers may be hesitant to move beyond their comfortable, routine use ("I've just gotten comfortable with this skill, why would I want to modify it?").

A risk of routine implementation is false clarity. According to Fullan (2001), false clarity "occurs when change is interpreted in an oversimplified way; that is, the proposed change has more to it than people perceive or realize" (p. 77). When we have false clarity, we know less than we think we do. We aren't implementing an innovation as effectively as we think we are. That means we probably aren't having the impact that we desire.

Innovations ultimately need to be adapted to respond to the unique strengths and needs of teachers and students. However, change just for the sake of change probably isn't the best strategy. The best outcomes occur when educators make informed, intentional adaptations—informed because the educator deeply understands the principles and nuances of innovations (which often comes from coaching and diverse experiences) and intentional, because educators use their knowledge to make good decisions about how to adapt strategies for better student outcomes. This kind of modification of an innovation is really only possible during the proficient stage.

Reflection Questions for "Moving From Talk to Action in Professional Learning"

1. What stage of implementation reflects your system currently?

2. Is there false clarity in your system?

3. Do you think your system is willing to adapt as needed to respond to meet desired outcomes?

NOTES

The Life-Changing Magic of Going In-Depth

In supporting educators' learning, resist pressure to skim the surface.

Originally published in *Educational Leadership, 79*(8). April 27, 2022.

 Zhu Xiao-Mei is one of my favorite classical pianists. What I love about the way she performs is that she commits to deeply understanding every piece she plays so she can uncover its fundamental beauty, then communicates that beauty so clearly that listeners are deeply moved by her playing. Her goal as an artist, she says, is to work "tirelessly, with no other goal than the truth of the music . . . I never force it or try to grasp its meaning too quickly. I do this until I experience love for each passage and note, until I reach a state of natural and intuitive understanding" (Zhu, 2012).

Zhu Xiao-Mei's in-depth approach stands in contrast to the way many of us operate in the modern world. We surf the web, skim books, speed date, and "like" or "block" friends with the swipe of a finger. If this tendency toward the superficial spills over into how we support children's—and adults'—learning, it can have serious consequences. If those leading PD lack a deep understanding of the strategies and ideas they share, for example, their explanations will be shallow and inadequate. Teachers won't learn what they need to, to implement strategies effectively—so students won't benefit from the changes teachers are trying to make. Everyone suffers when we stay on the surface.

Avoid "Shiny Object Syndrome"

We stay on the surface in learning for many reasons. Going deep may not seem like it's worth the effort, especially when we're asked to learn more strategies than anyone has time to. Often, we don't go deep because the children and adults we support have many urgent and important needs; we feel we need to learn so many things to help them that we never have the time to truly understand what we're learning. And in some settings, coaches and other educational leaders are exclusively rewarded for immediate action, leaving little time for the reflection required for deep understanding.

Some of us stay on the surface because we're drawn to new ideas before we develop an in-depth understanding of whatever it is we just recently learned. There is even a word for the tendency to be attracted to the new or novel: neophilia. Our work environments are also victims of neophilia. School leaders are often drawn to the next new thing, and educators may find themselves pushed to learn about new strategies and ideas before they've absorbed the previous new thing—then they are asked to drop that new thing when another one comes along. Management consultants call this "shiny object syndrome." Leadership changes can exacerbate this tendency.

In addition, because leaders must save time and money, they may feel they have to opt for overview workshops rather than deeper professional development, like coaching. Workshops are valuable because they can give educators an awareness of practices (I lead them all the time), but they rarely provide the deep support needed for real change in professional practice. Too often, PD is too much information, presented too superficially, when what people really need is someone who helps them implement practices in their classrooms. And when funds are limited, they shouldn't be spent on PD that doesn't lead to change.

Commit to Looking Deeper

We don't have to live on the surface. The most powerful step we can take toward deeper understanding of ideas and strategies in teaching may be to simply commit to looking deeper. Here are five strategies that can help us keep that commitment:

1. **Identify priorities.** The biggest barrier for individuals and organizations is trying to do so many things that nothing gets the focused attention it deserves. People need to make time to focus on what matters most for their learning. For example, I suggest coaches focus on getting comfortable with the basics and proficiently implementing a simple, three-stage coaching cycle (Knight et al., 2021)—to ensure that their coaching has an unmistakably positive impact on student learning and well-being.

2. **Say no to some demands on your time.** Not every "no" needs to be justified, but thanking others for inviting us to collaborate and explaining why we can't do so makes it easier for others to accept a negative response: "I'm honored you feel I have something to contribute to your committee, but I'm knee-deep in writing our instructional playbook now and need to focus my attention on that task." Saying no to your supervisor can be especially complex. I suggest coaches sit down with their supervisor with a list of tasks, asking which tasks absolutely need to be done and which are optional, and what percentage of time should be dedicated to each task. Administrators can also support deep learning by proactively ensuring that coaches have the time they need to learn what they need to learn.

3. **Make it real.** Coaches can deepen their knowledge of strategies by creating "instructional playbooks" of 15–20 of the highest-impact teaching strategies they share with teachers, including a one-page summary and checklist for each strategy. They can encourage teachers to deepen their knowledge by experimenting with these strategies in real-life situations (Knight et al., 2021).

4. **Adopt a learner's mindset.** We must ensure that our preconceptions—and sense of our own expertise—don't interfere with our learning. I suggest we adopt a learner's mindset, setting aside our preconceived notions and felt truths, to open our preconceived notions and felt truths, to open ourselves to what others are willing to teach us. Sōtō Zen monk Shunryū Suzuki's description of a "beginner's mind" comes close to describing what I mean. He writes, "In the beginner's mind, there are many possibilities; in the expert's mind there are few" (Suzuki, 2020).

5. **Be courageous.** A final barrier to going deep may be doubt about our own abilities. Researchers in psychology have pointed to imposter syndrome, a tendency to doubt our abilities and feel we don't deserve our accomplishments. If we feel like imposters, we may resist asking questions and seeking help from mentors for fear of being exposed. However, the best way to ensure that we aren't imposters is to have the courage to ask questions and learn from others. As coaches and professional developers, we may not "experience love" for each strategy and idea we share in the way Zhu Xiao-Mei experiences love for each note she plays. But deeper knowledge will lead to better PD and better teaching. Real learning only comes from real depth.

Reflection Questions for "The Life-Changing Magic of Going In-Depth"

1. Do people in your system have a learner's mindset?

2. Do you think that developing a partnership mindset can create deeper learning opportunities as coaches support teachers in your system?

3. How often do coaches in your system have an opportunity to learn professionally?

NOTES

THE IN CLOSING ACTIVITY

 Purpose: to share final thoughts about a text and to build on those ideas by hearing diverse perspectives.

Process:

1. Select a text for this protocol, and have all participants read the text.

2. Once everyone is done reading, give them time to go back through the text and find three big ideas that resonated with them.

3. On a piece of paper or sticky note, have participants write those three big ideas.

4. Then, invite participants to reread all three of the big ideas and come up with one sentence that captures the essence of those big ideas. In other words, summarize what stood out to them the most with one sentence.

5. Once everyone has their summary sentence, the rounds begin. Here are the three steps for each round:

    a. To begin, one person (the speaker) will read aloud their summary sentence.

    b. Then, the rest of the group will take turns sharing what that person's summary sentence means to them by building on their ideas.

    c. Once anyone who is interested has shared their ideas about the speaker's summary sentence, it is the speaker's turn again. At this time, the speaker will say, "In closing . . . " and share the final thought they have after hearing from the group.

6. The rounds continue for each person in the group to share their summary sentence and follow the three steps for sharing.

    a. This can be modified for large groups by creating smaller groups to ensure efficient use of time and increased voice equity.

END OF CHAPTER REFLECTION

Now that you have explored learning opportunities about System Support, take time to reflect on this Success Factor overall. Use the reflection questions below, or reflect in your own way, and fill the lines with your ideas.

REFLECTION QUESTIONS

1. On a scale of 1 to 10, 1 being not at all and 10 being significant, what impact did these learning paths have on your practice? What led you to choose the rating you did?

2. What is a major aha you had as you learned about System Support as a Success Factor?

3. What will you do next with your ideas?

NOTES

Conclusion

Dear Reader,

We want to take this opportunity to personally thank you for joining us in this growth expedition. *The IC Toolkit* was written just for you: the coach who is looking to improve their craft, the group of coaches who form a community of practice, the Coach Champion or administrator who is supporting a group of instructional coaches, and everyone in between. As we put this book together, we talked about the hope we had for its potential: that it would inspire, motivate, empower, and make lives easier as you worked toward being a coach or supporting coaches. In each chapter, learning paths were created in an effort to bring you evidence-based research, meaningful activities, and avenues for reflection. You all served as our empathy anchors as we strove for easy access to significant experiences. We believe in you and as Liz Wiseman says, you are "instrumental" in your place of work.[1]

Our team hopes that you have found joy and purpose in the pages you have explored throughout this book. What we know is that, just by being here, you are invested in the professional development of yourself and others. We also know that while the work is important, it is also complex, and to be truly meaningful, the professional development pathway we choose must be ongoing. As you read these words, we encourage you to continue developing a plan to learn more. Perhaps you go back through this book in a new way. Maybe you have questions about next steps and want to talk to someone. You might have discovered a Success Factor that resonated strongly with you and others or a particular topic in which you want to explore further. Our Instructional Coaching Group Consultants are here for you. We would love to partner with you and bring even more learning to your school or district. Mostly, we are so dedicated to this work and its impact and importance, and we want to hear all about how it is going for you in your district, school, province, county, or parish. We value you all so much and are so grateful for our partnerships.

---

[1] Wiseman, L. (2021). *Impact players: How to take the lead, play bigger, and multiply your impact*. Harper Business.

Finally, reader, we want to invite you to share your thoughts on our toolkit. Did you and others experience powerful moments of learning and discovery together? How did you use the book? What would you want more of as you continue learning? We would love to hear from you. Email us at hello@instructional coaching.com to tell us more or invite us to be your learning partner.

With gratitude,

Jim, Jessica, Michelle, and Amy

References

Introduction

Collins, J. (2001). *Good to great: Why some companies make the leap and others don't.* HarperCollins.

Knight, J. (2011a). *Unmistakable impact: A partnership approach for dramatically improving instruction.* Corwin.

Knight, J. (2011b). What good coaches do. *Educational Leadership, 69*(2), 18–22.

Knight, J. (2013). *High impact instruction: A framework for great teaching.* Corwin.

Knight, J. (2014). *Focus on teaching: Using video for high-impact instruction.* Corwin.

Knight, J., Elford, M., Hock, M., Dunekack, D., & Bradley, B. A. (in press). The instructional coaching cycle: Essential skills for instructional coaches. *Journal of Staff Development.*

Marzano, R. J. (2007). *The art and science of teaching: A comprehensive framework for effective instruction.* ASCD.

Saphier, J., Haley-Speca, M. A., & Gower, R. (2008). *The skillful teacher: Building your teaching skills* (6th ed.). Research for Better Teaching.

Sutton, R., & Pfeffer, J. (2000). *The knowing-doing gap.* Harvard Business School Press.

Chapter 1

Amabile, T., Conti, R., Coon, H., Lazenby, J., & Herron, M. (1996). Assessing the work environment for creativity. *Academy of Management Journal, 39*(5), 1154–1184.

Block, P. (1993). *Stewardship: Choosing service over self-interest.* Berrett-Kohler.

Buckingham, M., & Goodall, A. (2019, March–April). The feedback fallacy. *Harvard Business Review, 97*(2), 92–101.

Deci, E. L., & Ryan, R. M. (2000). Self-determination theory and the facilitation of intrinsic motivation, social development, and well-being. *American Psychologist, 55*(1), 68–78.

Dickson, J. (2011). *Humilitas: A lost key to life, love, and leadership.* Zondervan.

Freire, P. (2017). *Pedagogy of the oppressed.* Penguin.

Glouberman, S., & Zimmerman, B. (2002, July). *Complicated and complex systems: What would successful reform of Medicare look like?* (Discussion Paper No. 8). Commission on the Future of Health Care in Canada.

Grashow, A., Heifetz, R. A., & Linsky, M. (2009). *The practice of adaptive leadership: Tools and tactics for changing your organization and the world.* Harvard Business Review Press.

Heifetz, R., Grashow, A., & Linsky, M. (2009). *Adaptive leadership: Tools and tactics for changing your organization and the world.* Harvard Business Press.

Knight, J. (2007). *Instructional coaching: A partnership approach to improving instruction.* Corwin Press.

Knight, J. (2013). *High impact instruction: A framework for great teaching.* Corwin.

Knight, J. (2018). *The Impact Cycle: What instructional coaches should do to foster powerful improvements in teaching.* Corwin.

Knight, J. (2022). *The definitive guide to instructional coaching: Seven factors for success.* ASCD.

Neff, K. (2012). *Self-compassion: The proven power of being kind to yourself.* William Morrow.

Pink, D. H. (2009). *Drive: The surprising truth about what motivates us.* Riverhead Books.

Schairer, S. (2019, November 23). *What's the difference between empathy, sympathy, and compassion?*

chopra.com/articles/whats-the-difference-between-empathy-sympathy-and-compassion

Seligman, M. E. P. (2012). *Flourish: A visionary new understanding of happiness and well-being*. Free Press.

Sparks, D., & Malkus, N. (2015). *Public school teacher autonomy in the classroom across school years 2003–04, 2007–08, and 2011–12. Stats in brief. NCES 2015-089*. National Center for Education Statistics.

Wheatley, M. J. (2009). *Turning to one another*. Berrett-Koehler.

Chapter 2

Frank, B. D. (2018, September 26). *1 in 3 U.S. adults are lonely, survey shows*. AARP.

Hasbrouck, J., & Michel, D. (2021). *Student-focused coaching: The instructional coach's guide to supporting success through teacher collaboration*. Brookes.

Heifetz, R., Grashow, A., & Linsky, M. (2009). *Adaptive leadership: Tools and tactics for changing your organization and the world*. Harvard Business Press.

Kaiser Family Foundation. (2018). *Loneliness and social isolation in the United States, the United Kingdom, and Japan: An international survey—Introduction*.

Knight, J. (2015). *Better conversations*. Corwin.

Knight, J. (2016). *Better conversations: Coaching ourselves and each other to be more credible, caring, and connected*. Corwin.

Knight, J. (2022). *The definitive guide to instructional coaching: Seven factors for success*. ASCD.

Murphy, K. (2019). *You're not listening: What you're missing and why it matters*. Celadon Books.

Murthy, V. H. (2020). *Together: The healing power of human connection in a sometimes lonely world*. Harper Wave.

Percy, W. (1999/1980). *The second coming*. Picador.

Pink, D. (2009). *Drive: The surprising truth about what motivates us*. Riverhead Books.

Rosenberg, M. (2015). *Non-violent communication: A language of life*. Puddle Dancer Press.

Schein, E. (2009). *Helping: How to offer, give, and receive help*. Berrett-Koehler.

Seidman, I. (2013). *Interviewing as qualitative research: A guide for researchers in education and the social sciences* (4th ed.). Teachers College Press.

Turkle, S. (2015). *Reclaiming conversation: The power of talk in a digital age*. Penguin Books.

Chapter 3

Amabile, T., & Kramer, S. (2011). *The progress principle: Using small wins to ignite joy, engagement, and creativity at work*. Harvard Business Review Press.

Bradford, D., & Robin, C. (2021). *Connect*. Currency.

Bricusse, L., & Newley, A. (1965). Feeling good. I put a spell on you [Recorded by N. Simone]. On *I Put a Spell on You*.

Campbell, J., & van Nieuwerburgh, C. (2018). *The leader's guide to coaching in schools: Creating conditions for effective learning*. Corwin.

Eberhardt, J. L. (2019). *Biased: Uncovering the hidden prejudice that shapes what we see, think, and do*. Viking.

Eyal, N. (2019). *Indistractable: How to control your attention and choose your life*. Bloomsbury.

Fogg, B. J. (2020). *Tiny habits: The small changes that change everything*. Houghton, Mifflin, Harcourt.

García, H., & Miralles, F. (2016). *Ikigai: The Japanese secret to a long and happy life*. Penguin Books.

Grant, A. (2014). *Give and take: Why helping others drives our success*. Penguin Books.

Halvorson, H. G. (2012). *Nine things successful people do differently*. Harvard Business Review Press.

Heath, C., & Heath, D. (2010). *Switch: How to change things when change is hard*. Random House.

Jackson, P. Z., & McKergow, M. (2002). *The solutions focus: The simple way to positive change*. Nicholas Brealey.

Kendi, I. X. (2019). *How to be an antiracist*. Penguin Random House.

Knight, J. (2013). *High-impact instruction: A framework for great teaching*. Corwin.

Knight, J. (2022). *The definitive guide to instructional coaching: Seven factors for success*. ASCD.

Leider, J. (1997). *The power of purpose: Creating meaning in your life and work*. Berrett-Koehler.

Lopez, S. (2013). *Making hope happen: Create the future you want for yourself and others*. Atria.

Miller, W. R., & Rollnick, S. (2013). *Motivational interviewing: Helping people change*. Guilford Press.

Neff, K. (2011). *Self-compassion: The proven power of being kind to yourself.* Harper Collins.

Palmer, P. J. (2004). *A hidden wholeness: The journey toward an undivided life.* Jossey Bass.

Portman, J., Bui, T. T., Ogaz, J., & Treviño, J. (n.d.). *Microaggressions in the classroom.* University of Denver Center for Multicultural Excellence.

Prochaska, J. O., Norcross, J. C., & DiClemente, C. C. (1994). *Changing for good: A revolutionary six-stage program for overcoming bad habits and moving your life positively forward.* Harper Collins Publishers.

Project Implicit. (2011). *Implicit associations test.* https://implicit.harvard.edu/implicit/

Rosenberg, M. (2015). *Nonviolent communication.* Puddle Dancer Press.

Seligman, M. E. P. (2011). *Flourish: A visionary new understanding of happiness and wellbeing.* Free Press.

Snyder, C. R. (1994). *The psychology of hope: You can get there from here.* Free Press.

Stevenson, S. (2016). *Sleep smarter: 21 essential strategies to sleep your way to a better body, better health, and bigger success.* Rodale Books.

Sue, D. W. (2010). *Microaggressions in everyday life: Race, gender, and sexual orientation.* John Wiley and Sons.

U.S. Army. (2004). *The US Army leadership field manual.* McGraw Hill.

Wood, W. (2019). *Good habits, bad habits: The science of making positive changes.* Farrar, Straus, and Giroux.

Chapter 4

Amabile, T., & Kramer, S. (2011). *The progress principal: Using small wins to ignite joy, engagement, and creativity at work.* Harvard Business School Publishing.

Bradley, B., Knight, J., Harvey, S., Hock, M., Knight, D., Skrtic, T., Brasseur-Hock, I., & Deshler, D. (2013). Improving instructional coaching to support middle school teachers in the United States. In T. Plomp & N. Nieveen (Eds.), *Educational design research—Part B: Introduction and illustrative cases* (pp. 299–318). SLO. http://international.slo.nl/publications/edr/contents/c15

Colvin, G. (2008). *Talent is overrated: What really separates world-class performers from everybody else.* Penguin Group.

Danielson, C. (2007). *Enhancing professional practice: A framework for teaching.* ASCD.

Edmondson, A. C. (2012). *Teaming: How organizations learn, innovate, and compete in the knowledge economy.* Jossey-Bass.

Fox, L., & Diaz, D. (2018, January 22). Susan Collins had senators in bipartisan meetings using talking stick. *CNN News.*

Fritz, R. (1984). *The path of least resistance: Learning to become the creative force in your own life.* Ballantine Books.

Gallup. (2016). *First break all the rules. What the world's greatest managers do differently.* Gallup Press.

Gallwey, T. (1974). *The inner game of tennis.* Random House.

Gawande, A. (2011, October 3). Personal best. *The New Yorker.* www.newyorker.com/magazine/2011/10/03/personal-best

Glouberman, S., & Zimmerman, B. (2002, July). *Complicated and complex systems: What would successful reform of Medicare look like?* (Discussion Paper No. 8). Commission on the Future of Health Care in Canada.

Halvorson, H. G. (2012). *9 things successful people do differently.* Harvard Business Review Press.

Halvorson, H. G. (2015). *No one understands you and what to do about it.* Harvard Business Review Press.

Hargrove, R. (2008). *Masterful coaching.* Jossey-Bass.

Heath, C., & Heath, D. (2010). *Switch: How to change things when change is hard.* Random House.

Heifetz, R. A., & Linsky, M. (2002). *Leadership on the line: Staying alive through the dangers of leading.* Harvard Business Press.

Heifetz, R. A., Linsky, M., & Grashow, A. (2009). *The practice of adaptive leadership: Tools and tactics for changing your organization and the world.* Harvard Business Review Press.

Ibarra, H. (2015). *Act like a leader, think like a leader.* Harvard Business Review Press.

Knight, J. (2007). *Instructional coaching: A partnership approach to improving instruction.* Corwin.

Knight, J. (2011). *Unmistakable impact: A partnership approach for dramatically improving instruction.* Corwin.

Knight, J. (2013). *High-impact instruction: A framework for great teaching.* Corwin.

Knight, J. (2014). *Focus on teaching: Using video for high impact instruction*. Corwin.

Knight, J. (2018). *The Impact Cycle: What instructional coaches should do to foster powerful improvements in teaching*. Corwin.

Knight, J. (2022). *The definitive guide to instructional coaching: Seven factors for success*. ASCD.

Liu, E. (2006). *Guiding lights: How to mentor and find life's purpose*. Ballantine Books.

Lopez, S. (2013). *Making hope happen: Create the future you want for yourself and others*. Atria.

Patterson, K., Grenny, J., Maxfield, D., McMillan, R., & Switzler, A. (2008). *Influencer: The power to change anything*. McGraw-Hill.

Pink, D. H. (2009). *Drive: The surprising truth about what motivates us*. Riverhead Books.

Pink, D. H. (2018). *When: The scientific secrets of perfect timing*. Penguin.

Prochaska, J. O., Norcross, J. C., & DiClemente, C. C. (1994). *Changing for good*. Avon Books.

Stone, D., & Heen, S. (2015). *Thanks for the feedback: The science and art of receiving feedback well*. Penguin.

Stone, D., Patton, B., & Heen, S. (1999). *Difficult conversations: How to discuss what matters most*. Penguin.

Chapter 5

Amabile, T., & Kramer, S. (2011). The power of small wins. *Harvard Business Review*. hbr.org/2011/05/the-power-of-small-wins

Buckingham, M., & Goodall, A. (2019, March–April). The feedback fallacy. *Harvard Business Review*.

Centers for Disease Control and Prevention. (2009). *Fostering school connectedness*. www.cdc.gov/healthyyouth/protective/pdf/connectedness_administrators.pdf

Finn, J. D. (1993). *School engagement and students at risk*. National Center for Education Statistics.

Finn, J. D., & Rock, D. A. (1997). Academic success among students at risk of school failure. *Journal of Applied Psychology, 82*(2), 221–234.

Hattie, J. (2009). *Visible learning: A synthesis of over 800 meta-analyses relating to achievement*. Routledge.

Kegan, R., & Lahey, L. L. (2001). *How the way we talk can change the way we work: Seven languages for transformation*. Jossey-Bass.

Knesting, K. (2008). Students at risk for school dropout: Supporting their persistence. *Preventing School Failure: Alternative Education for Children and Youth, 52*(4), 3–10.

Knight, J. (2007). *Instructional coaching: A partnership approach to improving instruction*. Corwin.

Knight, J. (2013). *High-impact instruction: A framework for great teaching*. Corwin.

Knight, J. (2018). *The Impact Cycle: What instructional coaches should do to foster powerful improvements in teaching*. Corwin.

Knight, J. (2019). Students on the margins. *The Learning Professional, 40*(6), 28–32.

Knight, J. (2022). *The definitive guide to instructional coaching: Seven factors for success*. ASCD.

Knight, D., Hock, M., Skrtic, T. M., Bradley, B. A., & Knight, J. (2018). Evaluation of video-based instructional coaching for middle school teachers: Evidence from a multiple-baseline study. *The Educational Forum, 82*(4), 425–442.

Knight, J., Hoffman, A., Harris, M., & Thomas, S. (in press). *The instructional playbook: The missing link for translating research into practice*. One Fine Bird Press.

Lopez, S. (2013). *Making hope happen: Create the future you want for yourself and others*. Atria.

Quaglia, R., & Corso, M. J. (2014). *Student voice: The instrument of change*. Corwin.

Schlechty, P. (2011). *Engaging students: The next level of working on work*. Jossey-Bass.

van Nieuwerburgh, C. (2017). *An introduction to coaching skills: A practical guide* (2nd ed.). Sage.

Whitmore, J. (2017). *Coaching for performance: The principles and practice of coaching and leadership* (5th ed.). Nicholas Brealey.

Chapter 6

Knight, J. (2019). Students on the margins: How instructional coaching can increase engagement. *Learning Professional, 40*(6), 28–32.

Knight, J. (2022). *The definitive guide to instructional coaching: Seven factors for success*. ASCD.

Stanier, M. B. (2016). *The coaching habit: Say less, ask more and change the way you lead forever*. Box of Crayons Press.

Whitmore, J. (2017). *Coaching for performance: The principles and practice of coaching and leadership* (5th ed.). Nicholas Brealey.

Chapter 7

Block, P. (1993). *Stewardship: Choosing service over self-interest.* Berrett-Koehler.

Bloom, G., Castagna, C., Moir, E., & Warren, B. (2005). *Blended coaching: Skills and strategies to support principal development.* Corwin.

Bulgren, J. A., Deshler, D. D., & Schumaker, J. B. (1993). *The concept mastery routine.* Edge Enterprises.

Bush, R. N. (1984). Effective staff development. In *Making our schools more effective: Proceedings of three state conferences.* Far West Laboratory.

Collins, J. (2001). *Good to great: Why some companies make the leap . . . and others don't.* Harper Business.

Cornett, J., & Knight, J. (2008). Research on coaching. In J. Knight (Ed.), *Coaching: Approaches and perspectives* (pp. 192–216). Corwin.

Costa, A., & Garmston, R. (2002). *Cognitive coaching: A foundation for renaissance schools.* Christopher-Gordon.

Csikszentmihalyi, M. (1993). *The evolving self: A psychology for the third millennium.* HarperCollins.

Davenport, T. H. (2005). *Thinking for a living: How to get better performance and results from knowledge workers.* Harvard Business School Press.

Edwards, J. L. (2001). *Cognitive coaching: A synthesis of the research.* Center for Cognitive Coaching.

Fisher, D., & Frey, N. (2008). *Better learning through structured teaching: A framework for the gradual release of responsibility.* ASCD.

Freire, P. (1970). *Pedagogy of the oppressed.* Continuum.

Fullan, M. (2001). *Leading in a culture of change: Being effective in complex times.* Jossey-Bass.

Fullan, M., & Hargreaves, A. (1996). *What's worth fighting for in your school* (2nd ed.). Teachers College Press.

Gawande, A. (2010). *The checklist manifesto: How to get things right.* Metropolitan.

Gladwell, M. (2001). *The tipping point: How little things can make a big difference.* Little, Brown, and Co.

Goldsmith, M., & Reiter, M. (2007). *What got you here won't get you there: How successful people become even more successful.* Hyperion.

Guskey, T. (1999). *Evaluating professional development.* Corwin.

Hall, G. E., & Hord, S. M. (2001). *Implementing change: Patterns, principles, and potholes.* Allyn & Bacon.

Hall, G. E., & Hord, S. M. (2015). *Implementing change: Patterns, principles and potholes* (4th ed.). Pearson.

Hall, G. E., & Hord, S. M. (2006). *Implementing change: Patterns, principles, and potholes* (2nd ed.). Pearson Education.

Hargreaves, A., & Fink, D. (2005). *Sustainable leadership.* Jossey-Bass.

Hargrove, R. (2008). *Masterful coaching* (3rd ed.). Pfeiffer.

Heifetz, R. A., & Linsky, M. (2002). *Leadership on the line.* Harvard Business School Press.

Kegan, R., & Lahey, L. L. (2001). *How the way we talk can change the way we learn.* Jossey-Bass.

Knight, J. (1998). *The effectiveness of partnership learning: A dialogical methodology for staff development* [Unpublished doctoral dissertation]. University of Kansas, Lawrence, KS.

Knight, J. (2000). *Another damn thing we've got to do: Teacher perceptions of professional development* [Paper presented]. American Educational Research Association, New Orleans, LA, United States.

Knight, J. (2007). *Instructional coaching: A partnership approach to improving instruction.* Corwin.

Knight, J. (2011). *Unmistakable impact: A partnership approach for dramatically improving instruction.* Corwin.

Knight, J. (2018). *The impact cycle: What instructional coaches should do to foster powerful improvements in teaching.* Corwin.

Knight, J. (2022). *The definitive guide to instructional coaching: Seven factors for success.* ASCD.

Knight, J., & Cornett, J. (2009). *Studying the impact of instructional coaching.* Manuscript. University of Kansas Center of Research on Teaching.

Knight, J., Hoffman, A., Harris, M., & Thomas, S. (2021). *The instructional playbook: The missing link for translating research into practice.* ASCD.

Lenz, B. K., Bulgren, J., Schumaker, J., Deshler, D. D., & Boudah, D. (1994). *The unit organizer routine.* Edge Enterprises.

Liu, E. (2004). *Guiding lights: The people who lead us toward our purpose in life.* Random House.

Miller, W. R., & Rollnick, S. (2002). *Motivational interviewing: Preparing people for change* (2nd ed.). Guilford Press.

Moran, M. C. (2007). *Differentiated literacy coaching: Scaffolding for student and teacher success.* ASCD.

Patterson, K., Grenny, J., Maxfield, D., McMillan, R., & Switzler, A. (2008). *Influencer: The power to change anything.* McGraw-Hill.

Prochaska, J. O., Norcross, J. C., & Diclemente, C. C. (1994). *Changing for good.* Quill.

Sarason, S. B. (1990). *The predictable failure of educational reform: Can we change course before it's too late?* Jossey-Bass.

Showers, B. (1984). *Peer coaching: A strategy for facilitating transfer of training.* Center for Educational Policy and Management.

Skrtic, T. M. (1991). *Behind special education.* Love.

Sprick, R., Knight, J., Reinke, W., & McKale, T. (2006). *Coaching classroom management: Strategies and tools for administrators and coaches.* Pacific Northwest.

Stone, D., Patton, B., & Heen, S. (2000). *Difficult conversations: How to discuss what matters most.* Penguin.

Suzuki, S. (2020). *Zen mind, beginner's mind: Informal talks on Zen meditation and practice: 50th anniversary edition.* Shambhala Publications.

Toll, C. A. (2005). *The literacy coach's survival guide: Essential questions and practical answers.* International Reading Association.

West, L., & Staub, F. C. (2003). *Content-focused coaching: Transforming mathematics lessons.* Heinemann.

Zhu, X.-M. (2012). *The secret piano: From Mao's labor camps to Bach's Goldberg Variations.* (E. Hinsey, Trans.). AmazonCrossing. (Original work published 2007)

Index

INSTRUCTIONAL COACHING GROUP

GO DEEPER
WITH AN ICG CONSULTANT

1. **Identify Current Reality**
Casual discussion to identify needs and budget

2. **Develop Customized PD Plan**
Customized learning plan based on your needs and budget

3. **Deliver Training & Resources**
Participate in training on-site or virtually

4. **Measure Effectiveness**
Continuous discussions and check-ins with your ICG consultant

5. **Set Goals**
Evaluate growth and successes, and identify next steps for improvement

Long-Term Partnership & Support

Jim Knight and the Instructional Coaching Group (ICG) offer professional development services focused on instructional coaching for educators. They provide training, resources, and support to help teachers improve their instructional practices, aiming to enhance student learning outcomes. Their approach includes workshops, institutes, and customized professional development, emphasizing evidence-based strategies and fostering collaborative, reflective teaching environments.

For a customized plan, contact us by visiting InstructionalCoaching.com

A Sage Company

> Helping educators make the greatest impact

CORWIN HAS ONE MISSION: to enhance education through intentional professional learning.

We build long-term relationships with our authors, educators, clients, and associations who partner with us to develop and continuously improve the best evidence-based practices that establish and support lifelong learning.

THE PROFESSIONAL LEARNING ASSOCIATION

Learning Forward is a nonprofit, international membership association of learning educators committed to one vision in K–12 education: Equity and excellence in teaching and learning. To realize that vision, Learning Forward pursues its mission to build the capacity of leaders to establish and sustain highly effective professional learning. Information about membership, services, and products is available from www.learningforward.org.